Information Systems Analysis & Design
Lecture Notes & Supplements

This document contains Lecture Notes and supplements, primarily PowerPoint presentations, for the class X422 Introduction to Information Systems Analysis and Design at the University of California Berkeley Extension. They are designed as a resource for students who take the class.

This is the first course in a series covering information analysis and logical specification of the system development process in an organizational context. It emphasizes the interactive nature of the analysis and design process.

Today, more than ever, it is important to formulate plans and ideas in some structured manner before attempting to develop a solution to a problem or procedure. Most everything we do in life is a part of some system. In order to understand any system, the system must be analyzed. By the same token, to be able to design any system, one must have extensive knowledge about what the design objectives are. This course explores systems analysis and design from the early days of second generation systems development up to and including graphical user interface design and development (GUI).

This course then, is intended to teach the beginning student to think in terms of the "big picture" in problem solving and designing systems by defining specific objectives. By the end of the course, students will be able to:

- The purpose of systems analysis and design: Feasibility study; Analysis; Design
- How to shape the solution from the problem definition
- How to simplify a system: Partitioning the system according to functions; Organizing the system into hierarchies
- The introduction to life cycle systems design
- The introduction to systems design tools
- Methods of communications between analyst and user department: How to obtain information to design a system; How to begin a systems analysis and design project
- The difference between a systems analyst and a programmer analyst

This document was produced on Sunday, August 14, 2011
Color edition: CreateSpace # 3583533 ISBN: 978-1-4610-2119-3 1-4610-2119-7
Black & White edition: CreateSpace # 3671573 ISBN: 978-1-4662-2882-5 1-4662-2882-2

Cover photo by Lilian Roberts

Information Systems Analysis & Design

Table of Contents

0. Hello, Worldly Analyst!
Recommended Reading Material

Block, Peter, *Flawless Consulting: A Guide To Getting Your Expertise Used, Second Edition*, San Diego, California: Pfeiffer & Company (0-7879-4803-9), 2000.

Justice, Tom & David W. Jamieson, Ph.D, *The Facilitator's Fieldbook, Second Edition*, New York: AMACOM American Management Association (0-8144-7314-8 978-0-8144-7314-6), 2006.

McDermott, Patrick, *Zen and the Art of Systems Analysis: Meditations on Computer Systems Development*, New York: iUniverse (0-595-25679-1 [Paper] 0-595-75230-6 [eBook], 2003 (2002).

Ouellette, L. Paul, *I/S Internal Consulting: The "Must Have" Skill For Every I/S Professional, Second Edition*, Dubuque, Iowa: Kendall/Hunt (0-7872-2087-6), 1996.

Rosenberg, Scott, Dreaming in Code: Two Dozen Programmers, Three Years, 4,732 Bugs, and One Quest for Transcendent Software, New York: Crown Publishers (978-1-4000-8246-9), 2007.

Weinberg, Gerald M., *Rethinking Systems Analysis & Design*, New York: Dorset House (0-932633-08-0), 1988.

Weiss, Alan, *How to Establish a Unique Brand in the Consulting Profession: Powerful Techniques for the Successful Practitioner*, San Francisco: Jossey-Bass / Pfeiffer (0-7879-5513-2), 2002.

Thinking Like an Analyst

1. Think Outside the Box.

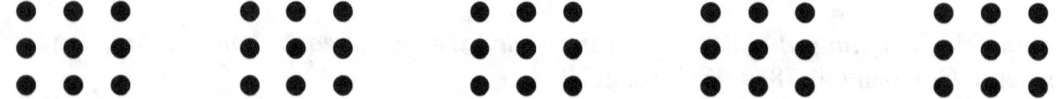

2. You Must Be Able To Answer *Every* Technology Management Question.

3. A Report Can Be A Solution, But *Not* A Problem: 5 *Why*'s will make You Wise.

4. Remember the Prime Directive: NO CULTURAL INTERFERENCE.

5. What Everybody Knows About Chicken Feed.

6. They Can't Always Get What They Want (But They'll Get What They Need).

7. Must Challenge the Process.

8. Of Problems and People.

9. If IT Doesn't Change Your Way Of Doing Business, Don't Bother.

You are *HERE*

The Answer to Every Question

The Answer to
Every
Technology or Management
Question…

IT

DEPENDS

1. The Role of the Analyst
Eight Skills

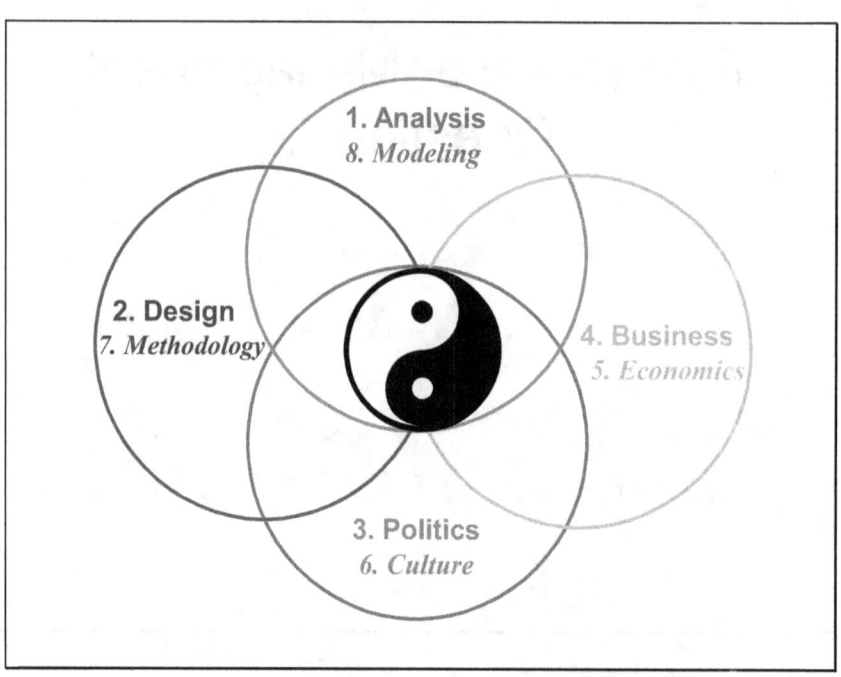

- 1. Analysis
- 8. *Modeling*
- 2. Design
- 7. *Methodology*
- 4. Business
- 5. *Economics*
- 3. Politics
- 6. *Culture*

Yin & **YANG**

陰陽
いんよう
Japanese: **In'yō**

- Everything has Both *Yin* & **Yang**
- *Y* & **Y**: Complements, not Opposites

太極
Chinese: Tai-Chi
Japanese: Taikyoku

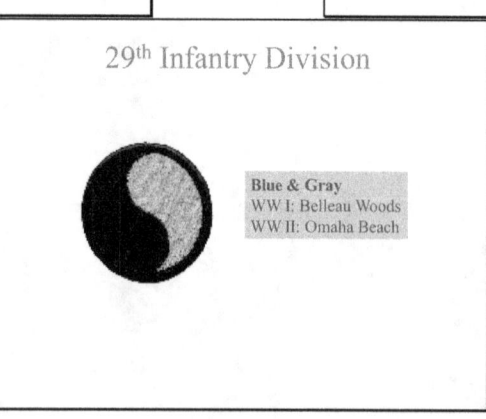

Republic of Korea

- Yin Yang
- *I Ching* Trigrams
- Liebniz Binary

29th Infantry Division

Blue & Gray
WW I: Belleau Woods
WW II: Omaha Beach

The Role of Information Systems in the Organization

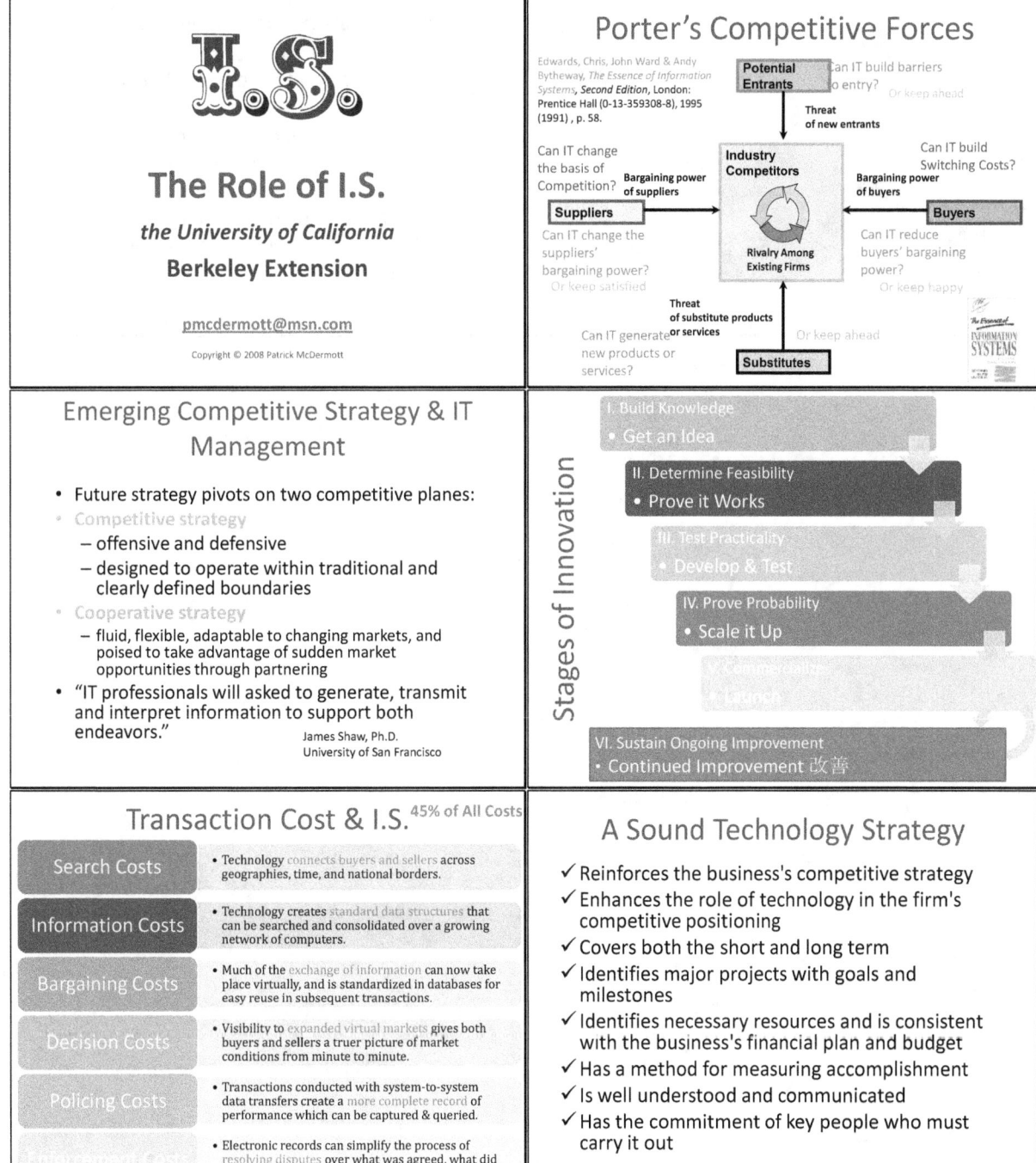

The Role of I.S.

the University of California
Berkeley Extension

pmcdermott@msn.com

Copyright © 2008 Patrick McDermott

Porter's Competitive Forces

Edwards, Chris, John Ward & Andy Bytheway, *The Essence of Information Systems, Second Edition*, London: Prentice Hall (0-13-359308-8), 1995 (1991), p. 58.

Potential Entrants — Can IT build barriers to entry? Or keep ahead

Threat of new entrants

Can IT change the basis of Competition? — Bargaining power of suppliers

Industry Competitors — Rivalry Among Existing Firms

Can IT build Switching Costs? — Bargaining power of buyers

Suppliers — Can IT change the suppliers' bargaining power? Or keep satisfied

Buyers — Can IT reduce buyers' bargaining power? Or keep happy

Threat of substitute products or services — Can IT generate new products or services? Or keep ahead

Substitutes

The Essence of INFORMATION SYSTEMS

Emerging Competitive Strategy & IT Management

- Future strategy pivots on two competitive planes:
- Competitive strategy
  - offensive and defensive
  - designed to operate within traditional and clearly defined boundaries
- Cooperative strategy
  - fluid, flexible, adaptable to changing markets, and poised to take advantage of sudden market opportunities through partnering
- "IT professionals will asked to generate, transmit and interpret information to support both endeavors."

James Shaw, Ph.D.
University of San Francisco

Stages of Innovation

- I. Build Knowledge
  - Get an Idea
- II. Determine Feasibility
  - Prove it Works
- III. Test Practicality
  - Develop & Test
- IV. Prove Probability
  - Scale it Up
- V. Commercialize
  - Launch
- VI. Sustain Ongoing Improvement
  - Continued Improvement 改善

Transaction Cost & I.S. 45% of All Costs

Search Costs	• Technology connects buyers and sellers across geographies, time, and national borders.
Information Costs	• Technology creates standard data structures that can be searched and consolidated over a growing network of computers.
Bargaining Costs	• Much of the exchange of information can now take place virtually, and is standardized in databases for easy reuse in subsequent transactions.
Decision Costs	• Visibility to expanded virtual markets gives both buyers and sellers a truer picture of market conditions from minute to minute.
Policing Costs	• Transactions conducted with system-to-system data transfers create a more complete record of performance which can be captured & queried.
Enforcement Costs	• Electronic records can simplify the process of resolving disputes over what was agreed, what did or did not occur.

A Sound Technology Strategy

- ✓ Reinforces the business's competitive strategy
- ✓ Enhances the role of technology in the firm's competitive positioning
- ✓ Covers both the short and long term
- ✓ Identifies major projects with goals and milestones
- ✓ Identifies necessary resources and is consistent with the business's financial plan and budget
- ✓ Has a method for measuring accomplishment
- ✓ Is well understood and communicated
- ✓ Has the commitment of key people who must carry it out

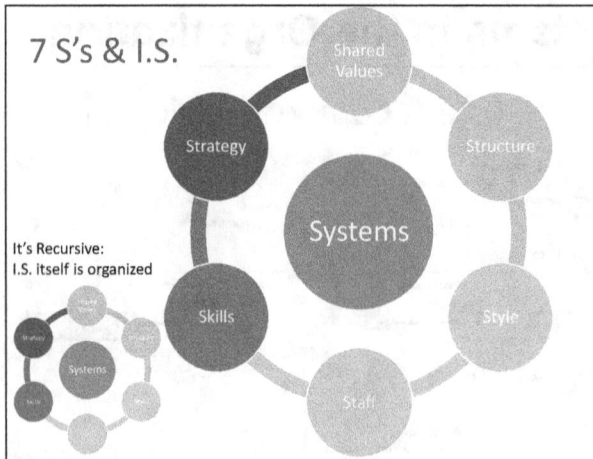

7 S's & I.S.

Shared Values

Strategy

Structure

Systems

It's Recursive:
I.S. itself is organized

Skills

Style

Staff

Exercise

1. What is a strategic information system?
2. What relationship does a strategic information system have to Michael Porter's competitive force model?
3. Which organization do you think has the best information technology and strategy and why?
4. Which organization do you think has the worst information technology and strategy and why?

Seven Habits for Effectiveness

Covey, Stephen R., *The Seven Habits of Highly Effective People: Restoring the Character Ethic*, New York: Fireside Book / Simon & Schuster (0-671-70863-5), 1990 (1989).

7 Habits

College of Alameda
ATLAS
pmcdermott@peralta.edu

Copyright © 2011 Patrick McDermott

1. Be Proactive

- Act, or be acted upon

- No one can insult you without your permission
- They can't take your self-respect unless you give it to them

Reactive vs. Proactive

Reactive	Proactive
1. There's nothing I can do	1. Let's look at our alternatives
2. That's just the way I am	2. I can choose a different way
3. He makes me so mad	3. I control my own feelings
4. I have to do that	4. I will choose my response
5. I can't	5. I choose
6. I must	6. I prefer
7. If only	7. I will

2. Begin with the End in Mind

In 2 Senses:

1. **Short-term:** Always plan ahead; decide where you want to be, then plan backward from there

2. **Contemplate:** What do you want people (family, friends, colleagues, etc.) to say about you at your funeral?

3. Put First Things First

Organize & Execute around Priorities
Generations of Time Management:
1. Notes & Checklists
2. Calendars & Appointment Books
3. Prioritize, Clarify Values, Compare Worth
4. Not Time Management, Self Management

Important/Urgent

	URGENT	NOT Urgent
Important	I. "Firefighting" Crisis Mode Pressing Problems Arbitrary Deadlines	II. BE HERE!!! Planning Prevention PC Production Capability
NOT Important	III. "Demands" Interruptions Some Calls Some Meetings Pressing matters	IV. "Trivia" Trivia, Busy Work Some Mail/Phone Time Wasters Pleasant Activities

4. Think Win-Win

- ...whenever possible/appropriate

- Abundance Mentality
- Positive-, Not Zero-Sum

- No Medieval Mind
  - "We can all have more potatoes"

5. Seek First to Understand, then to be understood

- We have 2 ears to listen and one mouth to talk

- Empathic Communication
- Diagnose before you Prescribe

6. Synergize

Synergy:
- The Whole is Greater than the Sum of its Parts
- $2 + 2 > 4$
- Doubled the Project, reduced the total load!

- "As a teacher, I have come to believe that many truly great classes teeter on the very edge of chaos"
  - I hope so!

7. Sharpen the Saw

- The Busy Woodcutter
- Physical
  - Exercise, Nutrition, Stress Management
- Spiritual
  - Values, Study, Meditation
- Mental
  - Reading, Visualizing, Writing
- Social/Emotional
  - Service, Empathy, Synergy

A Summary of Covey's 7 Habits

Covey, Stephen R., *The Seven Habits of Highly Effective People: Restoring the Character Ethic*, New York: Fireside Book / Simon & Schuster (0-671-70863-5), 1990 (1989).

Summary from Wikipedia
http://en.wikipedia.org/wiki/The_Seven_Habits_of_Highly_Effective_People
Retrieved April 11, 2011

7 Habits

College of Alameda
ATLAS
pmcdermott@peralta.edu

1. Be Proactive

Taking initiative in life by realizing your decisions (and how they align with life's principles) are the primary determining factor for effectiveness in your life. Taking responsibility for your choices and the subsequent consequences that follow. Getting things done.

2. Begin with the End in Mind

Self-discover and clarify your deeply important character values and life goals. Envision the ideal characteristics for each of your various roles and relationships in life. It is always better to try and foresee situations. Predict outcomes and then think of worst case scenarios, will help come up with informed decisions.

3. Put First Things First

Planning, prioritizing, and executing your week's tasks based on importance rather than urgency. Evaluating if your efforts exemplify your desired character values, propel you towards goals, and enrich the roles and relationships elaborated in Habit 2. Prioritization is the key to the success of any business or in any walk of life. Being proactive rather than being reactive leads to success.

4. Think Win-Win

Genuinely striving for mutually beneficial solutions or agreements in your relationships. Valuing and respecting people by understanding a "win" for all is ultimately a better long-term resolution than if only one person in the situation had gotten his way. Everyone will feel inclusive and involved. A better environment of trust and loyalty establishes.

5. Seek First to Understand, then to be understood

Using empathetic listening to be genuinely influenced by a person, which compels them to reciprocate the listening and take an open mind to being influenced by you. This creates an atmosphere of caring, respect, and positive problem solving. This can also avoid situations where the problem does not actually exist and it's just a matter of misunderstanding. It is always said that listen double to what you talk since we have 2 ears to listen and one mouth to talk.

6. Synergize

Combining the strengths of people through positive teamwork, so as to achieve goals no one person could have done alone. How to yield the most prolific performance out of a group of people through encouraging meaningful contribution, and modeling inspirational and supportive leadership. Everyone is a master of something and not everything. Positive potentials can be put together to achieve better results.

7. Sharpen the Saw

The balancing and renewal of your resources, energy, and health to create a sustainable long-term effective lifestyle. This is constant improvement of one's self in order to be a better human being and to sharpen one's skills in order to achieve better results.

Brainstorming

Brainstorming

Auguste Rodin (1840-1917)
The Thinker, c. 1879-89

Brainstorming

Copyright © 1999 Patrick McDermott

UC Berkeley

Extension

pmcdermott@msn.com

Since Alex Osborn of the advertising agency Batten, Barton, Durstine & Osborn came up with the idea of "brainstorming" in the late 1930s, business has been busy trying to wed creativity to commerce.

Your Goal

Quantity
not
Quality

Nothing is more dangerous than an idea
—if it's the only one you have.

The Right Mindset

☼ There's no Such Thing as a Bad Idea
☃ Break The Ice
♀ Creative Plagiarism
👁 Open Your Mind
🀫 Be Creative
? Take Risks
🔊 Shout! It! Out!!!
☺ Act Like a 3-Year Old

黙想 Mokusō

Brainstorming Rules

0. *Have Fun!!!*

1. No Criticism or Debate

2. No Self-Censorship

3. Piggyback

No idea, no matter how preposterous, expensive, irresponsible, or even stupid it may seem, is rejected at the time it's expressed.   Exercise

---

Brainstorming

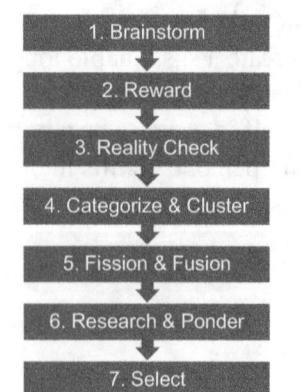

1. Brainstorm
2. Reward
3. Reality Check
4. Categorize & Cluster
5. Fission & Fusion
6. Research & Ponder
7. Select

Reward
✓ Most *Fun*
  – "Aha" is in "Ha-ha"
✓ Most Ideas
✓ Most Bizarre, Strange or Ridiculous Idea
• NOT: the Best Idea

How to Select
  – Consensus
  – Authority
  – Democracy…

Multi-Voting

• Each person gets multiple votes
• Votes can be "blocked"
  – You can put several votes on one choice
  – You can put all your votes on one choice
• Variation: vote aloud, explaining the vote in turn, allowing others to change their vote if convinced (avoids strategic voting)
• Or distribute $100

Brain Typhoon

Brainstorming is one of the most useful tools to stimulate creativity available to the Analyst. I use it almost daily in analysis and in all creative work. Brainstorming is a process you probably have done unconsciously, but it improves with some formal rules. I suggest you post them in a chart form in meeting rooms.

> **0. Have Fun!**
> **1. No Criticism**
> **2. No Self-Censorship**
> **3. Piggyback**

1. No Criticism

This is the most important rule of all. If someone offers the stupidest idea you ever heard in your life, the correct response is to say, "Fantastic!" Under no circumstances do you want to stop the creative flow by intimidating anyone. Some of the craziest ideas you've ever heard turn out to work once given a chance. But more important, a dumb idea can flow into another better idea if you give it a chance.

2. No Self-Censorship

This is almost as important. Don't hold back. If you think of the stupidest thing you've ever heard of in your life, blurt it out. Sometimes you are able to come up with an idea which is completely absurd, except that it works—because you look at a problem from the odd perspective—you "think different". This often lets you attack a difficult problem from another angle, one that leads to a surprisingly elegant solution. Even if it isn't adopted, it might start someone else thinking, or at a minimum will get a laugh and help to loosen up the group.

3. Piggyback

Hey, for once in life stealing is okay, in fact encouraged. Try to modify or expand on the ideas offered by the other participants. And if someone steals your idea, remember those who see farther are standing on the shoulders of giants, and that means you're a giant. Ideas feed on other ideas, and piggyback is not only okay, it's admirable. You want to take every idea to its illogical conclusion.

0. Have Fun

Although this one appears first on my chart, I have PowerPoint animated to have it appear last when I'm explaining the rules to a group. I explain that as a C++ programmer I naturally count from zero, not one. This rule is first because I've found that groups that are having fun usually do the best job.

I often use a silly brainstorming exercise as an icebreaker, a way to loosen a group of people up, especially if they don't know each other. You might consider something similar for a meeting of a new group, especially if you will be using brainstorming and need to warm up. Explain brainstorming, form the group into teams of four to eight people, and then pose a silly problem to the group, such as this one I often pose at my UC Berkeley Extension class:

> Berkeley is in a terrible fix. With the rainy season approaching, we decided to put coat racks and hangers in all the classrooms and offices. It seems a new employee went on to CoatHangers.com on the Internet, and like many UI's, this one was confusing, so she accidentally ordered not the 5,000 hangers wanted, but 5,000 cases of hangers, with 10,000 hangers in each case. There is no way to cancel this order. Your mission is to come up with as many possible uses for these hangers to get Cal out of this jam.

If asked "what kind of hangers, wood or wire?" Tell them "Every imaginable kind". This further opens the road to thought. You can vary the problem by using just about any item, although I tried it once with clothespins and it didn't work very well. Some of the students didn't know what a clothespin was!

Without telling them what I'm doing, I tally the number of times I hear laughter coming from each group. When we get to the reward phase (see below) the first behavior I reward is the "Fun Group", the one that laughed the most. In many learning situations, noise equals learning. For my course on systems analysis consulting, I consider the number of times the neighboring classes complain about the noise an indicator of how well things are going.

> *The Goal of Brainstorming is*
> # Quantity not Quality

Quality will come from the process. The point of the exercise, and of brainstorming, is to generate as many ideas as you can. With more options, you are more likely to come up with a good solution. It's easier to cross out the bad ideas than to come up with good ones.

The Process

1. Brainstorm

Discuss the rules, and perhaps do an icebreaker, such as the hanger exercise, or any from the *Games Trainers Play* series of books. Someone needs to be the scribe, and record all the ideas on a white board or flip chart. If your session is facilitated, the facilitator might be the scribe, and not participate. So just have the people shout the ideas out, with the caveat the scribe(s) need time to record them. With all meetings, especially freewheeling sessions with lots of ideas and decisions, this rule applies:

> **If it ain't recorded,**
> **It didn't happen.**

2. Reward

The next step is to reward the best performers. The reward can be a cheap gag toy, some candy, or just a pat on the back. In my class, the students in the rewarded groups get an extra point toward their final grade. All students receive one point for participating in the class exercise, plus each student gets an extra point for each category they "won" in. Often one group wins in more than one category—the fun group especially seems to win in one or both of the other categories.

These are the categories rewarded: 1. Most Fun—the group that laughed the most. 2. Most Ideas—the group with the greatest total number of ideas. 3. Most Bizarre, Strange or Ridiculous—the group with craziest idea. Note you should **NOT** reward the *best* idea, nor the one that is eventually chosen to work on. The best idea arises from the process, and everyone was part of that. This is to encourage the correct behavior. If you want people to think out of the box, reward them for escaping.

3. Reality Check

Now reality must raise its ugly head. If your boss has said, "Under no circumstances will you go to Hawai'i", then Hawai'i, alas, must be cut from the list. If you're doing brainstorming right, you will have come up with some things that are just plain impossible. But remember, what seems quite absurd can in fact be quite feasible. After all, if the infrastructure weren't built, the idea of the ubiquitous automobile would seem absurd. Not just to make the autos themselves, requiring materials from all over the world, but consider the requirements: You must build a ribbon of concrete from every place to every other place, with gas stations strategically located dispensing oil that comes from deep under ground in the far corners of the planet. It will never work! So only remove ideas that are patently absurd, illegal or clearly impossible given company policy or politics.

4. Clean the List Up

Categorize and combine items. By classifying them on some characteristic (brainstorm a list…), you'll find the same idea appears twice, or will see a hole or a whole. Try fusion and fission: some ideas combine, some split into two. Combine any two ideas that are the same, or split any cases where two ideas are posing as one.

5. Select

Hopefully you will have more ideas than you can possibly work on. So how to decide which merit further investigation? There are essentially three ways:

Autocracy—Some expert or authority shall decree the answer. Perhaps your assignment has been to come up with alternatives, not recommendations, and so you can pass the problem to the boss.

Democracy—or a modification of it. You could simply vote, or better, use a variation called *multi-voting*. In multi-voting, it's a weighted democracy, because each person gets multiple votes. How many? Usually three or four votes, but sometimes a good number is the number of alternatives you want to narrow down to. If you plan to look at six alternatives, you might give each participant six votes. Votes can be "blocked", i.e. you can cast several votes for the same choice, even cast all your votes on one choice if you really feel strongly about it. Multi-voting avoids several problems. Sometimes a lot of people are mildly in favor of an idea but a smaller number are very enthusiastic about another choice. Their enthusiasm can be registered by extra votes. Sometimes everybody's second choice is the best answer, which would be missed if everyone got only one vote.

Consensus—this involves getting broad agreement. It is covered in Chapter 3 on Consulting. Consensus is preferable when the success of the decision depends on cooperation and coordination.

Brainstorming works for either a group or an individual. Use it alone, use it with friends. Use it whenever you need to think out a problem or generate alternatives.

Excerpt from McDermott, Patrick, *Zen and the Art of Systems Analysis: Meditations on Computer Systems Development*, New York: iUniverse (0-595-25679-1), 2003 (2002), pp. 125-130.

Brainstorming Rules

0. *Have Fun!!!*
1. No Criticism or Debate
2. No Self-Censorship
3. Piggyback

Quantity
not
Quality

The Scribe's Role

- Record All Pertinent Facts & Events
    - Sometimes Minutes, But usually Better Organized
- Recordkeeper = Keeper of the Record
    - If the Scribe didn't record it, it didn't happen
    - Results, Decisions, Unresolved Issues
- For Exercises, make sure:
- ✓ Team Members get Credit (in this case, points)
- ✓ Teacher Knows the Score
    - If not, you didn't earn your extra point!

Walter Gould (1829-1893)
The Public Scribe, 1869
oil on canvas
43⅛" x 54¾" (109.2 x 139.1 cm)

2. Feasibility Study

Les Programeurs Miserables

We always hear how rarely computer projects are completed on time and within budget. Should we blame it on technologists? Here's the story of one "late and over budget project."

Scene 1: Manny the Programming Manager's office in a Fortune 500 firm.

Lily the Lead Programmer enters stage left. Manny looks up expectantly.

Lily: I have the estimate, Manny. It will take approximately 24 months to build that new system.

Manny: *Under his breath, but loud enough for Lily to hear:* Gee, I thought she was a better programmer than that! *To Lily:* Whew, that's two whole years! Dina the Director will never accept that. But wait! I know! What if I got you and your team brand new workstations, and a concierge service to handle some of your daily chores, and sent you all to that productivity seminar in Las Vegas so you can learn the latest programming techniques. Under those conditions, do you think you could do it in, say, 18 months?

L: *Hesitantly* Well, I suppose that might be possible....

M: Good, it's settled then! *Writes down: "18 Months". Does* not *write down workstations, or concierge, or Vegas.* I'll take this to Dina right away. *Exeunt, stage left.*

The Curtain Descends

Narrator: *On the way to Dina's office, through that phenomenon totally unexplained by science but frequently experienced by programming managers, a warp in the Universe causes the ink on the paper to re-arrange its molecules so that "18 Months" now reads "12 Months".*

Scene 2: Dina the Development Director's office.

Manny the manager enters stage left. Dina looks up expectantly.

Manny: I have the estimate, Dina. It will take approximately 12 months to build that new system.

Dina: *Under her breath, but loud enough for Manny to hear:* Gee, I thought he was a better manager than that! *To Manny:* Whew, that's a whole year! Vince the Vice President will never accept that. But wait! I know! What if I got you a bigger office, and a reserved parking space so you won't waste time trying to park, and sent you to that management seminar in Maui so you can learn the latest motivation techniques. Under those conditions, do you think you could do it in, say, nine months?

M: *Hesitantly* Well, I suppose that might be possible....

D: Good, it's settled then! *Writes down: "9 Months". Does* not *write down office, or parking space, or Maui.* I'll take this to Vince right away. *Gets up, they both exit, stage left.*

The Curtain Descends

This is one play you can safely leave during Intermission. We all know the outcome. A *six*-month project is approved and funded, a deadline set, and sure enough, *24* months later the project is eventually finished. Management decries the undependability of a programming staff that came in *Three Hundred Percent* over budget. They'll blame it on the miserable programmers. But in fact, we actually hit the programmer's original estimate right on the head. As Robert Glass points out in *Software Runaways*, "most cost and schedule targets are set by marketers or customers, next most often by managers, and least often by the technologists who will do the work."

In some cases, management reinforces this tendency to underestimate. When it's subtly clear a low estimate is expected, not surprisingly you'll get one. And when enough pressure is brought on technical employees to cave and agree to an unreasonable schedule, they'll probably do so.

In some cases, it's self-delusion of management, and to be fair, the programming staff as well, that leads to this problem: "We want it done by a certain date, therefore it must be possible to do it by that date." Or, "I really want to do this project, and if it can't be done within a certain cost it won't be approved, so I'm sure we can do it for that amount." The estimate is inversely proportional to the desire to do the project. This will be especially true if missed deadlines are easily forgiven; the corporate culture becomes "Tell them what they want to hear, the missed deadlines won't matter anyway."

In some cases, the management *uses* this tendency. In *I Sing the Body Electronic*, Fred Moody describes a project at Microsoft where the team agrees to an impossible schedule with an arbitrarily shortened schedule under pressure from Bill Gates himself. Moody concludes: "while giving his employees the means to win he also ensured that they would interpret their victory as defeat. There would be no laurels for them to rest upon; instead they would dive immediately into their next project hoping to redeem themselves." If Moody is right, this strategy might be cold-blooded, it might even be dishonest, but it's hard to argue it's not effective given Microsoft's commercial success.

And many deadlines are set arbitrarily with no actual relation to value, so overrunning the budget is really just missing a meaningless goal, anyway. American President Lines was developing a new computer system to track cargo in the early 1980s. The project got into the usual problems associated with a project in trouble: missed deadlines, cost overruns, and an overall lack of tangible progress. Eventually the manager was fired, and a consultant was interviewed to take over the project. After careful study, the consultant concluded the project was feasible, but that the schedule and budget would need some serious rework. At the meeting where he presented his proposal, the executives were pleased to hear the good news, and asked what modifications he would like. He replied: "Two, Two and Two." What did he mean by that? "Multiply the resources by two and the schedule by two, and divide the features by two." Naturally, pandemonium broke out, but after thing settled down, the executives ruefully agreed to the scheme. The consultant was as good as his word, and indeed delivered half the originally planned system with twice the staff in twice the time. But the results were great, and the system assured APL would be an industry leader for more than a decade. The original estimate had no relation to the eventual value, which was many times the actual cost even after accounting for the underestimate.

Prioritize

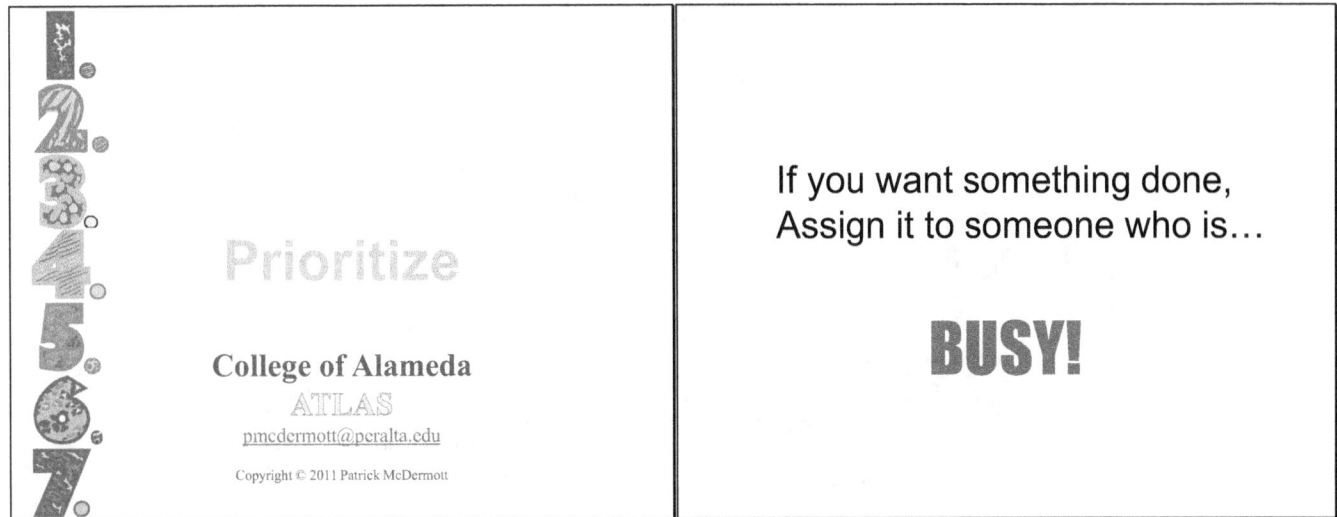

Prioritize

College of Alameda
ATLAS
pmcdermott@peralta.edu
Copyright © 2011 Patrick McDermott

If you want something done,
Assign it to someone who is…

BUSY!

What to Do?

1. The Difficult & the Unpleasant
2. Small × Many ➔ Big
3. Pareto's 80/20 Rule
4. In-Between Time
   - Do Something
   - Plan for it
   - BART to Breaks

Priorities

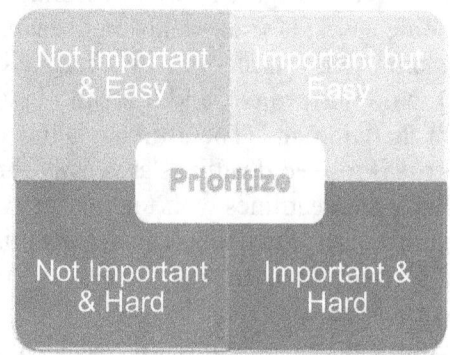

Not Important & Easy	Important but Easy
Prioritize	
Not Important & Hard	Important & Hard

cf. Stephen Covey's Important vs. urgent Time management Matrix

Pareto

- Vilfredo Pareto (1848-1923)
- Pareto Optimality

☞The Vital Few

versus

✋The Trivial Many

The Pareto Principle

- The 80%-20% Rule
- Vilfredo Pareto (1848-1923)
  - Italian Economist
- Income, Employment
- Bugs, Problems
- Input ➔ Output
- Effort ➔ Results
- Causes ➔ Consequences

- Maybe Even 90/10!

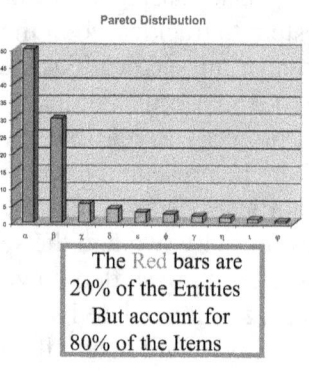

Pareto Distribution

The Red bars are 20% of the Entities But account for 80% of the Items

Pareto Chart of Injuries

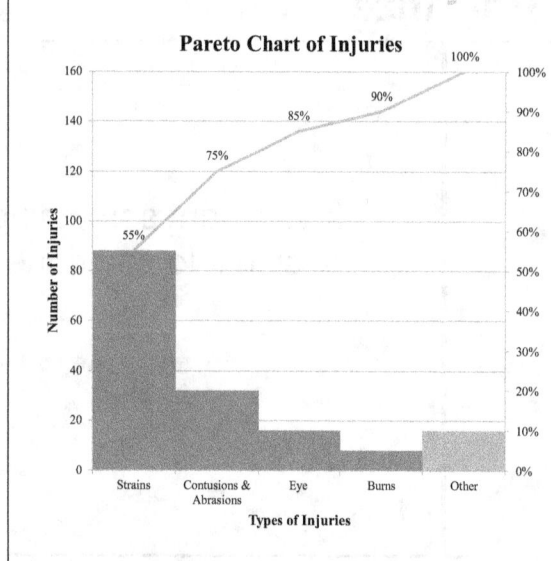

Pareto Chart of Injuries

Injury Type	Number
Strains	88
Contusions & Abrasions	32
Eye	16
Burns	8
Other	16

Project Overview Wizard

	Project Goals	**Description**
Project Overview **University of California** *Berkeley Extension* *pmcdermott@msn.com* **Copyright © 2008 Patrick McDermott** From an AutoContent Wizard 10/27/2007.	• Ultimate goal of project • Relationship to other projects • High-level timing goals	• Describe the project in non-technical terms. • Use following slides for discussing status, schedules, budget, etc. **FOR MORE INFO...** List location or contact for specification (or other related documents) here

Competitive Analysis
 	
• Competitors
  – (You may want to allocate one slide per competitor)
• Strengths
  – Your strengths relative to competitors
• Weaknesses
  – Your weaknesses relative to competitor
	Competitive Analysis, Cont.
	
	• Competitors
	• Strengths
	• Weaknesses
	
	FOR MORE INFO...
	List location or contact for competitive analysis (or other related documents) here
		Technology
		
		• New technology being used
		  – Benefits
		• Standards being adopted
		  – Benefits
		• Standards specifically being ignored
		  – Drawbacks & benefits
		DYA: define your acronyms!

Team/Resources
 	
• State assumptions about resources allocated to this project
  – People
  – Equipment
  – Locations
  – Support & outside services
  – Manufacturing
  – Sales
	Procedures
	
	• Highlight any procedural differences from regular projects of this type
	• Discuss requirements, benefits, and issues of using new procedures
	
	FOR MORE INFO...
	List location or contact for procedures document (or other related documents) here
		Schedule
		
		• Review high-level schedule milestones here
		
		Phase 1 Phase 2 Phase 3
		Jan Feb Mar Apr May Jun July Sep Oct Nov Dec
		
		FOR MORE INFO...
		List location or contact for detailed schedule (or other related documents) here

Current Status	**Related Documents**

• High-level overview of progress against schedule
  – On-track in what areas
  – Behind in what areas
  – Ahead in what areas
• Unexpected delays or issues
	• Marketing plan
	  – Location or contact name/phone
	• Budget
	  – Location or contact name/phone
	• Post mortem
	  – Location or contact name/phone
	• Submit questions
	  – Location or contact name/phone

Proposal
Edward R. Tufte

Edward R. Tufte

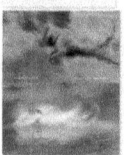

Copyright © 2006 Patrick McDermott

UCB Extension

pmcdermott@msn.com

Tufte, Edward R., *The Visual Display of Quantitative Information, Second Edition*, Cheshire, Connecticut: Graphics Press (0-9613921-4-2), (2001) [1983].

Tufte, Edward R., *Envisioning Information*, Cheshire, Connecticut: Graphics Press (0-9613921-1-8), 1990.

Tufte, Edward R., *Visual Explanations*, Cheshire, Connecticut: Graphics Press (0-9613921-2-6), 1997.

Tufte, Edward R., *Beautiful Evidence*, Cheshire, Connecticut: Graphics Press (0-9613921-7-7), 2006.

Tufte's Seminars

- I was Afraid might Cancel
  - 300 ✕ $360 = $108,000
  - Nothing to Worry about!
- Props
  - Olde Books
  - Space Shuttle Model
  - Dynamic Presenter
- Keep his objections in mind
  - Compensate

Tufte Hates PowerPoint

- Bullets Show
  - Sequence
  - Priority
  - Membership in a set
- Auto Content Wizard
- PowerPoint Phluff:
  - "A preoccupation with Form, not Content"

Chartjunk
- Over-produced layouts
- Cheerleader logotypes & branding
- Corny clip art

Irony: This is a PowerPoint about hating PowerPoint!

Napoleon's Army in Russia

"It may well be the best statistical graphic ever drawn—Edward Tufte"

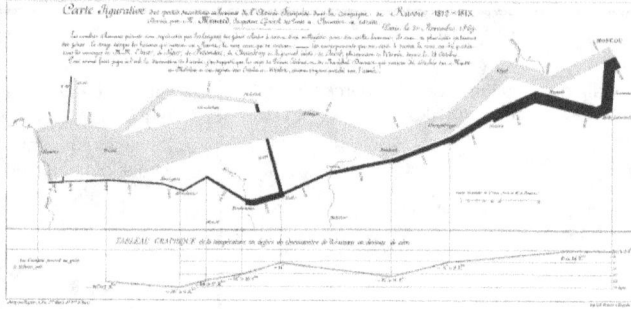

Charles Joseph Minard (1781-1870)
Russian Campaign of 1812, Napoleon's March to Moscow, 1861

In Defense of PowerPoint

Superficial analysis, rambling presentations and incoherent talks did not first appear with the advent of PowerPoint.

Printed versions were not the goal. Since it's available, the presenter shares it. Before PowerPoint, it simply wouldn't have been feasible to share it.

"PP presentations too often resemble the school play: very loud, very slow, and very simple."

- PMcD: Every school play I've ever seen were best described this way: The actors loved it! The students loved it! The parents loved it! The teachers loved it! Everybody loved it, except that grouch Edward Tufte! Frankly, if one of my talks was as successful as most school plays, I'd be delighted!
- Just Ask Disney about High School Musical!

Tufte's Advice

- He contrasts with magicians, and says do the opposite.
  - Magic works by indirection & distraction
  - We want to focus & clarify
- Never Tell Them what You're Going to Do
- Never Repeat Yourself

Why Are We Here?

1. Near the beginning of your presentation, tell the audience:
   - ✓ What the problem is
   - ✓ Why the problem is important
   - ✓ What the solution to the problem is

Jonier Marin, 1994

PGP

2. To explain complex ideas or data, use the method of PGP

Particular to General & back to Particular

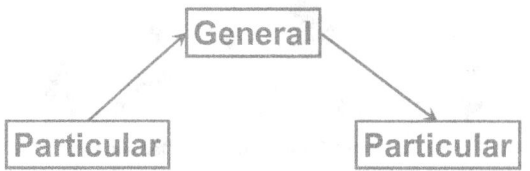

Handouts

3. No matter what, give everybody in the audience one or more pieces of paper, packed with material related to your presentation.

Practice

4. Analyze the details of your presentation; then master those details by practice, practice, practice.

The Earlies

5. Show up early. Something good is bound to happen.
6. Finish early.

Impression-Sunrise
Claude Monet
c. 1872

Instructor's Notes

- Mine are my Instructor Notes
- Head Start on Notetaking
- Take 'em or Leave 'em
- What's wrong with Corny Clip Art?!?

Presentation Tips

Presentation Tips

Copyright © 1999 Patrick McDermott

College of Alameda

pmcdermott@peralta.edu

Know

✓ Know your Audience
✓ Know Yourself
✓ Know your Purpose

Inspirational vs. Instructional

– Inform or Teach?
  - Expository (present information)
  - Narrative (explain a process or sequence)
  - Descriptive (describe)
– Inspire/Motivate
– Persuade (convince with logic and evidence)
  - ALL business presentations should persuade
    – At minimum: I'm good, I should get a raise!

Principles

- Assert Copyright © Year Name

  Copyright © 2010 Patrick McDermott

- Variety is the Spice of Life
- Clarity vs. Precision
  – "A little inaccuracy sometimes saves tons of explanation"—Saki
- Match Formality to the Situation
  – Sales should be *slick*
  – Layoff Notice should not be

How to Make Music

"Mozart is said to have conceived ideas and immediately known how every note would fall in a symphony.

Beethoven, on the other hand, would write a theme and then sit down at the piano and play different variations until he had one he liked just right."

Outline or Bricolage?

1. Stephen J. Gould's Outline [Mozart]
2. Sherry Turkle's Bricolage [Beethoven]
   – Harder to estimate: Chaos→Sudden Emergence
   – cf. Refactoring
- Cary Pepper's Russian Inn: People & Place
- Random re-arrangement
   – It might not matter as much as you think
   – CEOs, Mountain climbers, Tarantino & Juries

 The *bricole* was a medieval machine for throwing stones [Bricks]

How Much Preparation

Ben Franklin (1706-1790)

☐ 5 Minutes
☐ All Day

The key to avoiding *Nervousness*:

Be Prepared

When to Get There

Aim to Arrive at the Presentation Venue

ONE HOUR

Prior to the start time

"Show up early, something good is bound to happen."
—Edward Tufte

The Eyes Have It

- Find some Friendly Faces
  - Center
  - Left Front (or back)
  - Right Back (or front)
- Go for it!
- As you loosen up, find more faces

Never, Ever

Never Ever **Say:**

I Know You can't Read This

Don't Admit Nothin'

- If you make a presentation error, simply correct it.
- Don't accentuate the negative
  - "I forgot to tell you"
  - "I already told you"
  - "I'm really nervous"
  - etc.
- They don't know what you were going to say
  - They won't know you forgot
  - If it wasn't important, forget it!
  - I *always* forget *something*…
- That's my Story
  - & I'm Sticking to it!

Crisp Phrases

- Crows the Count 7; Typist type 5-7 ahead
- G.A. Miller's famous "7 plus or minus 2" hypothesis

$$7 \pm 2$$

- 6 by 6: No more than 6 Bullets of 6 Words

$$6 \times 6$$

- Excessively lengthy and pedantic bullet points are known to correlate negatively with valid comprehensional objectives.
- In other words...

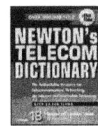

Keep It Simple, Stubid

Newton's Telecom Dictionary
It's not Just for Phoning!

Presentation Techniques

Presentation Techniques

Copyright © 2003 Patrick McDermott

UC Berkeley Extension

pmcdermott@msn.com

A Decision

Will your presentation stand on its own, suitable for use in an unnarrated kiosk, or to be sent to someone who did not attend the actual talk, so that they would understand the presentation completely despite not hearing you present it?

OR

Not there, tuff!

What We Retain

Source	Percent Retained
What we READ	15
What we HEAR	20
What we READ & HEAR	30
What we SEE	30
What we SEE & HEAR	60
What we SAY	70
What we STUDY	75
What we DO	90
What we TEACH	95

From the Institute of Urban Legends.

Content

- Bullets
- ☞ Examples
- " Quotes
- ✉ Charts
- ▓ Graphics
  - Drawings
  - Pictures
- ✂ Clipart
  - Decoration
  - Illustration
  - Anchor the Thought

- Animation
- Flowcharts
- Design Templates
- Sound
  - Sound card, Speakers
- Movie Clips
- Short Subjects

Variety is the Spice of Life. But don't over-season it!

Persuasion

Ronald Reagan: Anecdote Closer then Connect Them

1. Hook
   - Benefit, or Danger
   - Question/Statement
   - Most Dramatic/Humorous Item
3. Line
   - Logical progression from hook to sinker
   - Facts and statistics supporting your idea
2. Sinker: "The Close"
   - The Selling point
   - Call to Action
   - What do you want from Them? Ask!

What to Tell Them

1. Tell them what you're going to tell them.

2. TELL THEM.

3. Tell them what you told them.

- 1 Slide, 6 Slides, 1 Slide
- BUT don't emphasize **structure** over **substance**!

Audience

- Involvement
  - ✓ Get them thinking
  - ✓ Get them moving
- Expectation
- Questions
  - ✓ Interrupt
  - ✓ Save for end

> I hear, I forget.
> I see, I remember.
> I do, I understand.
> —Confucius

Mayer's Redundancy

In his book, *Beyond Bullet Points,* Cliff Atkinson cites Mayer's Redundancy Principle

- "which states that people understand a multimedia explanation better when the words are presented as verbal narration alone, instead of both verbally and as on-screen text".
- He suggests placing only a graphic on the slide, then read from fully written notes
- Note this slide, and my style, is the opposite of Atkinson's advice
- Mayer studied Diagrams & Illustrations!

Notes Pages

- To whom are they directed?
  - Author (Notes to me)
  - Speaker
  - Audience
- It can be a Handout Book
  - Somewhat crude, but effective
  - Ties to your presentation

Storyboard

- A la Hollywood & Madison Ave
- PowerPoint ® Slide Sorter
- Keynote ® Light Table
- Mortar Boards
- Flipcharts
- Whiteboards
- Notecards

- Outline

The Middle Way

- I think of it as making my notes available
  - I need them anyway & can print, so do
  - Head Start on Note Taking
    - NOT a substitute for being there
      - A conscious decision
  - Separate notes don't work for me
    - Reading is too stilted, I prefer spontaneity
- Even Atkison agrees
  - Technical Terms
  - Non-native Speakers

> **Lecture:** A process wherein notes go from a notebook of a Professor to a notebook of a student without passing through the mind of either.

Problems

- One Presentation, Several Versions
  - The familiar clone/synchronization nightmare
  - Many uses for a certain Slide
- `Copy of`, WIP, DIM, HOLD, ERASEME
- `- Copy`, WIP, DIM, HOLD, ERASEME
- Keeping Backup/Source Material Together
  - Quotes
  - Reports & Articles
  - Charts
  - Worksheets, etc.

Stickiness of Presentations, WebPages & Documents

Sticky, *adj.,*
1. Likely to stick in memory.
2. Likely to encourage web surfers to stick (return) to an online attraction, such as a website or blog.

"Stickiness"
University of California
Berkeley Extension

pmcdermott@msn.com

Copyright © 2010 Patrick McDermott

"I once learned a sure-fire memory technique, but I've forgotten it."

Atkinson, Mayer

Atkinson, Cliff, *Beyond Bullet Points: Using Microsoft Office 2007 PowerPoint® to Create Presentations That Inform, Motivate, and Inspire*, Redmond: Microsoft Press (978-0-7356-2387-3 0-7356-2387-2), 2008. [Cliff, not Robert]
Clark, Ruth Colvin & Richard E. Mayer, *e-Learning and the Science of Instruction: Proven Guidelines for Consumers and Designers of Multimedia Learning, Second Edition*, San Francisco: Pfeiffer (978-0-7879-8683-4), 2008.

Mayer's Redundancy

❀ In *Beyond Bullet Points,* Cliff Atkinson cites Mayer's Redundancy Principle
  – "which states that people understand a multimedia explanation better when the words are presented as verbal narration alone, instead of both verbally and as on-screen text".
❀ He suggests placing only a full-sentence headline & a graphic on the slide, then recite from fully written, then memorized, notes.

➢ Note this slide, and my style, is the opposite of Atkinson's advice.

(Clark &) Mayer

Do Not Add On-Screen Text to Narrated Graphics

☞ If you are planning a multimedia program consisting of graphics (such as animation, video, or even static pictures or photos) explained by narration, should you also include on-screen text that duplicates the audio?

☞ Based on research and theory in cognitive psychology, we recommend you avoid e-learning courses that contain redundant onscreen text presented at the same time as onscreen graphics and narration.

Mnemonic

• Mnemonic, named after Mnemosyne
  – The only English word that starts "MN"
    • Column ends that way
• Why is the word that means "Easy to remember" so hard to remember?

Mnemosyne, Mother of the Muses
Calliope, Clio, Erato, Euterpe, Melpomene, Polymnia, Terpsichore, Thalia & Urania
Goddess of Memory & ???????

Dante Rossetti (1828–1882)
Mnemosyne, 1881

Pix to Fix (in memory)

• Memory trick says more bizarre the better
• The Spectrum
  "ROY, Go Bring in Violet!"

♪a ka sa ta ♪ na ha ma ya ♫ ra wa n
♫ あかさた ♪ なはまや ♫ らわん
♪ Sing to Frère Jacques!

• POW List
  – Must re-wind to re-play

"A curious characteristic of many memory systems is that mnemonics work despite being (or possibly because of being) illogical or arbitrary."– Wikipedia

3. Data Dictionaries
CRAM/ERAT Babel

The Sour of Babel
CRAM: Class-Relationship-Attribute-Method
ERAT: Entity-Relationship-Attribute-Trigger

Context	Category	Thing	Connection	Fact	Behavior	Inheritance
CRC Cards	Class	N/A	Collaboration	(Attribute)	Responsibility	Superclass/Subclass
ERD	Entity (Type)	Entity	Relationship	Attribute	N/A *	Supertype/Subtype
Relational	Relation	Tuple	Foreign Key	Attribute	N/A	N/A
Database	Table	Row	Database Key	Column	Service, Procedure	3 Variations
Programmer	Layout, struct, class	Record	Pointer, Array, Containment	Variable	Function()	Base/Derived
UML	Class	Object	Association, Aggregation, Composition	Property	Method()	Generalization/Specialization
Etc., etc., etc..	Type, File, Structure	Occurrence, Instance	Has-a, Set, Pairing, Hierarchy, Parent/Child, Owner/Members	Field, Item, Element	Message, Operation, Algorithm, Trigger, Routine, Subroutine, Process, Macro	Is-a, Extension, Root/Branch/Leaf, Parent/Child, General/Specific

* Behavior in traditional Systems Analysis is tracked in a DFD (Data Flow Diagram)

CRC: Class-Responsibility-Collaborator
ERD : Entity-Relationship Diagram
UML : Unified Modeling Language

"The various OO methods use different (and often conflicting) terminology for these concepts. This is extremely frustrating but inevitable, given that OO languages are just as inconsiderate. It is in this area that the UML will bring some of its greatest benefits...."—Martin Fowler, *UML Distilled*, p. 53.

CRAM/ERAT Babel

CRAM: Class-Relationship-Attribute-Method
ERAT: Entity-Relationship-Attribute-Trigger

College of Alameda
pmcdermott@peralta.edu

Copyright © 2000 Patrick McDermott

Ha!

"The various OO methods use different (and often conflicting) terminology for these concepts. This is extremely frustrating but inevitable, given that OO languages are just as inconsiderate. It is in this area that the UML will bring some of its greatest benefits...."—Martin Fowler, *UML Distilled*, p. 53.

Context or "Camp"

- CRC Cards: Class-Responsibility-Collaborator
- ERD: Entity-Relationship Diagrams
  - SAD: Traditional Systems Analysis & Design
- Relational: Relational Database Theory
- Database: A Physical DB Table
- Programmer: In the Code
- UML: Unified Modeling Language
  - OOAD: Object/Oriented Analysis & Design
- Etc., etc., etc...: Any & All others

Category

- CRC Cards: Class
- ERD: Entity (Type)
- Relational: Relation
- Database: Table
- Programmer: Layout, struct, class
- UML: Class
- Etc., etc., etc...: Type, File, Structure

Thing

- CRC Cards: N/A
- ERD: Entity
- Relational: Tuple
- Database: Row
- Programmer: Record
- UML: Object
- Etc., etc., etc...: Occurrence, Instance

Connection

- CRC Cards: Collaboration
- ERD: Relationship
- Relational: Foreign Key
- Database: Database Key
- Programmer: Pointer, Array, Containment
- UML: Association, Aggregation, Composition
- Etc., etc., etc...: Has-a, Set, Pairing, Hierarchy, Parent/Child, Owner/Members

Fact

- CRC Cards: (Attribute)
- ERD: Attribute
- Relational: Attribute
- Database: Column
- Programmer: Variable
- UML: Property
- Etc., etc., etc...: Field, Item, Element

Behavior

- CRC Cards: Responsibility
- ERD: N/A (it's in the DFD)
- Relational: N/A
- Database: Service, Procedure
- Programmer: Function()
- UML: Method()
- Etc., etc., etc...: Message, Operation, Algorithm, Trigger, Routine, Subroutine, Process, Macro

Inheritance

- CRC Cards: Superclass/Subclass
- ERD: Supertype/Subtype
- Relational: N/A
- Database: 3 Variations
- Programmer: Base/Derived
- UML: Generalization/Specialization
- Etc., etc., etc...: Is-a, Root/Branch/Leaf, Parent/Child, Extension

CRUD

Caspar David Friedrich (1774-1840)
The Stages of Life, c. 1835

CRUD

College of Alameda
pmcdermott@peralta.edu

Copyright © 2008 Patrick McDermott

Create

✓ Required Entries
✓ Default Values
✓ Valid Values
  ? Look up Tables
- Constraints on Relationships
  - Insertion
  - Connection to Parents

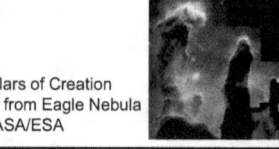

Pillars of Creation
from Eagle Nebula
NASA/ESA

Read

- Find it
  - Pick List
  - Index
  - Key Fields
- See it
- Read Only?
- Reports

Update

Always need, because To Err is Human
  - … but to really mess things up requires a computer
  - Maintenance of facts difficult, expensive
    - School contact: phone, email, snail mail all fail!
  - To Error is Computing

Delete

- Logical Delete
- Deletion of Parents
- Need Record
  - Bad Guy
  - Re-construct

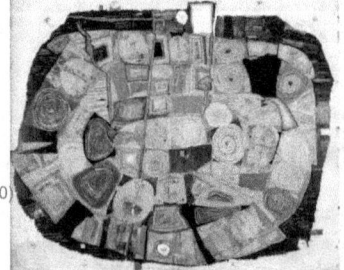

Friedensreich Hundertwasser (1928-2000)
Der Garten der glücklichen Toten
The Garden of the Happy Dead
August 1953

Purge

- Clutter
- Legal
  - If you have it, Produce it!
  - Legal Requirements
    - You SHOULD have it
    - Proof goes both ways!

Frans Hals (c.1580-1666)
Young Man With A Skull
1626-28

Data Dictionaries

Data Dictionaries

College of Alameda
pmcdermott@peralta.edu
Copyright © 1999 Patrick McDermott

One cannot give what one does not have

Nēmō dat qua nōn habet.

One cannot have what one has no place to keep

The Objects

- File ~> Database
- Things ~> Records
- Classes ~> Tables
- Relationships ~> Foreign Keys, Indexes
- Attributes ~> Columns, Fields
- Forms ~> Screens, Dialogs; One, On-line
- Reports ~> Usually: Many, Printed
- Queries ~> → Another Table

Conventions

- Make up your own, then stick to it.
- Table names are singular (except possibly collections)
- Programmers put no spaces in any name
- Short descriptive phrase
- CalledHumpNotation, CamelNotation

Fact

- CRC Cards: (Attribute)
- ERD: Attribute
- Relational: Attribute
- Database: Column
- Programmer: Variable
- UML: Property
- Etc., etc., etc....: Field, Item

Attributes

An attribute or variable or field is a fact about an object. It can hold only one value at a time. Attributes and relationships do not have attributes; if there is a fact to be kept, it is an object in its own right, not an attribute.

Attribute (Field) Properties

- `Identifier` (Name and Primary Key)
- `Data Type`
  - Min, Max or other range
  - Default Value or Algorithm
  - Validation Rule
  - Only Certain Values Allowed?
- `Format`
  - Decimal Places
  - Structure (e.g. phone number, SSN)
- `Required` or `Optional`?

"Repository"

- If it goes beyond data it's a "Repository"
- Zachman framework items, e.g.

MetaData

In human language, "One word can mean more than one thing. This flexibility provides a deep well of nuance and beauty; it is a foundation of poetry. But it leads only to trouble when you are trying to build software."—Scott Rosenberg, *Dreaming in Code*

"Data is, Data are."

I never met a data I didn't like.—PMcD

MetaData

"Data about Data"

College of Alameda

pmcdermott@peralta.edu

Copyright © 1999 Patrick McDermott

One cannot give what one does not have

Nēmō dat qua nōn habet.

One cannot have what one has no place to keep

The Sour of Babel

Camp	Category	Thing	Connections	Fact	Behavior	Inheritance
CRC Cards	Class	N/A	Collaboration	Attribute	Responsibility	Subclass/Superclass
ERD	Entity Type	Entity	Relationship	Attribute	N/A	Supertype/Subtype
Relational	Relation	Tuple	Foreign Key	Attribute	N/A	N/A
Database	Table	Row	Database Key	Column	Service, Procedure	3 Variations
Programmer	Layout	Record	Pointer	Variable	Function	Base/Derived
UML	Class	Object	Association	Property	Method	Generalization/Specialization
Etc., etc., etc...	Type, Structure	Occurrence, Instance	Pairing	Field, Item	Message, Operation, Algorithm, Trigger, Routine	Parent/Child, Is-a, Root/Branch/Leaf, Extension

Illustrates the Metadata obstacle
to the Semantic Web:
We need to call the Same thing
by the Same name,
Different things
by Different names

Pietr Brueg(h)el (the Elder)
The Tower of Babel, 1563

Attribute or Entity?

Attributes Don't have Attributes

Attributes are "OF" a class

Jean Tinguely
Self-Propelled Meta-Mechanical Machine
1954

Object

An object (business object) is a thing the business needs to know about. Classes are groups (classifications) of objects.

In most discussions, "class", "object" and "entity" can be used interchangeably.

In addition to business objects, there are infrastructure objects. During analysis, you should only discuss business (entity) objects.

Attribute

An attribute or variable is a fact about an object. It can hold only one value at a time. Attributes and relationships do not have attributes; if there is a fact to be kept, it is an object in its own right, not an attribute.

An attribute is a piece of information about an object needed in your business.

CRUD: Create, Read, Update, Delete

Attribute (Field) Properties

✓ IDentifier (Name and Primary Key)
✓ Data Type
  – Min, Max or other range
  – Default Value or Algorithm
  – Validation Rule
  – Select Values (Lookup)
✓ Format
  – Length
  – Decimal Places
✓ Required or Optional?

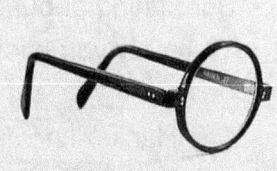

Marcel Marien
That which Cannot be Found, 1937

Class in UML

CLASS

CLASS
Attribute1
Attribute2
Attribute3
Method1()
Method2()

UML: Unified Modeling Language
Associated with "The Three Amigos"
(Spanish: "Los Tres Buddies")
  Grady Booch
  James Rumbaugh &
  Ivar Jacobson

Mnemonics

Mnemonics

College of Alameda
pmcdermott@peralta.edu

Copyright © 2008 Patrick McDermott

Mnemosyne, Muse Mother

- Mnemonic, named after Mnemosyne
  - The only English word that starts "MN"
    - Column ends that way
- Why is the word that means "easy to remember" so hard to remember?

Mnemosyne (*Μνημοσύνη*)
Mother of the Muses
Goddess of Memory & ???????

Dante Rossetti (1828–1882)
Mnemosyne, 1881

Hi!

*I've never seen a purple cow
I never hope to see one.
But one thing I will tell you now:
I'd rather see than be one*

- 🚢 APL Vessels
  - FDR, JFK
  - 321, 213
- ROY & Violet: RO**Y** GBIV
- Frère Jacques & 日本語 Dictionary Order
  - あかさた, なはまや, らわん
- You know the words to *hundreds* of Songs
- How we remember
  - Child Learning Grammar

Password Dilemma

- Easy to remember
- Hard to guess

- Something about Yourself
- That only you know…

- The Hacker knows…

Naming Standards

René Magritte (1898-1967)
The Tomb of the Wrestlers
1961

Naming Standards

College of Alameda
pmcdermott@peralta.edu

Copyright © 2008 Patrick McDermott

Name is Key

- A good name is easy to find!
- Name XL B4 Animate
- Name Controls
- Call it what they call it
  - NOT `AttorneyFirm`

Standardize Abbreviations

- Always or Never Abbreviate
- Singular Name for Entities
- Standard Short Name

Man at arms with a Standard
1483
from A Critical Inquiry into Antient Armour (1842)

Class/Type

- AMOUNT
- UNIT
- CODE
- DATE
- HOUR
- PERCENT
- CONSTANT

- COUNT
- NAME
- NUMBER
- TEXT
- ADDRESS
- TIME
- ID
- etc.

No Trace of Space

- Is you'll be programming, don't put spaces in names, even if they are allowed.
- Break Character: _ or –
  - The_Name or The-Name
- Group [The Name] or "The Name"

Identifiers "Variable Names"

- Long Enough to give a descriptive name
- **caSe SeNsItivE**
- No spaces: break character is underbar _
- No initial numeral: start with letter or _
- **lower_case**
- **UPPER_CASE**
- **HumpNotation** ("CamelCase" "Pascal case")
  - Initial Cap Each Word (no break character)

"If you cannot choose a concise name that expresses a method's task, your method might be attempting to perform too many diverse tasks. It is usually best to break such a method into several smaller methods."—The Deitels

Hungarian

- **typeHungarianNotation**
  - Charles Simonyi, Microsoft via Hungary
  - **type** is:
    - **int**   i- or n-
    - **double**   d-
    - **char**   ch-
    - **string**   s- or str-
    - **bool**   b-
- "conjBut pronI vrbLike nHungarianNotation! qWhat's artThe adjBig nProblem?"—Scott Rosenberg, *Dreaming in Code*

PMcD's Convention

- HumpNotationDescriptiveName
  - Brush, Dialog, etc., need type:
    - **brPurple**
    - **PurpleBrush**   Kernigan: "Use descriptive names for globals, short names for locals."
- Program control variables, such as loop counters, get 1- or 2-character lower-case names, initial of what they track.
- CONSTANTS ARE ALL_UPPER_CASE
- Don't like mine?
  - Choose Your Own, but be consistent!

Nulls: A Show about Nothing

```
bool GotMilk = true
if (GotMilk) // Same as GotMilk==true
    EnjoyCookies("ChocolateChip");
if (!GotMilk) // Same as GotMilk==false
    GoGetMilk();
```

A Show about Nothing

College of Alameda
pmcdermott@peralta.edu

Copyright © 2009 Patrick McDermott

There's No Such Thing as Nothing

- A Space [x20 or d32] is *not* Nothing
- The Numeral zero [x30 or d48] is *not* 0

- When you ask your S.O.* "What's wrong?" and the answer is "Nothing", *it's SOMETHING!*
- When you ask your kid "What are you doing?" and hear "Nothing", *it's NOT nothing!*
- The Rest is (never) Silence

- XL & SQL handle Nulls Unexpectedly...

* S.O. == "Significant Other"

Excel®

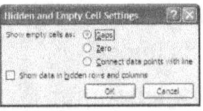

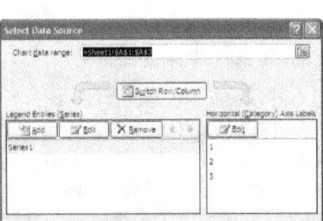

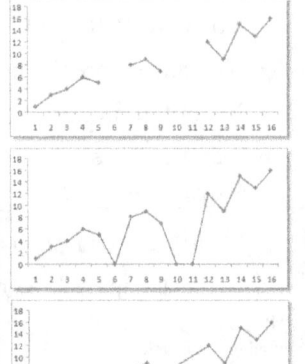

The Meaning of NULL

⊘ Missing
⊘ N/A: Not Applicable
⊘ Don't Know
⊘ Don't Care
⊘ Equals Zero
⊘ Rounds to Zero
⊘ There are None
⊘ There are some, but they total Zero
⊘ It was Left Blank, don't know why

The Null Symbol

The Unkown

Mysteries
? Whereabouts Unknown
? Date of Birth Unknown
? Status Uncertain
? Speaker to be Announced
? TBA: To Be Assigned
? TBD: To Be Determined

? Who wrote Shakespeare??

Customer Name
- We Don't Know
- Has No Name
  - Newborn, Not yet Named
- Unlisted Name
  - Secret Witness
  - Anonymous
  - Keyser Söze
- We Don't Care
  - Enough to Record
  - Enough to Bother
    - APL Port Charges
- Design Error!
- System Error!

Paper Forms

- On a paper form, you can write in an explanation
  - "Don't Know"
  - "Unknown"
  - "Not Applicable"
  - "None of your Business"
- In a computer system, you'll get a type error
- Computers have never been good at accepting text into a numeric variable

Sir System Word

The System Word is 4 bytes == 32 bits long.

As an* historical anomaly, Windows ® calls it a DWORD, short for *double word*, because the System Word used to be 16 bits.

It's used for system addresses, `ints` and `bools`.

The system is built around it, so it's the most efficient size.

1011	1111	0110	1001	0000	0011	1011	1000
Byte 0	Byte 1	Byte 2	Byte 3

* If you're Cockney, My Fair Lady, or a programmer, you'll say it in 'ex—**xBF6903B8**

Put a Hex on It

Because there are 16 combinations, each half-byte ("nybble") can be expressed conveniently (in a single digit) using Hexadecimal representation. 0-9 are expressed as in decimal, 11-15 as A-F.

xBF6903B8

xB	xF	x6	x9	x0	x3	xB	x8
1011	1111	0110	1001	0000	0011	1011	1000

Byte 0   Byte 1   Byte 2   Byte 3

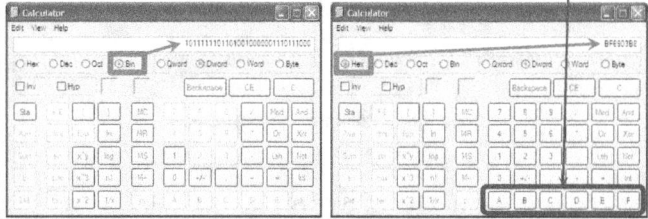

Meet Mr. NULL Ø!

You've probably known someone like this:
ALL ZEROES!!!

x00000000

x0	x0	x0	x0	x0	x0	x0	x0
0000	0000	0000	0000	0000	0000	0000	0000

Byte 0   Byte 1   Byte 2   Byte 3

Alias "Binary Zeroes"; "Low-Values"*; `false`.

* COBOL

Double Reverse Logic

- "It ain't no lie that nothing I don't say is not untrue."
  - Am I telling the Truth?
- No Password
  - The Password is NO PASSWORD
  - Not *any* password, *no* password
  - Not "NO PASSWORD"
    - Enter nothing
    - Who's on First?
    - The password is the Null value
    - The Automaton Typist

Leap Year

```
if (year%4)
    return false;
    // It's NOT a leap year!
```

- `year%4` can return 0, 1, 2, or 3
  - 0 is `false`; 1,2,3 are `true`
  - By definition: 0 ≡ `false`; `true` ≡ `!false`
- "If, when you divide the year by 4, the remainder is not 0, it's not a Leap Year"
- "If there is a remainder when divided by 4, it's not a leap year"

Next Pointer

```
while (pCurrent->pNext)
    pCurrent = pCurrent->pNext;
```

We cleverly (?!?) used NULL to mean there is no item, and NULL is 0, so absent is `false`

"While the next pointer of the Current Item is not NULL, move to the next Item by making the Current Pointer point to the Next Item"

```
if (pFirst != NULL) ...
if (!(pFirst == NULL)) ...
if (!pFirst) ...
```

"If there is no First Pointer"

Object Ontology

The Ontology of Objects in Inheritance

Copyright © 2006 Patrick McDermott

UC Berkeley

Extension

pmcdermott@msn.com

Category

- CRC Cards: Class
- ERD: Entity Type
- Relational: Relation
- Database: Table
- Programmer: Layout, struct
- UML: Class
- Etc., etc., etc....: Type, Structure

Thing

- CRC Cards: N/A
- ERD: Entity
- Relational: Tuple
- Database: Row
- Programmer: Record
- UML: Object
- Etc., etc., etc....: Occurrence, Instance

Set Theory

- Russell's Paradox
  - Where does the set of all sets that do not contain themselves belong?
    - If IN the set, it contains itself so OUT.
    - If OUT of the set, it doesn't so IN.
- Bertrand was depressed for 6 months!
  - Me: like contradictions about Mermaids
  - I do not think the Universe is arranged as Sets

"This method is to define as the number of a class the class of all classes similar to the given class."—Bertrand Russell

How We Think

- How many Definitions go: _____ is a kind of _____ and circle on up....
- Windows Buttons
  - CCmndTarget???
  - Button, Radio, Checkbox
    - C++: All have check attribute
    - C#: Each is Different with appropriate attributes

Driver License at DMV

- Driver['s] License
  - Car, Motorcycle, Truck
  - School Bus: it's not a type of vehicle, it's how the vehicle is used
  - Chauffeur's License
- Often the rules are not made based on a classification; in fact, it's hard to tease out the reasons: "legislative intent"
- Why Chocolate, Strawberry and Vanilla?

Biological Taxonomy

- It is undeniably Useful, BUT
- If inheritance is so natural, why was the work of Linnaeus a breakthrough?
- Nature Doesn't Care
  - Why shouldn't a Mammal lay an egg?
  - Marine Mammals are Kool!

- Period Table Lucky Ignorance
  - Would have been harder if Dmitri Mendeleev knew more

Things That Fly

It's hard to list all things that Fly
It's easy to say whether something Flies

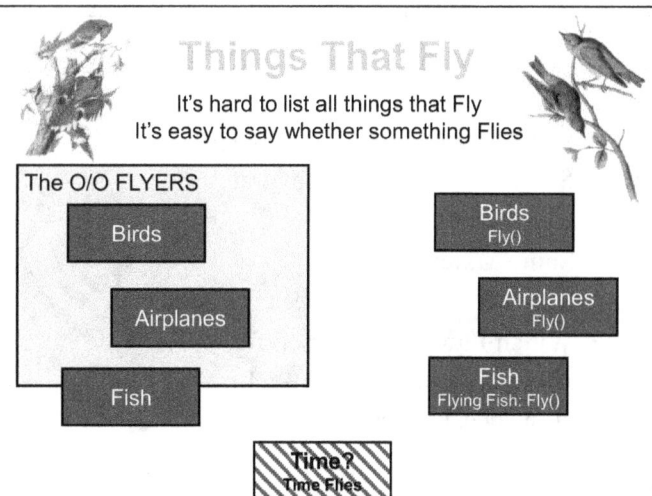

Deitels' School

Aren't Townies Community Members?

Deitels, *Simply C++*, p. 412.

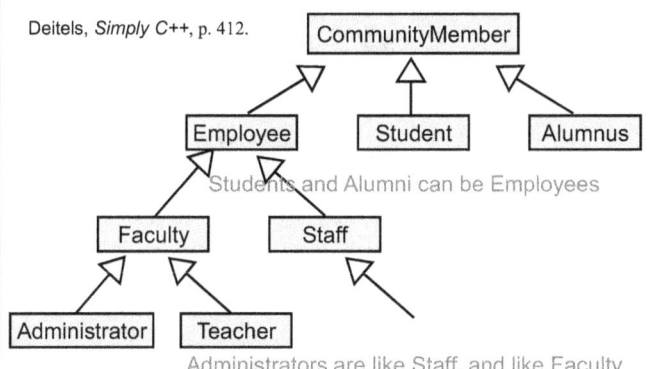

Students and Alumni can be Employees

Administrators are like Staff, and like Faculty

Deitel's

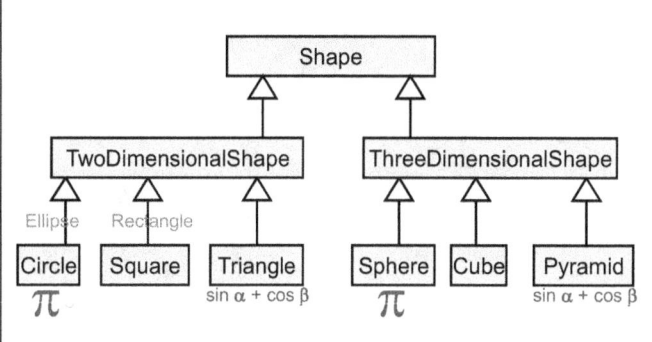

After Deitels, *Simply C++*, p. 413.   Should we exchange levels?

Multiple Inheritance

☹Can be A MESS

- Is possible in C++, But not C# (or Java)
  - Like pointers, removed & called "Improved"
- Is not Advisable to overuse
- But alas, the world does work that way
  - We each belong to many sub-classifications

Foods

Booch OOD, p. 111

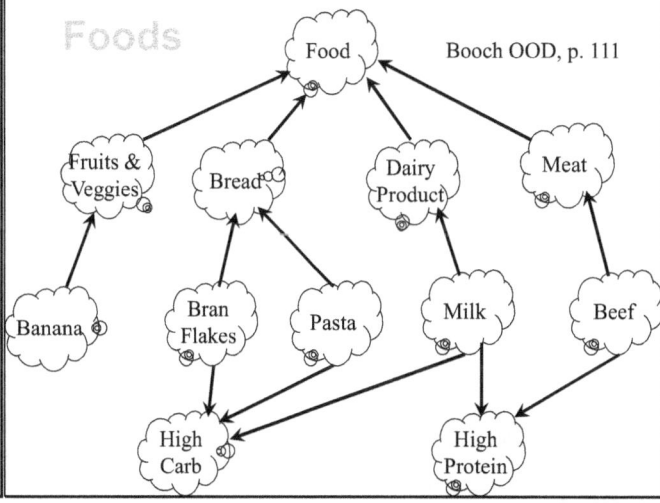

Which Way

- Plane & Solid, or Circle, Square
- Some Foods are Carbohydrates
  - Some CHO are Foods
- Same Males are Students
  - Some Students are Males
- Which Law is More Specific?
  - In Hazardous Material, Food
  - In Food, Poisons?

Payment?

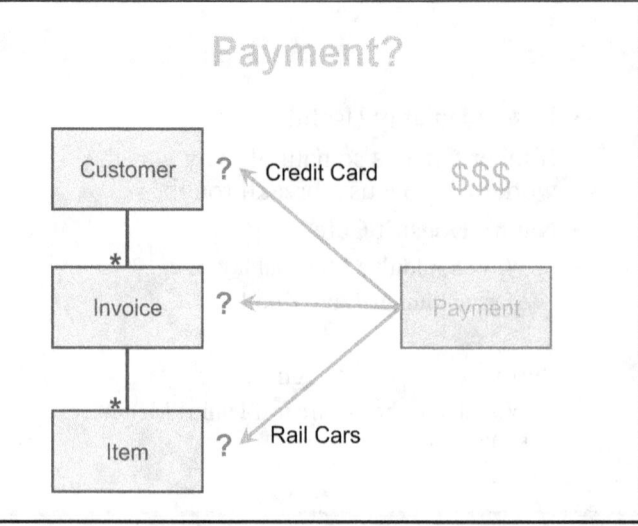

Software Quality

Software Quality

College of Alameda
pmcdermott@peralta.edu

Copyright © 2007 Patrick McDermott

Glass's Quality 7

1. Reliability
2. Usability (Human engineering)
3. Understandability
4. Modifiability
5. Efficiency
6. Testability
7. Portability

Glass, Robert L., *Facts and Fallacies of Software Engineering*, Boston: Addison-Wesley (0-321-11742-5), 2003, pp. 129-131.

➤ Order: "If any two software people agree, they probably constitute a majority. "

Glass: Quality !=

- Quality is *not*:

✓ User Satisfaction
✓ Meeting Requirements
✓ Meeting Cost & Schedule Targets
✓ Reliability

- It goes beyond those

The Great Law of Usability

- Goal: Reduce the Human Memory Load
- A System should be usable
  Without training, assistance or manuals
  By someone who knows the application
  but not the software

- Actually, an Ideal Goal ☺

Constantine, Larry L.
The Peopleware Papers: Notes on the Human Side of Software
Upper Saddle River, New Jersey: The Yourdon Press (0-13-060123-3), 2001.

Problem Solving

- Orderly Progression
  – Step By Step
- Solution by subdivision
  – Divide & Conquer
- Component independence

- Component integrity

- Structural fit
  – Model the World

Model The World

- Reflecting the "natural" structure of the problem domain in software saves us from solving problems that don't need solving.
- Instead of inventing whole new architectures, use the serviceable ones that already exist "out there".
- Software is simply structured the way people already think about the problem
  – Maintenance, expansion, reuse easier

Validation

Data Validation

College of Alameda
pmcdermott@peralta.edu

Copyright © 2007 Patrick McDermott

Quality Control???

GIGO

- Garbage In, Garbage Out
  - ✓ Check Entry after Entry
  - ✓ Restrict to Valid Entries
  - ✓ Warn
- "Editing"
- Standardize
  - – To avoid typing errors, avoid typing
- Consider the Consequences of an Error
- Can you Correct it Programmatically?
  - – Beware Artificial Stupidity

The Quality of system output is no better than the Quality of the input

Type I [α], Type II [β]

- If you decrease one, you will probably increase the other

	Computer says "Right"	Computer says "Wrong"
Right in the World	OK	Type I: **False Positive**
Wrong in the World	Type II: **Miss**	OK

- Bill's *Road Behind*
- Peralta Class Clash

Proper Form

- ✗ Type Errors—wrong Data Type
  - – Humans can Mix, Computers can't
- ✗ Numbers should be Numbers
  - – Appropriate Decimal Places
- ✗ Text should be Text
  - – But `any key` can defeat
  - – Proper Length
- ✗ Default Value
  - – Most Likely
  - ➡ Safest

Check For

- ✓ Required: Presence
  - ✓ Key Field
  - ✓ Critical Field
  - ✓ Can't proceed without it
- ✓ Reasonable Range
  - – Update with Inflation
- Lookup Table
  - – Hard Code `ifs`
  - – Array
  - – DataBase Record

Quality Control

The original meaning of QC:

"As good as it needs to be, and NO BETTER."

- What's a few Bugs between friends?
- Steve Ballmer's $2 million bug cleanup
- Yourdon's "Good Enough" Software
  - ⊘ Zero Defects, ⊘ 6 σ [sigma]

Yourdon, Edward, *Rise & Resurrection of the American Programmer*, Upper Saddle River, New Jersey: Yourdon Press (0-13-121831-X), 1996.

Do Them All!

- Every Last Stinkin' one!

- Try to Get a Rhythm

Bargehaulers on the Volga
Ilya Repin, c. 1870-73

Tedium

- Professional analysts spend much of their time deciding what to validate & how
- Professional programmers spend much of their time validating input
  - ☠Kill Your Patient
  - ⚱Wealthy Janitor
  - ⊗Overpaid PG&E Bill
  - ❓Pregnant Man

The Glass of Absinthe
Edgar Degas
c. 1876

Validation for Programmers

Vincent van Gogh (1853-1890)
The Langlois Bridge
March 1888

Programming
Data Validation

College of Alameda
pmcdermott@peralta.edu

Copyright © 2007 Patrick McDermott

Do Them All!

- <u>Every Last Stinkin' one!</u>

- Try to Get a Rhythm

Bargehaulers on the Volga
Ilya Repin, c. 1870-73

O E O!

Kinds of Garbage

- The Quality of system output is no better than the Quality of the input
- Problems of Type: Wrong type of data
  - Putting Phone Number in Credit Card
  - Text in a Numeric field
- Problems of Quality: Defective data
  - Wrong phone number
  - "Dirty Data"

Keeping Your Data Clean

✓ Restricting the Type of Data in a Field
✓ Restricting the Amount of Data in a Field
✓ Specifying the Format of Data in a Field
✓ Restricting Data by Using Validation Rules
✓ Creating a Simple Lookup List
✓ Creating a Multi-Column Lookup List
✓ Updating Information in a Table
✓ Deleting Information from a Table
✓ Preventing Database Problems

Program Structure

- Check all at Top of Module
  - Defensive Programming?
  - If Error, Report & `return`
- Violates Single-Entry-Single-Exit Rule

- Make Exception to 1E,1X
- Make a Big `if`
- Have Validation `Function()`

How Many Messages

? Just One, or Many?
- Make the Message Clear
  - Avd Mystrs Abrvtns
  - Word from User's Viewpoint

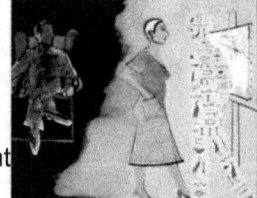

- Suggest Correction
  - Numbered, with Reference?

Joan Brown (1938-1990
The Message, ca. 1977

- Abused children can become abusers
  - Abused programmers write bad messages

Poka Yoke

- The Best Way to fix an Error is to not make it
- Mistake Prevention
  - Prevent the Errors
- Mistake Proofing
  - If you can't prevent all errors, at least catch them

Warnings?

- Compilers: Information, Warning, Error, Fatal
- Warn vs. Block vs. Audit trails
- Provide an Override
  - MoU: Master of Universe
  - POG: Power of a god

Warning! Extreme Danger!

Error Prevention

- Don't Let In
  - Menu, Radio Button, List
  - Look-Up Table
  - The Choice isn't there
  - You need to know all choices
- Let in, then Edit (Don't store)
- Correct Later
  - Report
  - Batch

Edit It

- If no direct use, gets dirty (good econ strategy—it don't matter)
- Warn versus forbid
- Once good, now bad (allow old to remain?)
- Flexible versus accurate
- Type I Type II

Complex Check

✓ Crosscheck Fields

  If Gender == Male, NOT Pregnant

  If Status == In Default, Credit Limit = 0

✗ Stop Error, or Correct it?

Table Maintenance

- If Item Removed
  - Are those on DB invalid
    - or "Grandfathered"
  - If Updated, it will Fail Edit
- If Item Added
  - Is it a split of an existing category?
- Validation Table
  - Are Values in Code, Table, or in UI?
  - Does User or Programmer Update Table?
- How Stable is The List?

Christo & Jeanne-Claude Wrapped Table, 1961

Zen & the Art of Oriented / Objects

René Magritte (1898-1967)
The Prince of Objects
Le Prince des objets
1927

With a tip of the hat to:
Herrigel, Eugen, R.F.C. Hull (translator from German),
Zen in the Art of Archery,
New York: Vintage Books (0-375-70509-0), 1953, 1989
(*Zen in der Kunst des Bogenschiessens*, 1948)

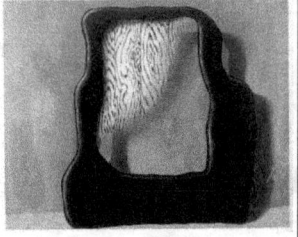

Zen & The Art of Oriented / Objects

College of Alameda

Data Processing

 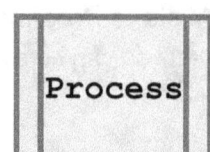

Tear down this Wall!!!

Data

Process

Name is "Pat"
Balance is $110
Payment is $50

Take Pat's Balance;
Subtract the Payment;
Make that the Balance;

Classes & Objects

CLASS: The descriptor for a set of objects that share the same attributes, operations, methods, relationships and behavior. A class represents a concept within the system being Modeled. Rumbaugh [3 Amigos], *Reference*, p. 185.

OBJECT: A discrete entity with a well-defined boundary and identity that encapsulates state and behavior; an instance of a class. Rumbaugh [3 Amigos], *Reference*, p. 360.

Separate the Essence **from the** Instance.

Class

A class is a category of *Things*. An object is one of those things. A instantiation of a class.

Encapsulation
Inheritance $$
Polymorp*hi*SM

Taxonomy is a taxing task:
Is a Grad student an employee?
Is Pluto a Planet?
Is Bill Gates human?

"Class" is perhaps Best defined by Examples...

- Tangible
- Intangible
- Conceptual
  - Cost Center, Account
- People
- Places
- Things
- Events
- Roles
- Organizations

- Collections of Objects
- Interface
  - Form or Dialog
- Infrastructure
  - Date, Money, Address
- Persistence: Database
- Control
- Reference Lists
- Other Systems
- Process
  - Currency Format?

They're Everywhere!

There must be a Class if
✓ ... there's a form
✓ ... there's a file
✓ ... there's a number
✓ ... there are multiple copies
✓ ... It's Important
- NOTE--
  - Sections and boxes on Forms
  - The name might not be obvious

Responsibilities
- Obligation or Contract
- Personification Helps

✓ Know Things
  - Invoice: Know the Customer
✓ Do Things
  - Invoice: Compute Total
✓ Get Organized
  - Abstraction

Class Diagram

Class Diagrams

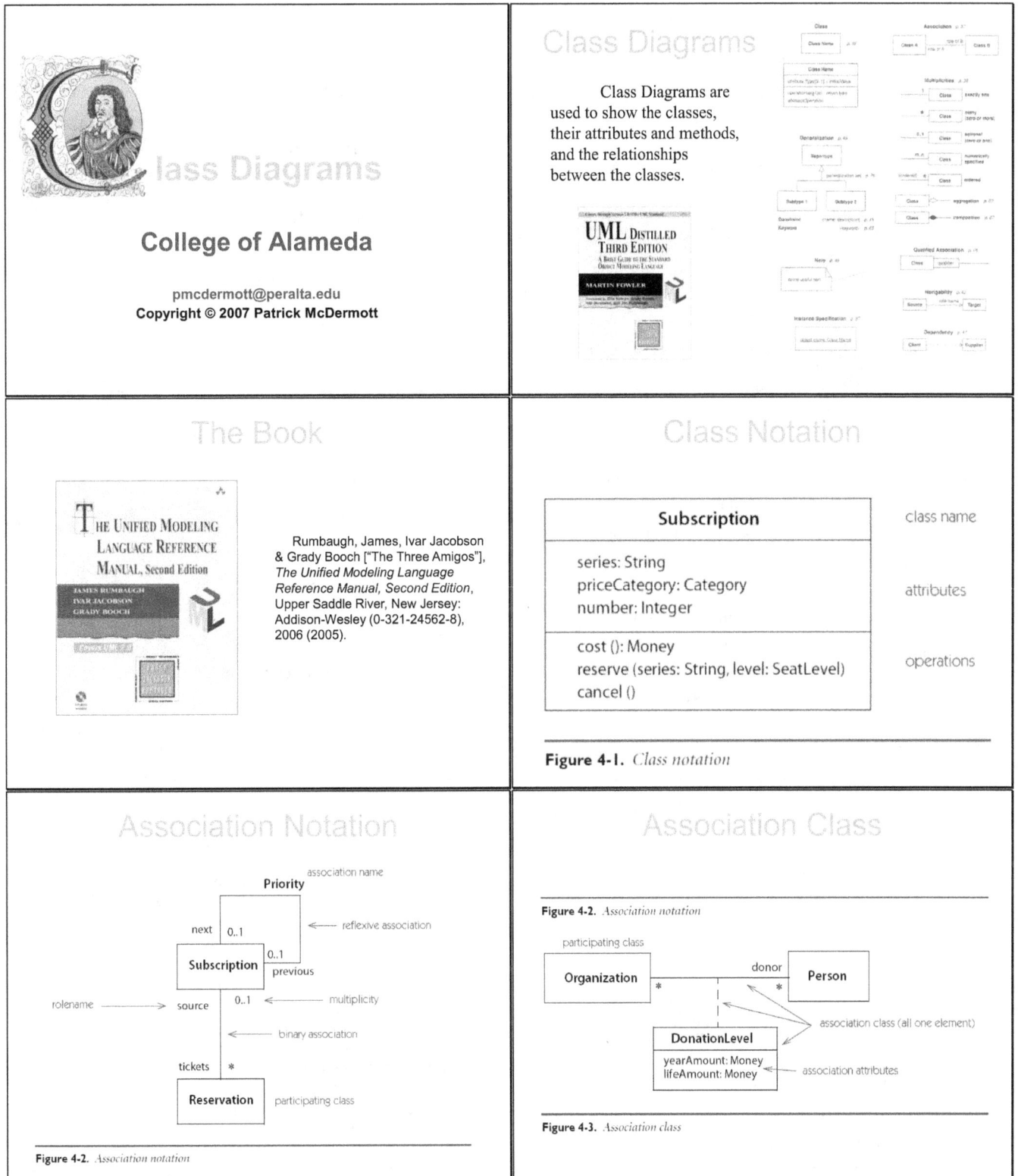

College of Alameda

pmcdermott@peralta.edu
Copyright © 2007 Patrick McDermott

Class Diagrams are used to show the classes, their attributes and methods, and the relationships between the classes.

The Book

Rumbaugh, James, Ivar Jacobson & Grady Booch ["The Three Amigos"], *The Unified Modeling Language Reference Manual, Second Edition*, Upper Saddle River, New Jersey: Addison-Wesley (0-321-24562-8), 2006 (2005).

Class Notation

| Subscription | class name |

series: String
priceCategory: Category
number: Integer — attributes

cost (): Money
reserve (series: String, level: SeatLevel)
cancel () — operations

Figure 4-1. *Class notation*

Association Notation

association name
Priority
next 0..1 ← reflexive association
0..1
Subscription
previous
rolename → source 0..1 — multiplicity
← binary association
tickets *
Reservation participating class

Figure 4-2. *Association notation*

Association Class

Figure 4-2. *Association notation*

participating class
Organization * — donor — * **Person**

DonationLevel
yearAmount: Money
lifeAmount: Money

association class (all one element)
association attributes

Figure 4-3. *Association class*

CRC Cards

CRC Cards

CRC Cards

Class • **R**esponsibility • **C**ollaborator

Copyright © 1999 Patrick McDermott

UC Berkeley

Extension

pmcdermott@msn.com

Although not strictly part of the UML, CRC (Class-Responsibility-Collaborator) Cards are often useful for learning requirements from users.

Class

- A *Thing* the Business needs to know about.
- At this stage, a business person should be able to understand every one of them.
- "Class" is best defined by examples…

Examples of Classes

- Tangible
- Intangible
- People
- Places
- Things
- Events
- Roles
- Organizations
- Other Systems

- Collections of Other Objects
- Conceptual: Cost Center, Account
- Interface: Screen
- Infrastructure: Date, Money, Address
- Persistence: Database
- Control

There Must be a **Class** if…

✓ … There's a file
✓ … There's a form
✓ … There's a number
✓ … There are multiple copies
✓ … It's Important
NOTE—
  – Sections and boxes on Forms
  – The name might not be obvious

They're Everywhere!

Classes have **Responsibilities**

- Personification Helps
  – What if a person, not a computer, does it?
  – Obligation or Contract

- Know Things
  – Invoice: Know who the Customer is
- Do Things
  – Invoice: Compute Total
- Get Organized
  – Abstraction

A Responsibility might use a **Collaborator**

- Some Relationship between two classes
- Another class that assists in fulfilling the Responsibility
  – Has information (Knows something)
  – Helps accomplish the Task
  – No need to List Both Directions (Reverse is implied)
- A verb should connect the two
  • A Customer Pays an Invoice
  • A Student Registers for a Class
- Personification (or messaging) can help
  – The Pathetic Fallacy is Preferred
  – Act Like the class is a Person
  – How was it done B.C.? [Before Computers]

A CRC Card

NAME	
A Responsibility	Collaborator
Another Responsibility	Collaborator
A Great Responsibility	Collaborator

Attributes

- Attributes are <u>facts</u> about classes
- Do not attempt to list all possible attributes
- List only attributes that are
  - Defining
  - Likely to be forgotten
  - Politically Important

- Do not make get/sets for all attributes

A CRC Card Session

1. Prepare the Group
   - Ice Breaker?
   - Choose a scribe
2. Brainstorm Class List
3. ACE it: Add, Combine, Eliminate
4. Make Cards
5. Write Descriptions
6. Brainstorm Responsibilities & Collaborators
7. Review
8. Sketch UML Class Diagram with Cards

Brainstorming Rules

0. Have Fun!!!
1. No Criticism or Debate
2. No Self-Censorship
3. Piggyback

Quantity
not
Quality

Steps

1. Brainstorm
2. Reward
3. Reality Check
4. Fuse & Fission
5. Categorize, Cluster & Combine
6. Select
   Consensus
   Multi-Vote

Purchase Order

A **Purchase Order (PO)** is prepared by a customer and sent to us to order goods or services. The term "Purchase Order" has a special legal meaning under the Uniform Commercial Code (UCC) and implies a huge volume of terms and conditions that are set out in the UCC.

LILY'S LILACS		23259

PURCHASE ORDER

TO MCD, INC.	DATE Oct. 1, 1999
ADDRESS P. O. Box 20689	DATE REQUIRED Oct. 15, 1999
CITY, STATE, ZIP Oakland, CA 94620	TERMS Net 30
SHIP TO Jane Rose	HOW SHIPPED Fed. Ex
ADDRESS 123 A Street	REQ. NO. OR DEPT W328
CITY, STATE, ZIP Alameda, CA 94501	FOR Violet Jones

	QUANTITY	DESCRIPTION	PRICE		UNIT
1	1	Red Widget	8	00	ea
2	2	Widget Oil	3	00	btl
3					
4					
5					
6					
7					
8					
9					
10					
11					
12					

IMPORTANT
PURCHASE ORDER NUMBER MUST APPEAR ON ALL INVOICES-PACKAGES, ETC
PLEASE NOTIFY US IMMEDIATELY IF YOU ARE UNABLE TO COMPLETE ORDER BY DATE SPECIFIED

PLEASE SEND 1 COPIES OF YOUR INVOICE WITH ORIGINAL BILL OF LADING.

PURCHASING AGENT Joe Black

Packing Slip

A PO is technically a legal offer to pay us a certain amount for the goods ordered. We can turn the PO into a contract by accepting the offer. The simplest way to accept an offer is to perform on it, in this case by shipping the goods. We prepare a **Packing Slip** as a record of the shipment.

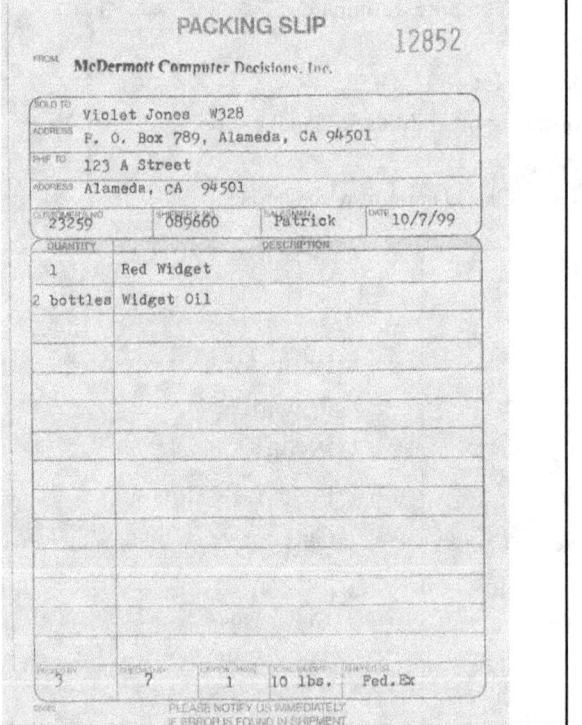

An **Invoice** is a demand for payment. The invoice is sometimes legally necessary but also shows the customer the calculation of the total.

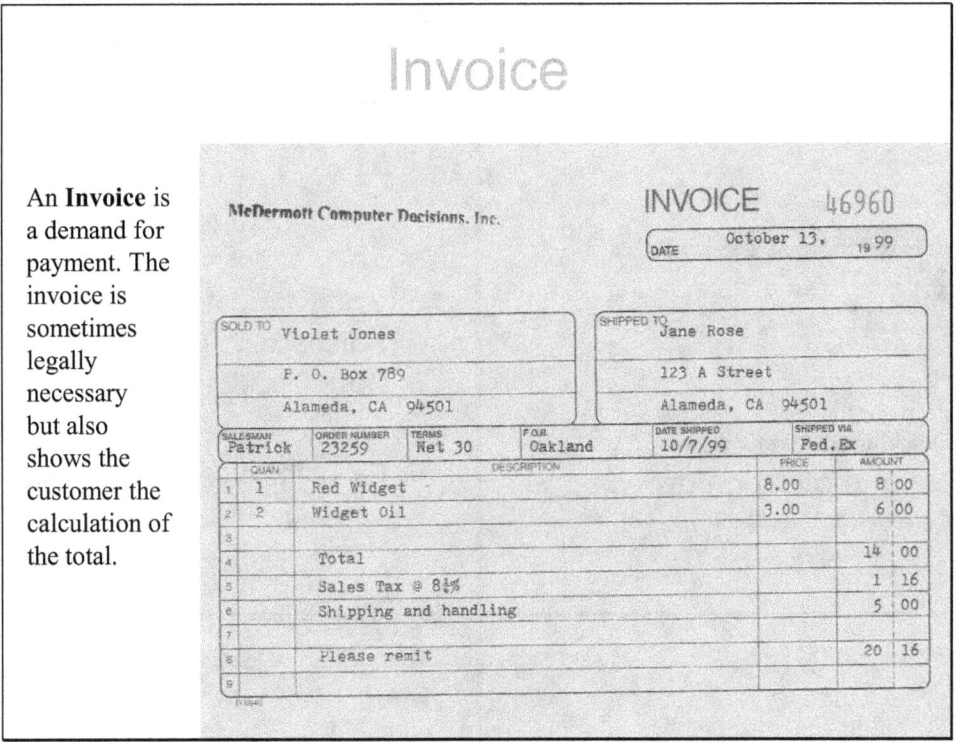

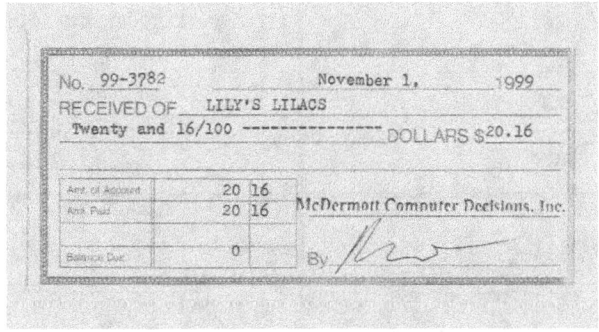

A **Receipt** is acknowledgement of payment. Receipts are usually only prepared when the payment is in cash; in other cases the customer's canceled check serves as the receipt.

Data Types

Data Types

Copyright © 2006 Patrick McDermott

College of Alameda

pmcdermott@peralta.edu

Fact

- ⊷ CRC Cards: (Attribute)
- ⊷ ERD: Attribute
- ⊷ Relational: Attribute
- ⊷ Database: Column
- ⊷ Programmer: Variable
- ⊷ UML: Property
- ⊷ Etc., etc., etc.…: Field, Item, Element

The Rules

- Allowed/Forbidden characters
  - Letters, Numerals, _
  - NO Spaces
    - Break_character: Underscore _
  - No initial numeral
- Length, Very Long
- Case SeNsItiVe
- Cannot be a Keyword (Keywords are Reserved Words)
- ➢ Nouns for Variables/Classes
- ➢ Verbs for Functions/Methods

Numbers, Text & Truth

- Numbers
  - `int` or `double`
- Text
  - `char` or `string`
  - C#: `char` is 2 bytes in C++ `wchar_t`
- Booleans
  - Logical: **true** or **false**.
    - We might not have beauty, but it does have truth.
- Decimal (.NET)
  - ± \$792,281,625,142,643,375,935,439,503.35m
  - ± 79,228,162,514,264,337,593,543,950,335M

2 Kinds of Numbers

Integers	Floating Point
• `int`	• `float`, but use `double`
• A counting number	• A measuring number
• A whole number	• A fractional number
• Discrete	• Continuous
• No fraction	• Fraction
• No decimal	• Decimal
• 2 3 9	• 2½ , 3.14159, 99.99
	• `3.0` too!

Numbers

- Integers: `int`
  - @ 4 billion
  - –2,147,483,648 to +2,147,483,647
    - 0-4.3 billion if `unsigned`
  - Not enough bils for Bill's fortune
- Double-Precision Floating-Point: `double`
  - Range: Big enough
    - You can enumerate all the atoms in the Universe.
  - Precision: at least 15 decimal digits
    - Just enough for \$Trillion to the cent.
    - \$1,234,567,890,123.45
    - Not quite enough for a credit card number

I Declare!

```
string s;
string s = "Hi";
int x = 0;
double x, y;
int x = 0, y = 1;
const int MYNUMBER = 0;
```
The Unchanging `constant`

ALLUPPERCASE or **ALL_UPPER_CASE**
```
extern int SOMEWHERE_NOT_HERE;
```

In compliment `extern`, 'tis not long after
But I will wear my heart upon my sleeve—Iago, *Otello* I.1.

Number versus Character Sort

> Numbers sort by value.
> Text sorts character by character.

#	Raw	Numbers	Text	Text Sort
1	1	1	1	1
2	111	2	11	11
3	2	11	111	111
4	49	17	123	123
5	423	22	17	17
6	11	49	2	2
7	22	111	22	22
8	313	123	313	313
9	17	313	423	423
10	123	423	49	49

You can be richer than Bill Gates!
As text, $9 is greater than $80,000,000,000!
So, just keep $9, and sort net worth as text!

As numbers, one & two & three are binary 1 and 10 and 11.
As text, 1 & 2 & 3 are ASCII characters 49 & 50 & 51.

Precision

- Values of type `float` have seven digits of precision.
- Values of type `double` have 15-16 digits of precision.
- Values of type `decimal` are represented as integer values that are scaled by a power of 10. Values between -1.0 and 1.0 are represented exactly to 28 digits.

Size not Standard

Type	Size
char, unsigned char, signed char	1 byte
short, unsigned short	2 bytes
int, unsigned int	4 bytes
long, unsigned long	4 bytes
float	4 bytes
double	8 bytes
long double	8 bytes

> Each computer system is different.
> Types are based on the system Word.
> We are on a 32-bit (4-byte) system,
> So `int` is a word (4 bytes),
> `double` is 2 words (8 bytes)…

The incredible Growing `int`

C Standard for `int`:
The `short` must not be longer than the `int`
The `long` must not be shorter than the `int`

Windows 3.11
(and earlier)
The 16-bit Windows
A 2-byte system word

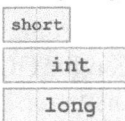

| short |
| int |
| long |

Windows 95
(and later)
The 32-bit Windows
A 4-byte system word

| short |
| int |
| long |

Alphanumeric Text **String**s

- Single character or a string of characters?
  - `'a'` is the single character known as a
  - `"a"` is a character string consisting of the letter a
- A C string is actually a null-terminated array
  - It needs a space for the null (binary zeroes)
  - `"a"` is 2 characters long: a + null
    - lpsz "long pointer to a null-terminated string" [yuck!]
- String Theory
  - Strings have been a sore point, with me & others
  - Unnecessarily overcomplicated
  - *What were they thinking*???

Data Names

René Magritte (1898-1967)
The Voice of the Absolute
1955

Data Names

College of Alameda
pmcdermott@peralta.edu

Copyright © 2006 Patrick McDermott

If you can't *Name* it
You don't *Understand* it!

"If you cannot choose a concise name that expresses a method's task, your method might be attempting to perform too many diverse tasks. It is usually best to break such a method into several smaller methods."—The Deitels

---

Identifiers "Variable Names"

- Long Enough to give a descriptive name
- caSe SeNsItivE
- No spaces: break character is underbar _
  - "a discussion on the placement of braces within a function or whether to use an underscore within variable and type name (the infamous isRight versus is_right debate)."—Stanley Lippman
- No initial numeral: start with letter or _

   lower_case   UPPER_CASE

HumpNotation ("CamelCase" "Pascal case")
   - Initial Cap Each Word (no break character)

---

1 Rose (Windows, VB), or 16 Roses (Unix, Cˣˣ)?

1. ROSE   9. rOSE
2. ROSe   10. rOSe
3. ROsE   11. rOsE
4. ROse   12. rOse
5. RoSE   13. roSE
6. RoSe   14. roSe
7. RosE   15. rosE
8. Rose   16. rose

Pierre-Auguste Renoir (1841–1919)
Les Roses dans un Vase, c. 1910–17

Windows is Case Insensitive; Unix (including C) is Case Sensitive
Visual Basic is Case Insensitive; The C family is Case Sensitive

---

Mnemonic

- Mnemonic, named after Mnemosyne
  - The only English word that starts "MN"
    - Column ends that way
- Why is the word that means "easy to remember" so hard to remember?

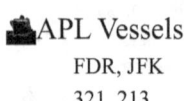APL Vessels
   FDR, JFK
   321, 213

Mnemosyne, Mother of the Muses
Goddess of Memory & ???????

Dante Rossetti (1828–1882)
Mnemosyne, 1881

---

t for Throwaway

- "Use a Set of Standard Names for 'Throwaway' Variables and Parameters"
  - Loop indices i, j, k (yuck!)
  - String s
  - Exception e or ex [y not x?]
- Name according to meaning not type BUT exception for GUI controls, often need to know/distinguish Textbox, Combo, Radio

<table>
<tr><td>

Hungarian

`typeHungarianNotation`

    • Charles Simonyi, Microsoft via Hungary

`type` is:

`int`	`i…` or `n…` `iCount`
`double`	`d…` `dCalculated`
`char`	`ch…` `chGrade`
`string`	`s…` or `str…` `sText`
`bool`	`b…` `bIsItTrue`

"conjBut pronI vrbLike nHungarianNotation! qWhat's artThe adjBig nProblem?"—Scott Rosenberg, *Dreaming in Code*

</td><td>

PMcD's Convention

• HumpNotationDescriptiveName
  – Brush, Dialog, etc., need type:
    • `brPurple`
    • `PurpleBrush`   Kernigan: "Use descriptive names for globals, short names for locals."

• Program control variables, such as loop counters, get 1- or 2-character lower-case names, initial of what they track.

• CONSTANTS ARE ALL_UPPER_CASE

• Don't like mine?
  – Choose Your Own, but be consistent!

</td></tr>
</table>

Data Types in Win32

The table lists the amount of storage required for fundamental types in Microsoft C++.

Table Sizes of Fundamental Types

Type	Size
char, unsigned char, signed char	1 byte
short, unsigned short	2 bytes
int, unsigned int	4 bytes
long, unsigned long	4 bytes
float	4 bytes
double	8 bytes
long double[1]	8 bytes

1 The representation of **long double** and **double** is identical. However, **long double** and **double** are separate types.

Data Types .NET

Type	Low	High
bool	false	true
char	\u0000 (0, null)	\uFFFF (65,535)
byte	0	255
sbyte	-128	127
short	-32,768	32,767
ushort	0	65,535
int	-2,147,483,648	2,147,483,647
uint	0	4,294,967,295
long	-9,223,372,036,854,775,808	9,223,372,036,854,775,807
ulong	0	18,446,744,073,709,551,615
float	Magnitude:	$1.40129846432481707E-45$ to $3.4028234663852886E+38$
	Positive 0.000 000 000 000 000 000 000 000 000 000 000 000 000 000 000 000 001 401 298 464 324 817 07	
		340,282,346,638,528,860,000,000,000,000,000,000,000
	Negative -340,282,346,638,528,860,000,000,000,000,000,000,000	
		-0.000 000 000 000 000 000 000 000 000 000 000 000 000 000 000 000 001 401 298 464 324 817 07
double		
	Positive 4.94065645841246544E-324 to 1.7976931348623157E+308	
	0.000 000 000 000 000 000 000 000 000 000 000 000 000 000 000 000 000 000 000 000 000 000 000 000 000 000 —	
	000 000 000 000 000 000 000 000 000 000 000 000 000 000 000 000 000 000 000 000 000 000 000 000 000 000 —	
	000 000 000 000 000 000 000 000 000 000 000 000 000 000 000 000 000 000 000 000 000 000 000 000 000 000 —	
	000 000 000 000 000 000 000 000 000 000 000 000 000 000 000 000 000 000 000 000 000 004 940 656 458 4124 65 44	
		179,769,313,486,231,570,000,000,000,000,000,000,000,000,000,000,000,000,000,000,
		000,000,000,000,000,000,000,000,000,000,000,000,000,000,000,000,000,000,000,000,000,000,
		000,000,000,000,000,000,000,000,000,000,000,000,000,000,000,000,000,000,000,000,000,000,
		000,000,000,000,000,000,000,000,000,000,000,000,000,000,000,000,000,000,000,000,000,
		000,000,000,000,000,000,000,000,000,000,000,000,000,000,000,000,000,000,000,000
	Negative -1.7976931348623157E+308 to -4.94065645841246544E-324	
decimal		
	Positive 0.000 000 000 000 000 000 000 000 000 000 100	
		79,228,162,514,264,337,593,543,950,335
	Negative -79,228,162,514,264,337,593,543,950,335	
		-0.000 000 000 000 000 000 000 000 000 000 100

COBOL Picture Clauses

Character	Description
A	Alphabetic character (A-Z, a-z, or blank)
B	Blank (space) character
CR	Sign indicator ('CR' if negative, blanks if positive)
DB	Sign indicator ('DB' if negative, blanks if positive)
E	Floating-point exponent
G	Double-byte (DBCS) graphic/alphanumeric character
N	Double-byte (DBCS) character
P	Implied scaling digit (not displayed)
S	Implied sign (not displayed)
V	Implied decimal point (not displayed)
X	Any character, alphabetic, numeric, or other symbols
Z	Numeric digit, but leading-zero-suppressed (replaced by a blank when equal to zero)
0	Inserted '0' digit
9	Numeric digit (0-9)
/	Inserted '/' character
,	Inserted digit group separator[2]
.	Inserted decimal point[2]
+	Sign ('-' if negative, '+' if positive)
-	Sign ('-' if negative, blank if positive)
$	Floating currency sign (blank for leading zeroes, '$' to the left of the most significant digit, otherwise digit 0-9)
*	Floating digit fill ('*' for leading zeroes, otherwise digit 0-9)

4. System Development Life Cycle
The Zachman Framework

People	Data	Activities	Networks	Technology

Zachman Framework

The University of California

Berkeley Extension
pmcdermott@msn.com

Copyright © 2008 Patrick McDermott

Classification Troubles

- Generates a lot of documentation, due to its completeness, which can be difficult to digest and sometimes of questionable utility
- In practice, one can ask how every question (why, what, how…) is related to every ingredient (data, function…).
- The questions are by no means as objective as they appear; one person's *how* is another person's *what* is another person's *why*.
- The rows conflate perspective with idealisation, allowing for the definition of each perspective (enterprise, system and technology) at each level of abstraction (high level, medium level and excruciating detail).

6 by 6

- Communication Interrogatives
  - What, How, Where, Who, When, and Why
- Stakeholder Groups
  - Visionary, Owner, Designer, Builder, Implementer, and Worker

Building Blocks

- People
- Data
- Activities—Biz or Systems Processes & Activities
- Networks—Geography or Networks
- Technology

People

People

1. System Owners
2. System Users
3. System Designers
4. System Builders

User View of Self

People

1. Executive Managers
2. Middle Managers
3. Project & Team Leaders/Supervisors
4. Technical & Professional Workers
5. Clerical Workers

- No Blue Collar???

Data

1. Business resources
2. Data requirements
3. Computer files & databases
4. Data programs

Activities

1. Functions
2. Business processes
3. Computer processes
4. Computer applications programs

Activities: Applications

1. Office automation
2. DSS / Expert systems
3. EIS
4. MIS

Networks

1. Geography
2. Business networks
   – aka Logistics Network
3. Computer networks
4. Network programs

Technology

1. Information Technology
2. It's the base, matches each of the other 4
   – Data Technology
   – Processing Technology
   – Communications Technology
   – Technical Specialists

Levels of Analysis

Purpose	Requirements	Specification	Implementation
Activity	Analysis	Design	Coding
Need	Business Need	Programmer's Need	User's Need

Entities	Subject Areas	Entities	Tables
Relationships	Plain Old Relationships	Generalizations	Aggregations
Multiplicity	Cardinality	Optionality	Implementational
Many-to-Many	Many-to-Many Okay	Many-to-Many Suspect	Many-to-Many Forbidden

Attributes	Defining Attributes	Attributes Detailed	Variables Detailed
Attributive Classes	No Attributive Classes	Detail	De-Normalize?
Normalization	Only Major Subjects	Normalize 3NF	De-Normalize?

Use Cases	Diagram	Scenarios	Test Cases
Methods	Major Responsibilities	Use Cases Detailed	Functions Written

If	What if	I wonder if	No ifs
Concern ... ... versus	What is vs. ... ... what must be	What is vs. ... ... what could be	What you need vs. ... ...what you want

House Analogy...

Artifact	Architect's Drawing	Blueprint	The House
Need	Builder	Contractor	Homeowner

SDLC

Salvador Dali (1904-1989)
Old Age, Adolescence, Infancy
(The Three Ages), 1940

The System Development
Life Cycle

Copyright © 1999 Patrick McDermott

UC Berkeley

Extension

pmcdermott@msn.com

Eleven Stages for an Evolutionary Circumbulation

Pancho Quilici, Eleven Stages for an Evolutionary Circumbulation, 1988.

💡 Light Reading 💡

 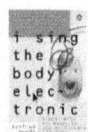  

Zachary, G. Pascal, *Showstopper: The Breakneck Race to Create Windows NT and the Next Generation at Microsoft*, New York: The Free Press (0-02-935671-7), 1994.

Moody, Fred, *I Sing the Body Electronic: A Year with Microsoft on the Multimedia Frontier*, New York: Penguin Books (0-14-017655-1), 1995.

Kidder, Tracy, *The Soul of a New Machine*, Boston: Little, Brown (0-316-49197-7), 1981.

Rosenberg, Scott, *Dreaming in Code: Two Dozen Programmers, Three Years, 4,732 Bugs, and One Quest for Transcendent Software*, New York: Crown Publishers (978-1-4000-8246-9), 2007.

Phases of a Development Project

Feasibility — Analysis — Design — Construct — Launch

System Life Cycle

"Waterfall"

$$Feasibility$$ — $$\$\$ Funding$$

Analysis — Requirements

Design — Specifications/ Prototype

Code

Test — System

Install

Maintenance

Thomas Wolfe was right:
You can't go
Home Again

System Life Cycle

Glass, Robert L.,
Facts and Fallacies of Software Engineering,
Boston: Addison-Wesley (0-321-11742-5), 2003.

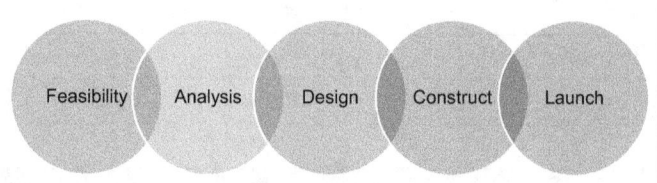

Facts and Fallacies of
Software Engineering

Robert L. Glass

Maintenance consumes 40-80%, average 60% of software costs.

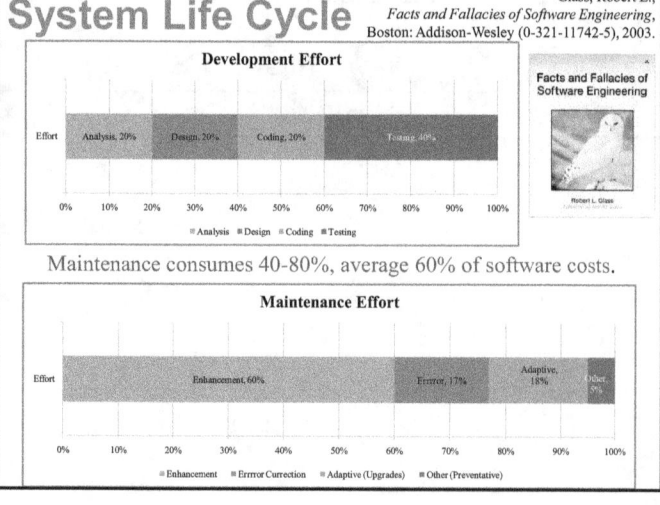

Staffing Over the Cycle

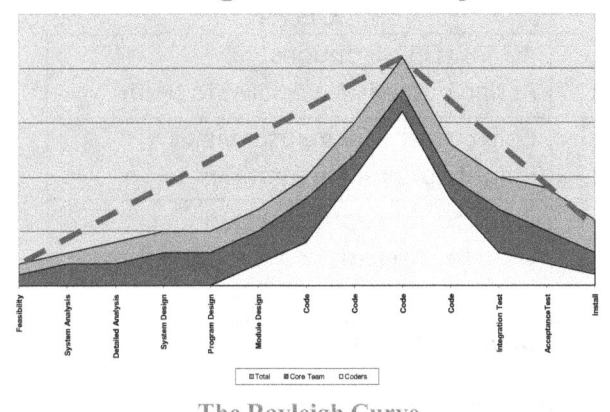

The Rayleigh Curve

The Boehm Curve
Cost to Fix a Bug

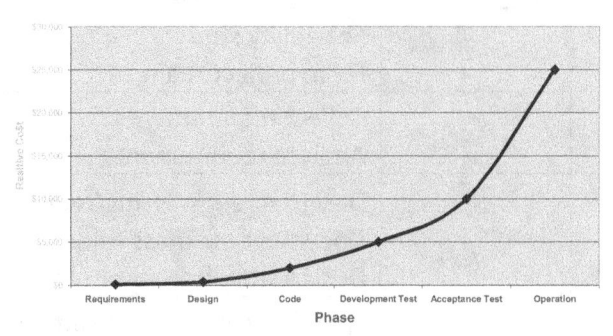

Sashimi

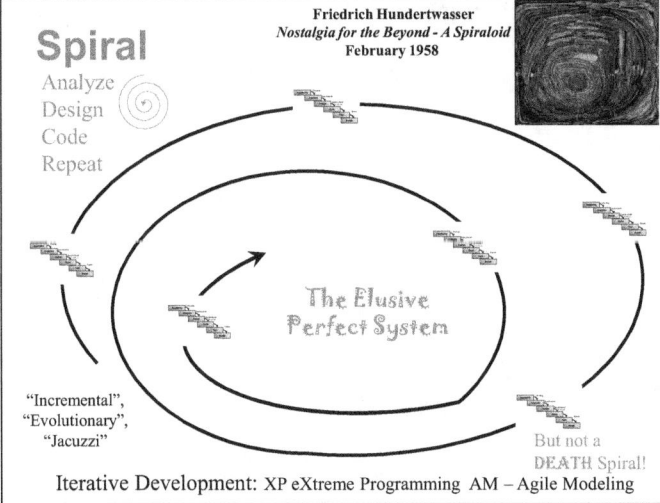

Go!
Analysis
Design
Prototype
Code/Test
Install

Nonaka Ikujiro & Nishiguchi Toshihiro (editors), *Knowledge Emergence: Social, Technical, and Evolutionary Dimensions of Knowledge Creation*, Oxford: Oxford University Press (0-19-513063-4), 2001. Takeuchi Hirotaka & Nonaka Ikujiro "The New New Product Development Game" *Harvard Business Review*, January-February 1986. Reprint 86116.

Rotoreliefs

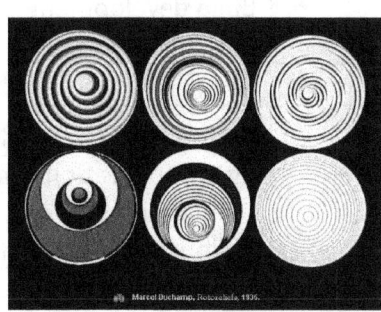

Marcel Duchamp, 1935

Spiral

Friedrich Hundertwasser
Nostalgia for the Beyond - A Spiraloid
February 1958

Analyze
Design
Code
Repeat

The Elusive
Perfect System

"Incremental",
"Evolutionary",
"Jacuzzi"

But not a
DEATH Spiral!

Iterative Development: XP eXtreme Programming AM – Agile Modeling

Wheels within Wheels

Programmers & DBAs in the SDLC

Phase	Programmer/Analysts	DBAs
Feasibility	Feasibility study Form project team	Review DBMS options Assign database specialist to team
Analysis	Collect requirements Analyze requirements	Collect and analyze user views Identity preliminary entities
Design	Design screens/forms/reports Document business rules Design story boards or screen flows	Develop conceptual data model Update enterprise conceptual model
	Specify logical system software Specify logical hardware	Develop logical data model Perform normalization
	Specify physical system software Specify physical hardware	Physical database design
Code	Construct application software Build development & test environments	Create development & test databases
Test	You'd Better!!!	Test any required data conversion
Install	Create production environment Install application components Train users Rollout to users	Create production databases Perform required data conversion
Maintenance	Respond to reported problems Apply mandated changes Respond to change requests	Database performance tuning Database software patches Schema changes to support application changes

The Analyst through the SDLC

Phase	Particular strength, Greatest contribution	The Particular Dangers
Feasibility		
	Look at tech & Business	Analysis Paralysis
	Scopes, milestones ROI, intangibles	
Analysis		
	Domain expertise	Too close to subject, biased
	Narrow the Scope	Written is Bible, Rigidity
	Documentation, living breathing used	Analysis Paralysis
	Perspective on the Lunacy	
Design		
	Technology support business	Not aware of all requirements
	Understand tech constraints & Capabilities	No user like an end user
	Independence	Inflexible, design s/b enhanceable maintainable
	Plain Brilliant	
Coding		
	Business expertise to programmers	Only as good as the prior analysis
	Resource for programmer	Can't communicate/not same language
	Interface with multiple groups	Meet reality
	Navigate and Audit Design	Lose detachment
	Head problems off	
Testing		
	Best to audit results, analyze good or bad	You believe you know it all, incorrectly
	Assist users in test scripts (repeatable)	Lose detachment
	Detachment	Not Black Box
Implementation		
	Compare before and after	Flaws
	Training	Sell current
	Multiple user groups, analyze	
	Plan for enhancements	
	Sell current, plan future	

5. Prototyping
Analytical Anomalies

Analytical Anomalies

Copyright © 2007 Patrick McDermott

College of Alameda

pmcdermott@peralta.edu

Ben Franklin

- He had a 50-50 Chance, and he blew it
  - "Negative" should have been "Positive"

- Don't waste brain cells on things that can only go 2 (or few) ways

Romeo & Ethel the Pirate's daughter

Henslowe: "Strangely enough, it all turns out well."
Shakespeare: "How?"
Henslowe: "I don't know—It's a mystery."

Ψ PseudoCode

- For Quick Thought
- For Communication
- Think before you Code
- Get it down before you forget it!

- Mick Jagger: Don't try to Rhyme while writing a song

First Edition

A Society of Gentlemen in Scotland, *Encyclopædia Britannica; or, A Dictionary of Arts and Sciences, Volume I: A-B; Volume II: C-L; Volume III: M-Z*, Edinburgh: Colin Macfarquhar / A. Bell & C. Macfarquhar, 1771.

Why is this Crane Articulated?

Programming Principles

Programming Principles

Copyright © 2007 Patrick McDermott

College of Alameda

pmcdermott@peralta.edu

Go For It

"Always make fresh mistakes"—Esther Dyson

Don't let not knowing what you're doing stop you

– I never have!

– The Beauty of Clouds

• Show you know what you don't know

"The corollary of constant change is ignorance. This is not often talked about: we computer experts barely know what we're doing. We're good at fussing and figuring out. We function well in a sea of unknowns. Our experience has only prepared us to deal with confusion. A programmer who denies this is probably lying, or else is densely unaware of himself."—Ellen Ullman, *Close to the Machine*

Boilerplate

• Just Get Used to Ambiguity

• Over Time, Learn Little by Little

• I Always have Some question or problem in the Back of the Mind
  – How Do You do that?
  – There Must be a Better Way!

Stochastic Methods

David Parnas: "Programming is a trial-and-error craft. People write programs without any expectation that they will be right the first time."

– He used this as an argument against "Star Wars", the Strategic Defense Initiative, since the first real test is the real thing

Positive Procrastination

• The Difficult & the Unpleasant

• "Always defer details as long as you can."—*H1st OOA&D*

• "Sometimes the way to write great code is to hold off on writing code as long as you can."—*H1st OOA&D*

Confidence

Raymond, *Cathedral & Bazaar*: "You also have to develop a kind of faith in your own learning capacity—a belief that even though you may not know all of what you need to solve a problem, if you tackle just a piece of it and learn from that, you'll learn enough to solve the next piece—and so on, until you're done."

I have that confidence, but I don't know how you develop it. For one thing, it must be true, at least most of the time.

It Probably Didn't Check

The machine wasn't smart enough to let you do it:
 It was dumb enough: It didn't check.
Maybe Manet didn't check the reflection
 He moved the reflection twice (x-rays show)

A Bar at the Folies-Bergère
Édouard Manet (1832-1883)
1881-82

Clutter

- The Clutter Effect
  - IRS: If You have it, we can hold it against you
- Real Estate
  - Get as much Real Estate as You Can
  - White Space
- Remove what's No Longer Needed
- Pretty Print

 Fowler, Martin with Kent Beck, John Brant, William Opdyke & Don Roberts, *Refactoring: Improving the Design of Existing Code*, Reading, Massachusetts: Addison-Wesley (0-201-48567-2), 2001 (2000).

- Refactor

Seat Belts, or Handcuffs?

　　The biggest debate in language design is probably the one between those who think that a language should prevent programmers from doing stupid things, and those who think programmers should be allowed to do whatever they want. Java is in the former camp, and Perl in the latter. (Not surprisingly, the DoD is big on Java.)
　　Partisans of permissive languages ridicule the other sort as "B&D" (bondage and discipline) languages, with the rather impudent implication that those who like to program in them are bottoms. I don't know what the other side call languages like Perl. Perhaps they are not the sort of people to make up amusing names for the opposition.

Graham, Paul, *Hackers & Painters: Big Ideas from the Computer Age*, Sebastopol, California: O'Reilly (0-596-00662-4), 2004, p. 151.

Eat Your Own Dogfood

- Microsoft
  - Word ® team uses Word-under-development whenever such a product is needed: memos, white papers, etc.
  - Visual Studio Team must use VS to develop VS
- In normal practice, not fully Practical
  - I don't do A/P or Load Ships
  - Could include Not having super-Duper computers
    - Display sizes, clarity not available for (some) users
    - Faster than users
  - Webpage development, always use your own links

Lazy == Good

A Good Programmer…

…is a Lazy Programmer

Why did John Backus Develop Fortran?

"Much of my work has come from being lazy."

Critique Yourself

- "One of the hardest things you will ever do is let go of mistakes you made *in your own design*."
- It's <u>HARD</u> to change something you thought was working.
- Pride kills good design: "Design is <u>iterative</u>… and you have to be willing to <u>change your own designs</u>, as well as those you inherit from other programmers."
- The more you invest in a mistake the less willing you are to admit it.

Bad Experience is Good

"Most good designs come from bad designs. Never be afraid to make mistakes and then change things around."—*H1st OOA&D*

Good judgment comes from experience. Unfortunately, experience comes from bad judgment.

An Experiment on a Bird in the Air Pump
Joseph Wright of Derby
1768

What They Want

"Customers don't pay you for great code, they pay you for great software."— *H1st OOA&D*

- You *can't* Work as a Diver
- You *can* Dive as a Worker

Gustav Klimt
Portrait of Adele Bloch-Bauer I
1907

How Much Does It Cost? $135,000,000

Programmers Control Freaks

- Don't Hide Nothin' Important
- In Access, I control the Key Fields
- In XL, I do my own %
- I hard code vs. use Control Properties
- Don't use the auto-dates

- Standard Shift on my car

Test Cases

David Low and Pater J. Wisoff conducting detailed Test Objective procedures
Space Shuttle Endeavour
Earth in background, 1993
NASA

Test Cases

College of Alameda
pmcdermott@peralta.edu

Copyright © 2008 Patrick McDermott

The Tests are the Requirements

- Testing Tools
  - "Look ma, no hands!"
- Can communicate Specs
- Regression test: make sure you didn't break something else.

Each Test Case should have…

1. … an ID & Name
2. … <u>one specific thing</u> that it tests
3. … an input you supply
4. … an output that you expect
5. … a starting state

When Someone says…

- This could not possibly cause a problem
- You can be sure:
- This could WILL cause a problem

Bruce McCandless II
Tests a Mobile Foot Restraint
Space Shuttle Challenger, 1984
NASA

Prototyping

Prototyping

Copyright © 2000 Patrick McDermott

McDermott Computer Decisions, Inc

Extension

pmcdermott@msn.com

Prototyping

- Building a Façade System to Gather Requirements
- Hi or Lo Tech
  - Mock-up
  - Flipchart
- Types
  - Throw Away
  - Base

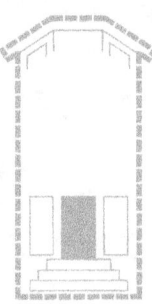

Use

- VB
- VC++
- Visio
- PowerPoint
- Paper
- Notecards
- Whatever!

Can Code

- Proof of Concept
- What XP calls a "spike"

GUI
UI Design

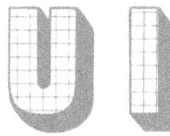

User Interface Design

College of Alameda
pmcdermott@peralta.edu

Copyright © 2008 Patrick McDermott

Interface Art

The most profound change ushered in by the digital revolution will not involve bells and whistles or new programming tricks. It will not come in the form of a 3-D Web browser or voice recognition or artificial technology. The most profound change will be with our own generic expectations about the interface itself. We will come to think of interface design as a kind of art form—perhaps the art form of the next century.—
STEVEN JOHNSON, 1997

Forgiveness

* Good Affordances
* Reversibility of Actions
* Safety Nets
* Confirmation
* Warnings
* Help

Word, Word, Icon

I miss the print icon because it's buried in other buttons with words…

Form & Control Sampler

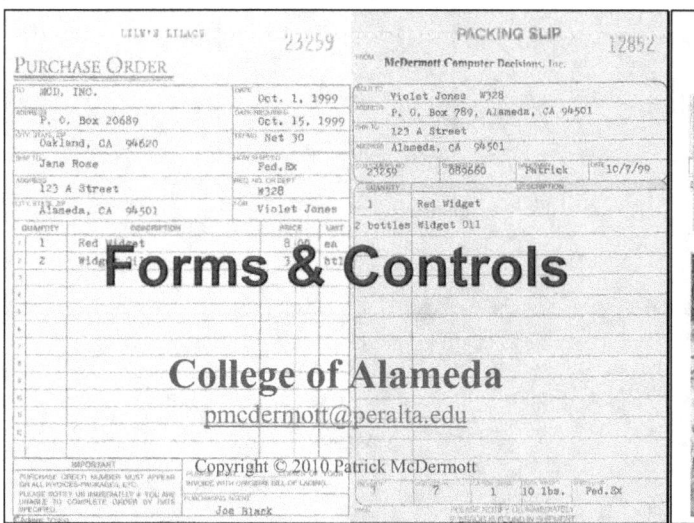

Forms & Controls

College of Alameda
pmcdermott@peralta.edu

Copyright © 2010 Patrick McDermott

"Controls"

"Doohickey"
"Thingamajig"
"Whatcha-ma-call-it"

Diego Rivera (1886-1957)
Man, Controller of the Universe
c. 1934

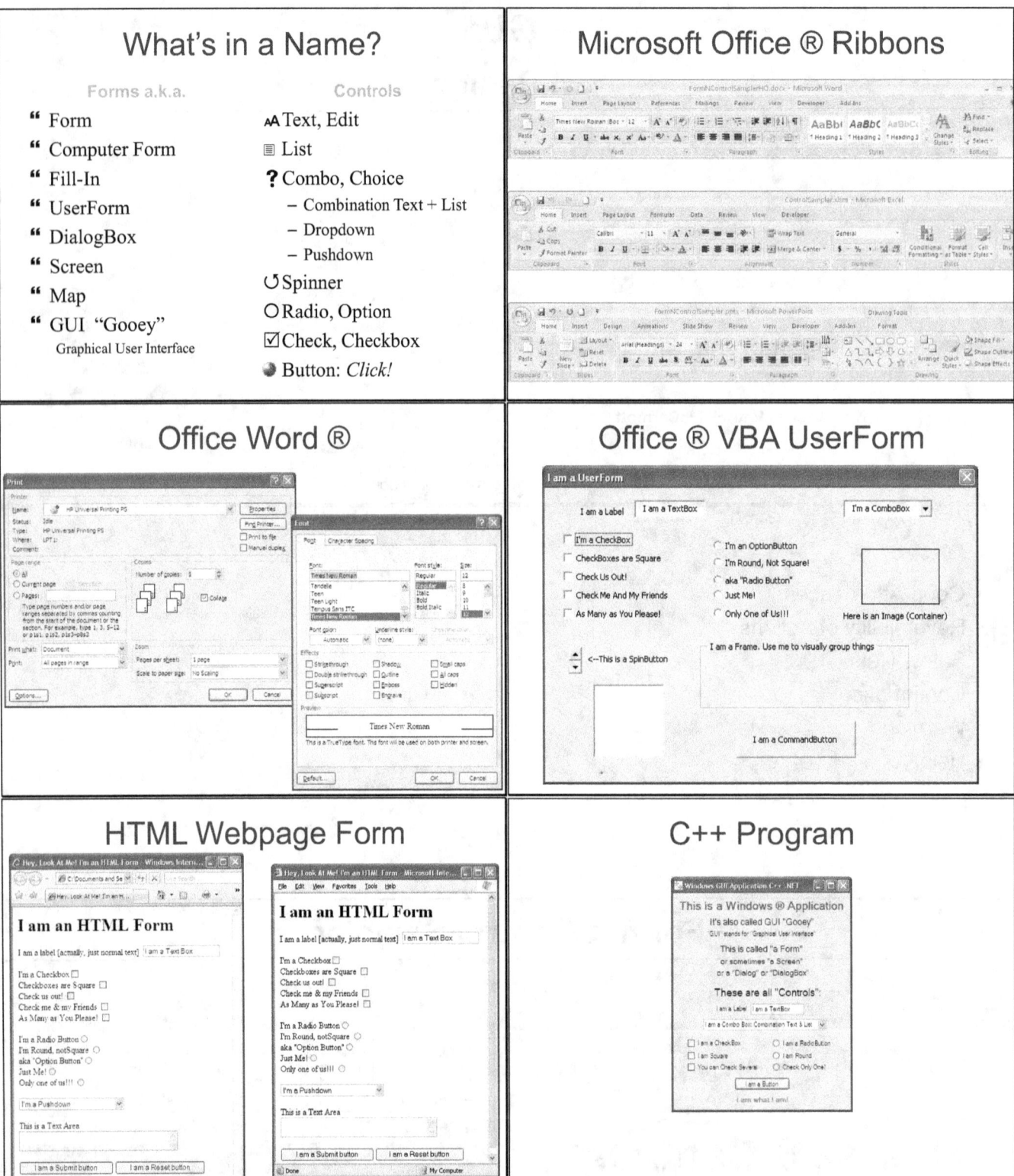

HTML Forms

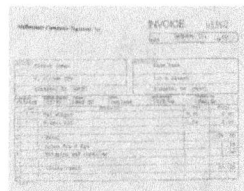

Put some substance in your Form!

HTML Forms

Berkeley City College
Copyright © 2007 Patrick McDermott

pmcdermott@peralta.edu

I am an HTML Form

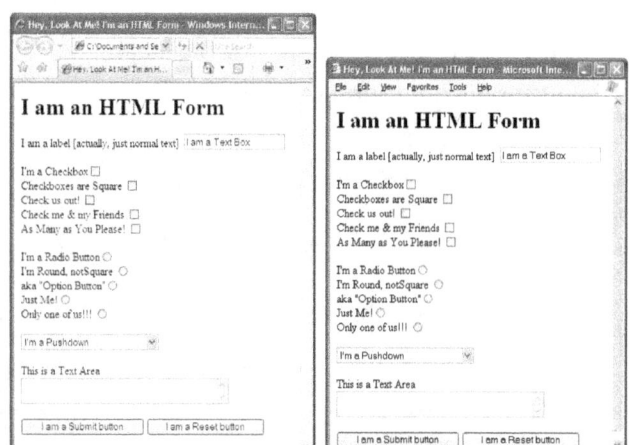

IMA Form Code

```
<h1>I'm in Very Good Form</h1>
<form method=post action=mailto:pmcdermott@peralta.edu>
What is your name? 
<input type="text" name="CustName" bgcolor="red" / >

What is your nickname? 
<input type="text" name="NickName" maxlength="5" size=10 / >
     <br /> <br />
Do you want:<br />
Money? <input type="checkbox" name="Money" />
Fame? <input type="checkbox" name="fame" />
Happiness? <input type="checkbox" name="Happiness" />
     <br /> <br />
Are you willing to:<br />
Work Hard? <input type="radio" name="WillDo" value="Work" />
Study Deeply? <input type="radio" name="WillDo"
     value="Study" />
Stick to it? <input type="radio" name="WillDo"
     value="Persevere" />
```

Brain Overload

- ⇥ Some are Keywords
  textarea, select / option
- ? Others are reserved attributes of input type
  text, checkbox, radio
  Buttons
  ↗ submit, or reset
      use value to label the button
- input type text has size, maxlength
  – I call them "MyX" to show name is chosen
- textarea has rows, cols, too

Colors of VWD

Inconsistent color code in Visual Web Developer since HTML is inconsistent!

Visual Web Developer Defaults:

- Attribute Name
- Attribute Value
- Comment <!-- Blab! -->
- Element Name
- Operator < > =

form

- post it

```
<form method=post
action=mailto:pmcdermott@peralta.edu>
Whatever boxes & buttons you like...
</form>
```

71

Label It

- a.k.a. "Prompt"
- There is no special control for the label
- Just use text as normal
- Not the same as the Name
- The Computer doesn't know it's associated

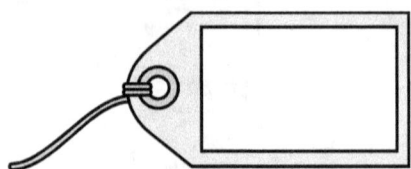

input a **text** Box

- ➢a.k.a. "Textbox"; "Edit Box"
- ➢A Place to put Text, i.e., Words
- ➢The default input type

```
<input type="text" name="MyText"
size=12 maxlength=25 / >
```

The **textarea**

- ❖Multi-Line text input
- ❖Browser set limit, typically 32K

```
<textarea name="MyTextArea"
 cols=25 rows=5>
It will Scroll automatically
</textarea>
```

It will Scroll
automatically

fieldset

- ❑Boxes it for Visual Grouping
```
<fieldset>
Field stuff
<textarea></textarea>
</fieldset>
```
Field stuff

- ❑Can have a legend
```
<fieldset>
<legend>
Legendary Field
</legend>
A legend in my own time
<textarea></textarea>
</fieldset>
```
Legendary Field
A legend in my own time

input a **checkbox**

- ☑Check it Out
- ☐Square (not radio round) Box
- ☑Binary: Yes or No
```
<input type="checkbox" name=
"MyCheckBox" />

<input type="checkbox" name=
"MyCheckedCheckBox" checked />
```
☐Plain text for label
☑

input a **radio** Button

- ◯Car radio metaphor
- ◯Round (not check square) Box
- ◉Only One Channel at a time in each Group
  - ◉Mutually Exclusive; "Option Button"
- ◯Grouped by the name
```
<input type="radio" name="MyGroup"
value="My1stChoice" />Plain text for label<br />

<input type="radio" name="MyGroup"
value="My2ndChoice" checked />
```
◯Plain text for label
◉

Prompt Before or After?

- Programming languages usually attach after
- Choose one way & stick to it!

- Make it Clear!

select an option

- a.k.a. "Dropdown"; "Pushdown"; "Drop List"
- Not a "Combo Box"
  - Combination List & TextBox

```
<select name="MySelection">
<option value="My1stChoice">
  First Choice</option>
<option value="My2ndChoice">Second
Choice</option>
</select>
```

Buttons

- Button it Up
- submit calls a Routine (program)
- reset clears entries (returns to defaults)

```
<input type="submit" value=
"My Submit Caption" name="GoForIt">
<input type="reset" value="My Reset
Caption" name="TryAgain">
```

| My Submit Caption | My Reset Caption |

Design Principles for Dialogs

van Vliet

van Vliet, Hans, *Software Engineering, Principles and Practices*, Chichester, England: John Wiley & Sons (0-471-93611-1), 1993. [1]

* Source: R. Molich & J. Nielsen, Improving a human-computer dialogue, *Communications of the ACM* 33,3 (1990) 338-348. Reproduced by permission of the Association for Computing Machinery, Inc.

Quote

1. **Simple and natural dialogue** Dialogues should not contain information that is irrelevant or rarely needed. Every extra unit of information competes with other relevant units for our attention. Information should appear in a logical and natural order.

2. **Speak the user's language** Dialogues should use concepts and phrases that are familiar to the user. The dialogue should not be expressed in computer-oriented terms.

3. **Minimize memory load** The user should not have to remember information from one part of the dialogue to another. There must be easy ways to find out what to do next, how to retrace steps, and get general instructions for use.

4. **Consistency** Users should not have to wonder whether different words or actions mean the same thing (but recall the above remarks against consistency as the one and only driving force).

5. **Provide feedback** The system should keep users informed about what is going on. Though certain processes may take quite a while, the user should not be left in the dark as to what is going on. A percent-done indicator for example informs the user about the progress towards the goal.

6. **Provide clearly marked exits** Users make mistakes and may choose inappropriate functions. There must be ways to leave the unwanted state without having to enter an extensive dialogue with the system.

7. **Provide shortcuts** Novice users may not be hindered by an extensive question-answer dialogue. It gives them a safe feeling and helps them learn the system. This is not optimal for experienced users, and the system should provide clever shortcuts to accommodate the experts.

8. **Good error messages** Error messages should be expressed in plain language and not refer to the internals of the system. They should precisely state the problem and constructively suggest a solution.

9. **Prevent errors** As with any piece of software, it is better to prevent errors from occurring in the first place.

Unquote

---

[1] van Vliet, Hans, *Software Engineering, Principles and Practices*, Chichester, England: John Wiley & Sons (0-471-93611-1), 1993, p. .

6. Information Gathering
Information Gathering

Jean-François Millet
(1814-75)
The Gleaners, 1857

Information Gathering

Copyright © 2001 Patrick McDermott
University of California
Berkeley Extension
pmcdermott@msn.com

Domain Analysis

"The process of identifying, collecting, organizing, and representing the relevant information of a domain, based upon the study of existing systems and their development histories, knowledge captured from domain exerts, underlying theory, and emerging technology within a domain."—*H1ˢᵗ OOA&D*

- The study of existing systems
- The systems' development histories
- Knowledge captured from domain experts
- The underlying theory
- Emerging technology

Techniques

1. Interviewing
2. Observation
3. Document Analysis
4. Facilitated Sessions (JAD)
5. CRC Card Session
6. Use Cases
7. User Stories
8. UML Modeling
9. Prototyping
10. User Test Cases
11. Reverse Engineering
12. Surveys
13. Research
14. WWW

1. Interviewing

- Gathering Information from the Stakeholders
  - Usually F2F (Face to Face)
  - Usually one by one
- ☞There is a Separate Presentation

2. Observation

- 👁Observe and Learn
- 🪰A Fly on the Wall
  - Beware Heisenberg
- A Day in the Life
- Co-Locate
- Walk a Mile

- 👁Doctor's Eye
- 👁Flight Engineer's Instruments

3. Document Analysis

- Current Reports
  - *Anything* the Computer Generates
  - And Manually Produced Reports
- Forms Analysis
  - Multipart Forms, Rainbow Colors
  - Boxes, Lines
  - The Box Misused: Manila Tax
  - Colored Check Marks
- Policy, Procedure, Training manuals

☹Be Careful—it could Lie

4. Facilitated Sessions

- JAD: Joint Application Design/Development
- Organized Group Meeting to Gain Information
- Hard to Schedule
- Needs a Good Facilitator

☞We'll have a Separate Presentation

5. CRC Card Session

- Class-Responsibility-Collaborator
- Great way to Get Started

☞Separate Class Exercise

A CRC Card

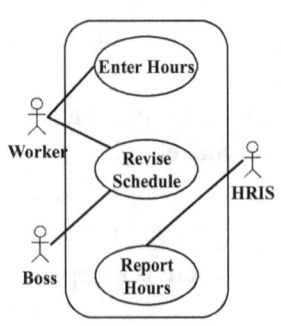

6. Use Cases

- Cases of the System in Use

- CRC
  - Class
  - Responsibility
  - Collaborator
- Other Models

7. User Stories

- XP Uses Them Extensively
- Business "Stories"
- A Promise to Discuss

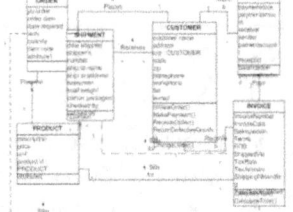

Edward Hopper
New York Movie
1939

8. UML Modeling

- Or other technique
  - ERD, DFD
- Capture
- Validate
- Communicate

☞See Separate Presentation

9. Prototyping

- Building a Façade System to Gather Requirements
- Hi or Lo Tech
  - Mock-up
  - Flipchart
- Types
  - Throw Away
  - Base

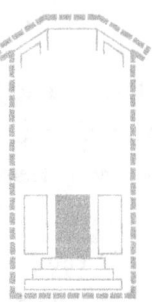

10. User Test Cases

- One System—User did test cases B4 we started programming
  - Requirements were clearly communicated thru the test cases
  - Wonderful!
  - But in another case…
  - It never worked

Detailed Test Objective procedures
Space Shuttle Endeavour
Earth in background, 1993

11. Reverse Engineering

✓ The Current System
✓ Old Physical/Old Logical
✓ Read/Convert the Code
✓ Data Mining—SAS

- Your Competitor

GNIREENIGNE

12. Surveys

- Formal
  - Gallup
  - Gartner Group
- Informal
  - Check Sheets

13. Research

- Benchmark
- Your Own Locations
- Books & Magazines
- $ Gartner &c.
- Vendors

☹Travel Boondoggles
  - L.L Bean

14. WWW

- Useful, But Beware
- Broken Links
- Stale Information
- Untrustworthy Information
- Volatile
☹Can be a Time Sink

Technique Comparison

#	Method	IT Time	User Time	Effectiveness	Notes
1	Interviewing	High	Medium	Excellent	Essential
2	Observation	High	Low	Excellent	Seeing is Believing
3	Document Analysis	Medium	Low	Good	Needs Context
4	Facilitated Sessions	Medium	Medium	Good OR Bad	Need the Right People
5	CRC Card Session	Medium	High	Good OR Bad	Hard To Schedule
6	Use Cases	High	High	Very Good	Can become Test Cases
7	User Stories	Medium	Medium	Good	Must follow through
8	UML Modeling	High	Medium	Very Good	Or other modeling techniques
9	Prototyping	High	High	Excellent	Great
10	User Test Cases	Medium	High	Wonderful	Great if they do it
11	Reverse Engineering	High	Low	Excellent	Out with the Old?
12	Surveys	Low	Low	Mixed	Don't Misinterpret
13	Research	Varies	None	Mixed	Can be Time sink
14	WWW	Medium	None	Mixed	Question it!

Information Gathering Comparisons

To do proper analysis you need information, information that is often stored inside people's heads. You need to get it out. In this section, we'll put requirements gathering in perspective. We'll talk about the various methods used by Systems Analysts to gather the information needed to design an effective system. We'll discuss these ten basic techniques used by analysts to gather information.

#	Method	IT Time	User Time	Effectiveness	Notes
1	Interviewing	High	Medium	Excellent	Essential
2	Observation	High	Low	Excellent	Seeing is Believing
3	Document Analysis	Medium	Low	Good	Needs Context
4	Facilitated Sessions	Medium	Medium	Good OR Bad	Need the Right People
5	CRC Card Session	Medium	High	Good OR Bad	Hard To Schedule
6	Use Cases	High	High	Very Good	Can become Test Cases
7	User Stories	Medium	Medium	Good	Must follow through
8	UML Modeling	High	Medium	Very Good	Or other modeling techniques
9	Prototyping	High	High	Excellent	Great
10	User Test Cases	Medium	High	Wonderful	Great if they do it
11	Reverse Engineering	High	Low	Excellent	Out with the Old?
12	Surveys	Low	Low	Mixed	Don't Misinterpret
13	Research	Varies	None	Mixed	Can be Time sink
14	WWW	Medium	None	Mixed	Question it!

Interviewing

Interviewing the Centenarian
M.-E. Chevreul, 1886
Paul Nadar

Interviewing

Copyright © 2001 Patrick McDermott
University of California
Berkeley Extension
pmcdermott@msn.com

Be sure that you carefully Plan Ahead

- Fail to Plan = Plan to Fail
- Plan
  - Who to interview
  - What to ask
  - Schedule
- Prepare
- Do It
- Follow up

Prepare

✓ Do your Homework
✓ Research
✓ Question Types and Structure
✓ Purpose
✓ Agenda
✓ Prepare the Interviewee

Do It

- Set the Stage
- Ask good questions
- Keep on track
- Listen
  - ☞ Practice Active Listening
  - ☞ Give them time to Answer
  - ☞ Be present in the Present
  - ☞ You're not there to show them how smart *you* are.

Follow up

- Document
- Give Feedback
  - As a Courtesy
  - For Clarification & Correction
- Don't let your notes Age
  - Schedule time afterward to document

Interview vs. Facilitated Session

- Scope and Objectives
  - More Candid
- Scheduling is easier
  - No need to get all at once

- For specific questions & Detail
  - Taken Off Line
- Small Projects
- Pre-session & Follow-up

Interviewing Pros

- Specific questions w/o boring group
- Honest confidential, not-in-front-of-boss
- Shy people avoid group exposure

Interviewing Cons

- Tag Team Interviewing
  - He said you said they said.
- No Public memory
  - Repeat info to get on same page
- Consensus, Convergence Hard
- Time
  - Repeat lots of material

Do

- ✓ Find a place away from phones
  - Their Place or yours? They have reference material there
  - No Phones, Interruptions
  - Cell Phones Off
- ✓ Keep separate 2do list
- ✓ Get to all levels: Managers & Workers
- ✓ Shift gears if progress stalls

Don't

- ⊘ Don't Over schedule yourself
  - Only 1 or 2 a day
  - The Fatigue Factor
  - You'll Ignore the Follow-up & Paperwork
- ⊘ Don't Interrupt
  - You're there so *they* can talk
- ⊘ No Double-Barreled Questions
  - 1 Question per Question
- ⊘ No Leading Questions
  - Don't confirm your own misapprehensions
  - You might be surprised...

Interviewing Tips*

1. Save the big cheese for last - get a lay of the land first
2. Find a comfy nest - not in someone's office
3. Prepare, prepare, prepare
4. "Please give me an example"
   - The 5 most important words to utter
5. Don't stop digging until you understand
6. Think small - get the details
7. Get out of executive row
   - Talk to people who do the work
8. Picture a day in the life - what did you do yesterday?
9. Practice and observe - team up with a partner

from Tom Peters, Canadian Airlines Magazine, January 1995

Tricks of the Trade

- Intelligent Ignorance
  - Real or Feigned
  - Lt. Columbo

- Friendly Disbelief

- Reinforcing Repetition
  - Playback for confirmation

William Merritt Chase
(1849–1916)
A Friendly Call, 1895

Poignant Pause

- Let the tension rise

  Tom DeMarco, speaking about a job interview, but applies to any interview: "she was prone to allowing long, uncomfortable silences. During this time, she would sit calmly, looking at the interview subject. At the end, the candidate would invariably break and begin to speak. What was said at such points was almost always the most useful part of the interview."

Closed vs. Open Questions

- A *closed* question elicits facts and has a specific answer.
  - How many do you do each month?
  - Who Gets This?

- An *open* question elicits ideas and even feelings and has no specific answer.
  - What problems are you having?
  - How do you do this?

Closed

- Faster—to the Point
- Easier to compare positions
- Keeps Control—on track (your track)

- Miss ideas
- Doesn't Build Rapport
- Boooorrrring

Open

- Interviewee is at Ease
- Vocabulary, attitudes and belief come out
  - Detail
- Spontaneity leads to Serendipity

- Irrelevant Detail
- Lose Control
- Time

Interviewing the
Centenarian M.-E. Chevreul
Paul Nadar, 1886

Probing

- A *Probing* question is an open question searching for feelings and motivations.

- What they Really think
- Get it off their chests and then concentrate

- Brian Lamb of CSpan is the Master
- Can be irritating
- Cultural Differences

DANGER
WATCH YOUR STEP

Probing Examples

- Why?
- Give me an example
- This contradicts someone else
- This contradicts Yourself
  - Be careful how you word this…

John James Audubon (1785-1851)
Long-billed Curlew
The Birds of America, 1840-1844

Interview Challenges

Suggested by a Comment by Jeremy on July 17, 2007 2:42 AM on Charlie Rose's website:
http://www.charlierose.com/shows/2007/07/16/1/a-conversation-with-dennis-ross.

Direct the shape of the interview
Provide context for viewers less familiar with the topic
Focus and condense responses for clarity and conciseness
Clarifying responses that are unclear
Challenging responses that are contradictory
Challenging responses that sidestep the issue

Lee Rogers: Bringing out specific points
Sean Hannity: Getting the guy to admit to something embarrassing

All while staying out of the interview and letting the guest speak

BUT interviewee might have an agenda, too
For TV, also must entertain; inform ⌐ always ≡ entertain
Control, versus Horizon effect

Modeling
Models

Models

College of Alameda
pmcdermott@peralta.edu

Copyright © 2008 Patrick McDermott

Paradigm

- Paradigm: a generally accepted model of how ideas relate to one another, forming a conceptual framework within which scientific research is carried out
  - Microsoft Word dictionary

- So sez (CHECK) Byte Wars p. 3

Various Kinds

- Economic
- Econometric
- Revel Kits
- Meteorological
- Fashion
- Role Models
- "Computer Model"

It's Only Words

- Model
- Analogy
- Metaphor
- Simile
- Allegory
- Parable
- Paradigm
- Prototype
- Symbol
- Theory

2 Types

- Polncaré's 2 types of Mathematicians
  - "If mathematics was not quickly brought in terms of equations, [von Neumann] thought it could quickly become insufficiently rigorous, insufficiently logical, very liable to mislead."
- Visual
  - Visualize chess moves
  - "See" numbers
- Auditory
  - See list of moves
  - Manipulate symbols

Makes U Think

"The justification of all mathematical models is that, oversimplified, unrealistic and even false as they may be in some respects, they force analysts to confront possibilities that would not have occurred to them otherwise."

A Realistic Model?

- Does it help us to understand the real world?
- Does it make predictions that can be tested?

Kata as Model

 型 【かた(P); がた】 (n) (1) (がた when a suffix) type; style; pattern; (2) model; mold (mould); (3) kata (standard form of a movement, posture, etc. in martial arts, sport, etc.); (4) form (i.e., customary procedure); (5) standard size (i.e., of shoes)

8 Levels of Reality

The Real World
Business Model
Business Workflow
Analysis Models
User Interface
Application Logic
Data Organization
Machine Representation

Nature's Models

"Nature has some sort of arithmetic-geometrical coordinate system, because nature has all kinds of models. What we experience of nature is in models, and all of nature's models are beautiful. It struck me that nature's system must be a real beauty, because in chemistry we find that the associations are always in beautiful whole numbers—there are no fractions."—R. Buckminster Fuller

MVC

- Model-View-Controller
- Model vs. View
  - UI: Console, Windows, HTML, & Unix
  - "Display" is quite dif
- Cf. MVP: Model-View-Persistence

MVC

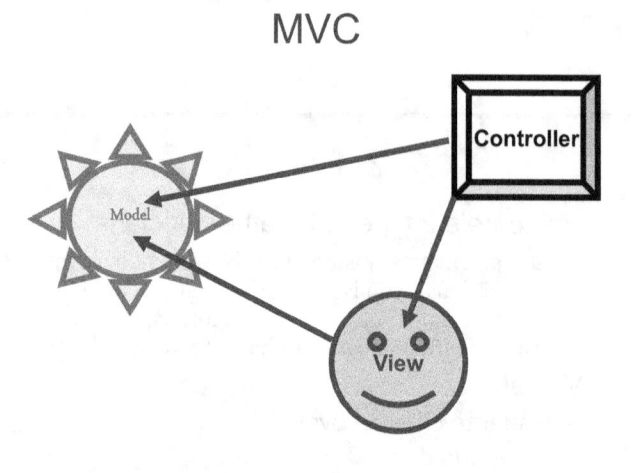

Intro to Models & the UML

Not really Unified…
Not a Language…
But you *CAN* Model!

An Introduction to

Models & The UML
The Unified Modeling Language

Copyright © 2007 Patrick McDermott
College of Alameda

pmcdermott@peralta.edu

Why Model?

Business modeling is an important skill for the analyst: not only is it a powerful tool for conducting analysis and design, but frequently coders receive specifications as models and therefore must be able to read them.

"We decide which details are irrelevant for the questions of interest and proceed to ignore them. This has the effect of collecting into a category things that differ only in the abandoned details; the category becomes a building block for the model." —John Holland

The UML

UML unified three competing Object Oriented (O/O) methodologies into a single methodology-independent modeling technique. UML is has gained wide acceptance within the O/O community and has become a standard tool for O/O development. It has been adopted by the largest players in the software industry (IBM, Microsoft, Oracle and Hewlett Packard, for example). The major O/O modeling techniques include: Use Cases, CRC (Class-Responsibility-Collaborators) sessions, Static Structure (Class and Object) diagrams, Interaction (Sequence and Collaboration) diagrams, and State and Activity diagrams.

The Twins

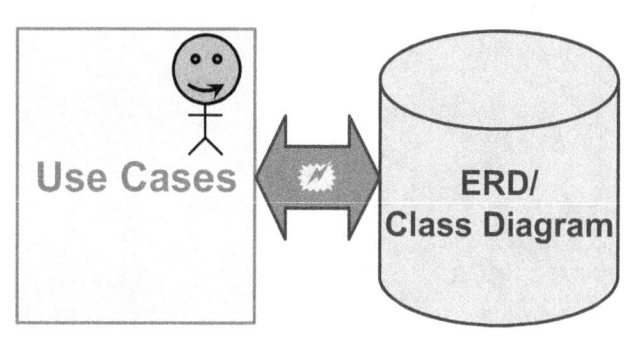

The Notorious 13

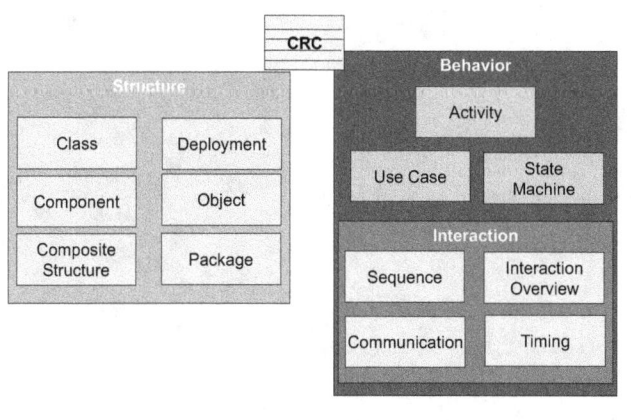

The 3 Amigos

Español: Los Tres Buddies

Booch, Grady, James Rumbaugh & Ivar Jacobson ["The Three Amigos"], *The Unified Modeling Language User Guide, Second Edition*, Upper Saddle River, New Jersey: Addison-Wesley (0-321-26797-4), 2005.

Rumbaugh, James, Ivar Jacobson & Grady Booch ["The Three Amigos"], *The Unified Modeling Language Reference Manual, Second Edition*, Upper Saddle River, New Jersey: Addison-Wesley (0-321-24562-8), 2006 (2005).

Jacobson, Ivar, Grady Booch & James Rumbaugh ["The Three Amigos"], *The Unified Software Development Process*, Reading, Massachusetts: Addison-Wesley (0-201-57169-2), 1999.

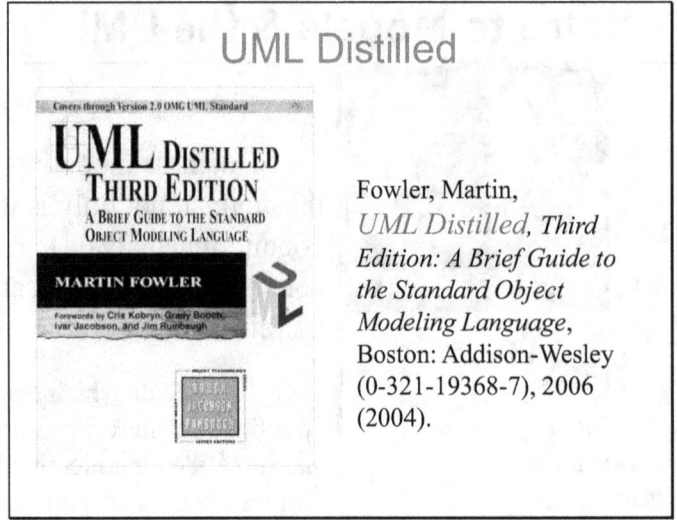

UML Distilled

Fowler, Martin, *UML Distilled, Third Edition: A Brief Guide to the Standard Object Modeling Language*, Boston: Addison-Wesley (0-321-19368-7), 2006 (2004).

Models & the UML

An Overview/Review of

Models & The UML
Unified Modeling Language

Copyright © 2007 Patrick McDermott
Berkeley Extension

pmcdermott@msn.com

Why Model?

Business modeling is an important skill for the analyst: not only is it a powerful tool for conducting analysis and design, but frequently coders receive specifications as models and therefore they bridge business and technology.

"We decide which details are irrelevant for the questions of interest and proceed to ignore them. This has the effect of collecting into a category things that differ only in the abandoned details; the category becomes a building block for the model." —John Holland

The UML

UML unified three competing Object Oriented (O/O) methodologies into a single methodology-independent modeling technique. UML is has gained wide acceptance within the O/O community and has become a standard tool for O/O development. It has been adopted by the largest players in the software industry (IBM, Microsoft, Oracle and Hewlett Packard, for example). The major O/O modeling techniques include: Use Cases, CRC (Class-Responsibility-Collaborators) sessions, Static Structure (Class and Object) diagrams, Interaction (Sequence and Collaboration) diagrams, and State and Activity diagrams.

The Twins

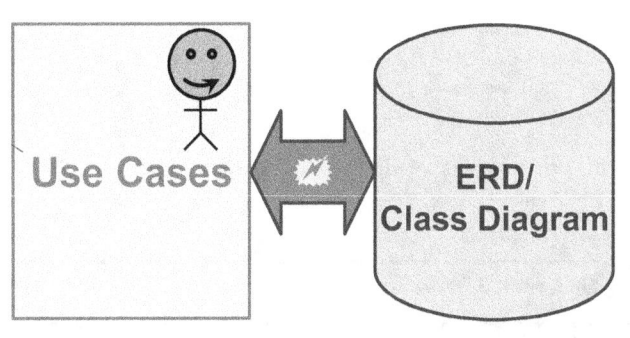

The Notorious 13

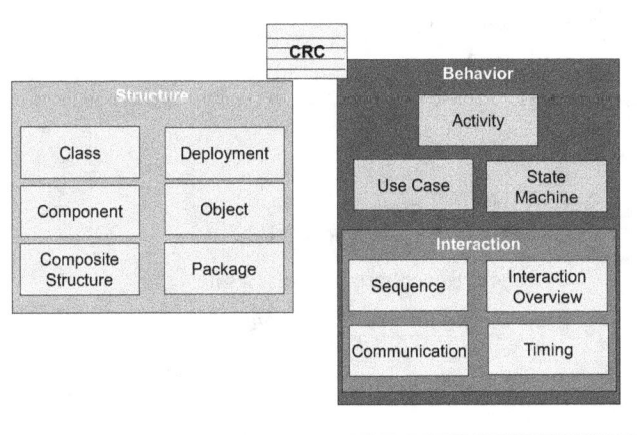

Relationships between various UML Diagrams

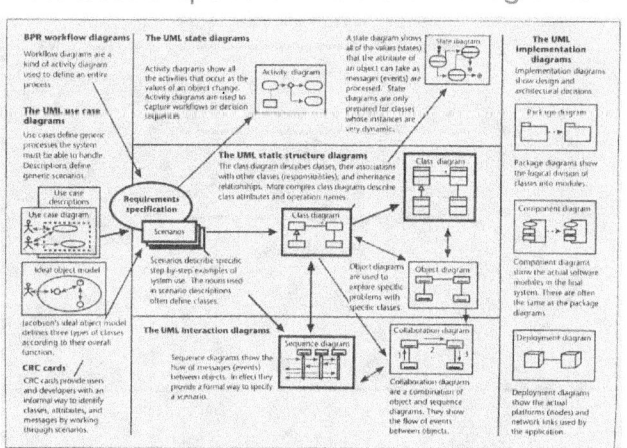

The 3 Amigos

Español:
Los Tres Buddies

Booch, Grady, James Rumbaugh & Ivar Jacobson ["The Three Amigos"], *The Unified Modeling Language User Guide, Second Edition*, Upper Saddle River, New Jersey: Addison-Wesley (0-321-26797-4), 2005.

Rumbaugh, James, Ivar Jacobson & Grady Booch ["The Three Amigos"], *The Unified Modeling Language Reference Manual, Second Edition*, Upper Saddle River, New Jersey: Addison-Wesley (0-321-24562-8), 2006 (2005).

Jacobson, Ivar, Grady Booch & James Rumbaugh ["The Three Amigos"], *The Unified Software Development Process*, Reading, Massachusetts: Addison-Wesley (0-201-57169-2), 1999.

Class Diagrams

Class Diagrams are used to show the classes, their attributes and methods, and the relationships between the classes.

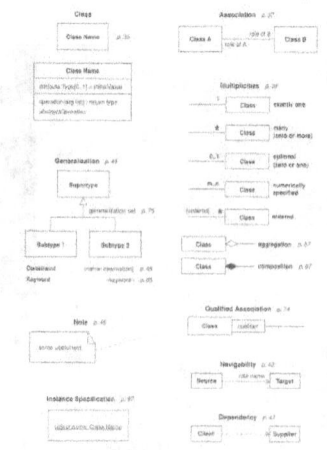

Fowler, Martin, *UML Distilled, Third Edition: A Brief Guide to the Standard Object Modeling Language*, Boston: Addison-Wesley (0-321-19368-7), 2006 (2004).

Class Notation

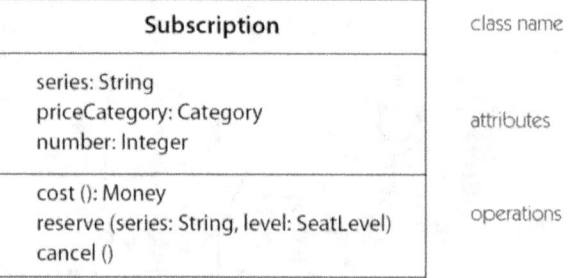

class name

attributes

operations

Figure 4-1. *Class notation*

Association Notation

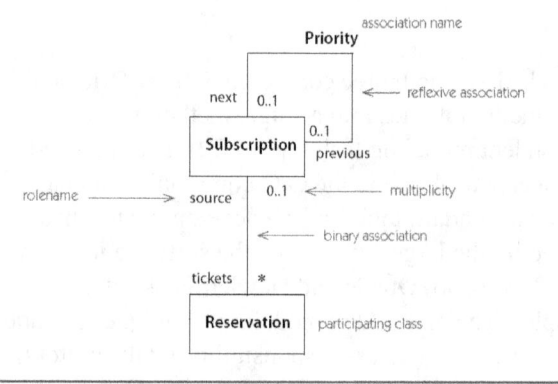

Figure 4-2. *Association notation*

Cardinality

Of Hottentots, Russians & Systems Analysts

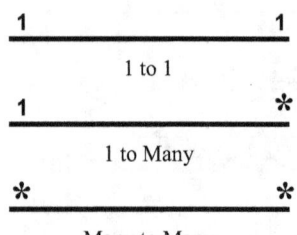

1 to 1

1 to Many

Many to Many

Use Connector (Not Line)

We are Driven

- Procedure Driven
- Data Driven
- Object Driven
- Business Rules Driven
- Workflow Driven
- Test-Driven
- Use Case Driven [OOSE]
  – Booch, Rosenberg, Deitels, Agile, etc.
- Real Goal: _____ -Driven

Discovery

- Brainstorm
- Events
- Document Analysis
- CRUD your Classes
- CRUD your Relationships
- Key Attributes
- Methods…

Use Case Diagrams

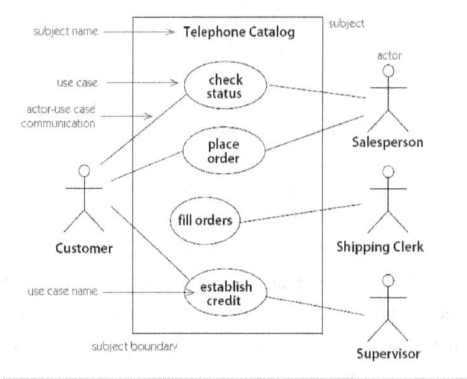

Figure 6-1. *Use case diagram*

A Use Case Diagram

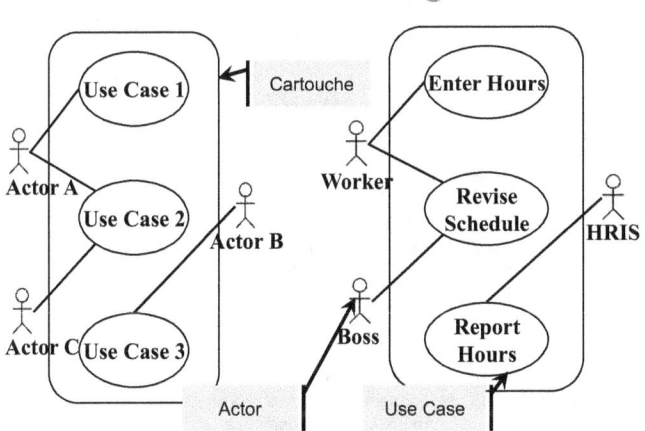

Chart Form

	Actor 1	Actor 2	Actor 3	Actor 4	Actor 5
Use Case 1	X				
Use Case 2	X				
Use Case 3	X	X			
Use Case 4			X		
Use Case 5					X
Use Case 6		??		X	

	Worker	Boss	HRIS
Enter Hours	X		
Revise Schedule	X	X	
Report Hours			X

Why I Recommend

- **Scenario-Driven**
- Can become Test Cases
- Can become User Manual
- Better yet, can come FROM user Manual:
  - *"Write the user manual, then write the code."*
    —Doug Rosenberg

Words & Pictures

- Eventually Pictures fail, Words are Needed
- Pictorial diagrams become too complex (e.g., trying to show every decision point and path in an event-driven interface), and don't illustrate desired system functions
- Flowchart is no better than code
  - Once you grasp it, no longer need it
- Access Query no Better than Code
- Like storyteller with unnecessary detail
  - It was 5 years ago, Or maybe 6. No, wait, it was 4½ years ago, or was it?

What's a Use Case Scenario?

Use Case Scenarios are a powerful tool to specify requirements, and can also serve as test case scenarios to assure those requirements are met. They are often used as design or coding specs. They can even evolve into the User Manual. Use brainstorming techniques to help come up with Use Cases and Use Cases Scenarios to better understand the problem.

A use case scenario is a specific example—an instance of a use case. The sunny-day scenario is the normal case: What happens if the user does exactly what is expected and completes the transaction? The rainy-day scenarios (of which there are usually many) are variations on the use case (e.g., the user tries to perform a task for which she isn't authorized).

Use Case Scenario

- Note that one use case is a collection of several use case scenarios. A use case might be Register Vehicle. Four scenarios: Register New Vehicle, Register Out-of-State Vehicle, Re-Register Existing Vehicle, Register Stolen Vehicle.

- We'll use "step" to refer to the lower level items: they are called steps on our diagrams and are portrayed as boxes, but the individual workers often call them tasks, or activities.

A Scenario

Worker Enters Time: Sunny Day Scenario		
When...	**Then...**	**Objects**
Worker logs in	System displays current schedule	**Schedule**
Worker selects Week	System displays current schedule	**Task**
Worker selects Task	System displays task	**Task**
Worker enters hours for task	System edits task entry for reasonableness	**Task**
Worker indicates "Finished"	System edits schedule for reasonableness	
Worker logs out	System informs Boss of completion	

Instance

Use case behavior for parent **Verify Identity**:

The parent is abstract, there is no behavior sequence.
A concrete descendant must supply the behavior as shown below.

Use case behavior for child **Check Password**:

Obtain password from master database
Ask user for password
User supplies password
Check password against user entry

Use case behavior for child **Retinal Scan**

Obtain retinal signature from master database
Scan user's retina and obtain signature
Compare master signature against scanned signature

Figure 14-288. *Behavior sequences for parent and child use cases*

Use Case Instance
The execution of a sequence of actions in a specified use case.
An instance of a use case.

Quick Draw

M.C. Escher (1898-1972)
Drawing Hands
1948

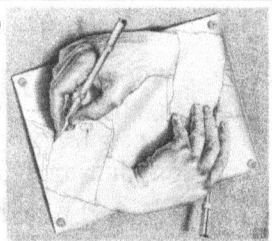

Quick Draw

Shapes

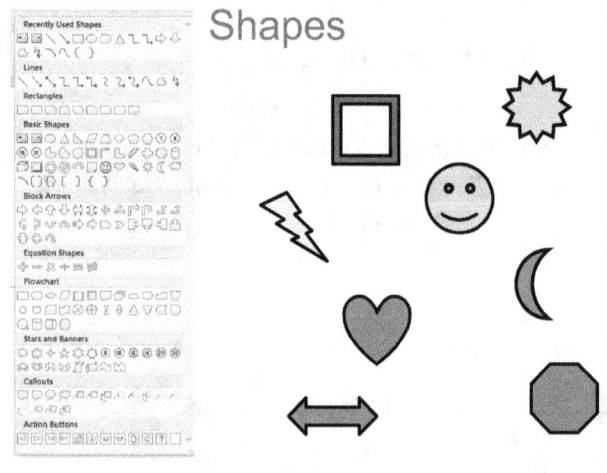

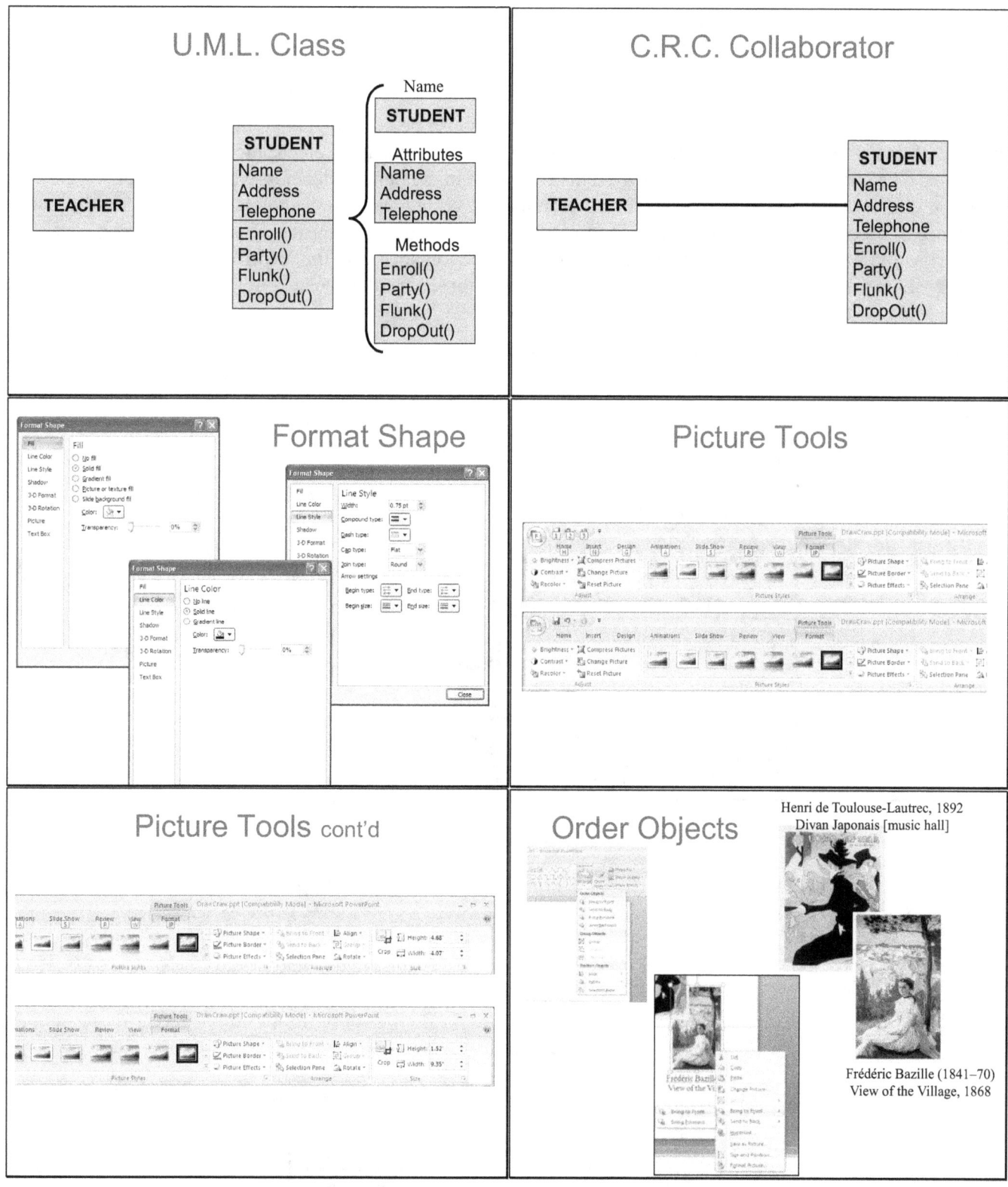

7. Business Strategy

Porter's Competitive Forces

Information systems not only help cut costs; they can also be used to gain competitive advantage. An example of this is the ability to gain control over distribution channels using electronically linked suppliers and customers. The application of information systems can result in greater efficiencies, which can improve the quality of the product, expand the market, or differentiate the company from the competition. Michael Porter's five external forces model can help identify competitive advantages for the business. Strategies in research, engineering and design, lower manufacturing costs, improved logistics, and the identification of customer desires are also important. In service-oriented businesses, information flows can be refined through better decision tools for managers. [1]

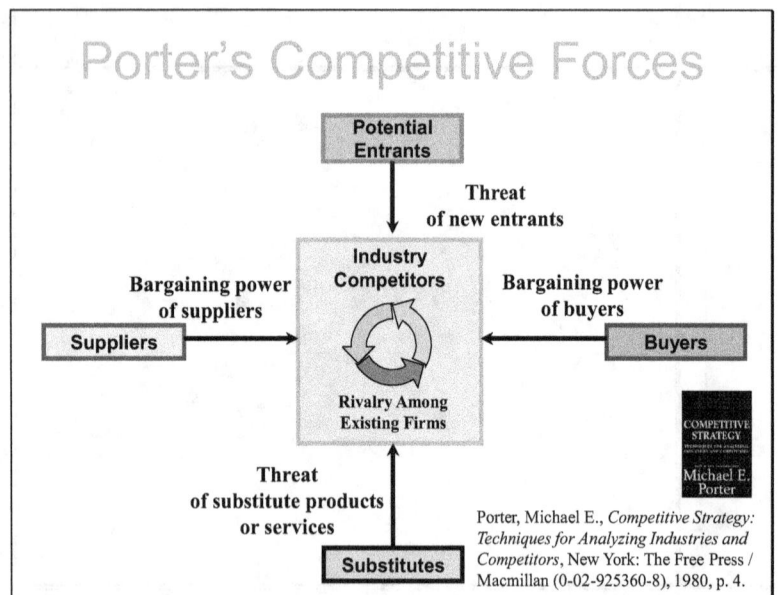

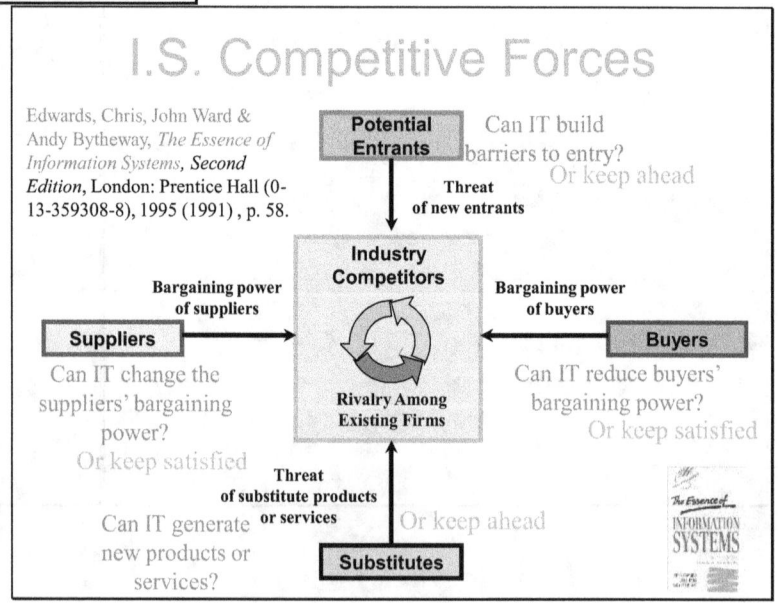

[1] Anderson, David, *Managing Information Systems: Using Cases within an Industry Context to Solve Business Problems with Information Technology*, Upper Saddle River, New Jersey: Prentice Hall (0-201-61176-7), 2000, p. 292.

Business Strategy

Business Strategy

Copyright © 2006 Patrick McDermott

The University of California

Berkeley Extension

pmcdermott@msn.com

Strategy
versus
Tactics

Understand the industry, market, customers, competitors, suppliers, partners and capabilities of the business. Identify opportunities and threats, and actively identify trends and future scenarios.

I.S. Competitive Forces

Edwards. Chris, John Ward & Andy Bytheway, *The Essence of Information Systems, Second Edition*, London: Prentice Hall (0-13-359308-8), 1995 (1991), p. 58.

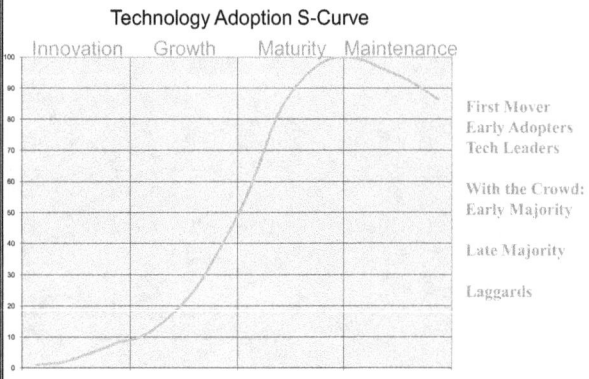

Can IT build barriers to entry? Or keep ahead

Can IT change the suppliers' bargaining power? Or keep satisfied

Can IT reduce buyers' bargaining power? Or keep satisfied

Can IT generate new products or services? Or keep ahead

3 Disciplines

The Three Strategic Disciplines			
Michael Porter	**Overall Cost Leadership**	**Differentiation**	**Focus**
Treacy & Wiersema	**Operational Excellence**	**Product Leadership**	**Customer Intimacy**
Core Business Processes that...	Sharpen distribution systems and provide no-hassle service	Nurture ideas, translate them into products, and market them successfully	Provide solutions and help Customers run their business
Structure that...	Has strong, central authority and a finite level of empowerment	Acts in an ad-hoc, organic, loosely knit, and ever-changing way	Pushes empowerment close to the point of Customer contact
Management Systems that...	Maintain standard operation procedures	Reward individuals' innovative capacity and new product successes	Measures the cost of providing service and of maintaining Customer loyalty
Culture that...	Acts predictably and believes "one size fits all"	Experiments and thinks "out of the box"	Is flexible and thinks "have it your way"

Porter, Michael E., *Competitive Strategy: Techniques for Analyzing Industries and Competitors*, New York: The Free Press / Macmillan (0-02-925360-8), 1980.

Treacy, Michael & Fred **Wiersema**, *The Discipline of Market Leaders: Choose Your Customers, Narrow Your Focus, Dominate Your Market*, Reading, Massachusetts: Addison-Wesley (0-201-40719-1), 1995.

Don't Make an *S* of Yourself

Technology Adoption S-Curve

Innovation   Growth   Maturity   Maintenance

First Mover
Early Adopters
Tech Leaders

With the Crowd:
Early Majority

Late Majority

Laggards

Why an Curve?

"A slow gestation giving way to rapid alterations in youth, followed by a lengthy and substantially unchanging adulthood, followed by decline and eventual death, seemed to be a nearly universal pattern among living things."

Warsh, David, *Knowledge and the Wealth of Nations: A Story of Economic Discovery*, New York: W.W. Horton (978-0-393-05996-0 0-393-05996-0), 2006, pp. 67-68.

Growth / Share Matrix

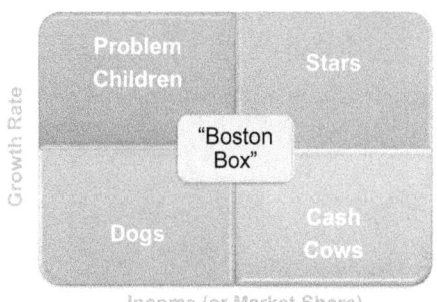

Growth Rate

Problem Children   Stars

"Boston Box"

Dogs   Cash Cows

Income (or Market Share)

The Boston Box

Bruce Henderson of BCG: Boston Consulting Group, 1970

Kaizen

改善

– Microsoft Spellchecker accepts as English word

- McDonalds or Chez Panisse?
- Bigger Small Cars

- My PowerPoints

What to Maximize

- ROI Return on Investment
- Total Profit
- Market Share

$ ROI
$ Total Profits
$ Market Share

- College: Greatest Number of Classes
  – Dean, too
- Tech Leadership
- This Quarter versus the Long Term
- The First-Mover Advantage

Paradoxes

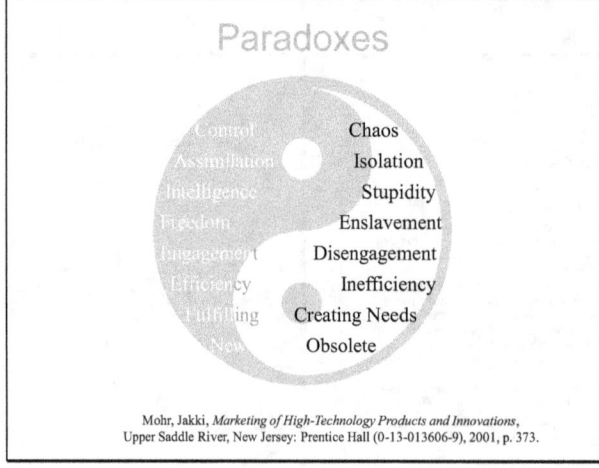

Control	Chaos
Assimilation	Isolation
Intelligence	Stupidity
Freedom	Enslavement
Engagement	Disengagement
Efficiency	Inefficiency
Fulfilling	Creating Needs
New	Obsolete

Mohr, Jakki, *Marketing of High-Technology Products and Innovations*,
Upper Saddle River, New Jersey: Prentice Hall (0-13-013606-9), 2001, p. 373.

The Mission

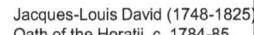

Jacques-Louis David (1748-1825)
Oath of the Horatii, c. 1784-85

The Mission

The University of California

Berkeley Extension
pmcdermott@msn.com

Copyright © 2008 Patrick McDermott

Mission Q's

1. "How would you describe the purpose of your organization to a client?"
2. "What would you say is the purpose of your organization?"
3. "What is the major function of your organization?"
4. "How would you describe what your organization does?"
5. "Will you define the single most important reason for the existence of your organization?"
6. "What is the main focus of your organization?"

Hernandez, Michael J., *Database Design for More Mortals: A Hands-On Guide to Relational Database Design*, Reading, Massachusetts: Addison-Wesley (0-201-69471-9), 1999 (1997), p. 85.

Mission Format

We exist to:	• Business engaged in & Primary Purpose
... for:	• Customers or Clientele served in order of significance
...in order to:	• Core Services provided
... so that:	• Key Outcomes for success (CSFs)

Drawn from Justice, Tom & David W. Jamieson, Ph.D., *The Facilitator's Fieldbook, Second Edition*, New York: AMACOM American Management Association (0-8144-7314-8 978-0-8144-7314-6), 2006, pp. 335-339.

Mission Examples

- A PC on every desk, running MicroSoft
- Our company strives to support improvements in education and make a positive difference in students' lives by providing software tools that help students learn to think.—Inspiration Software®, Inc
- To continuously improve our customer's ability to efficiently manage the lifecycle of data, information, and knowledge.—EIM
- To ensure equal access to education and to promote educational excellence throughout the nation.—U.S. Department of Education

User Mission ➜ DB Mission

- "We supply entertainment services to our clientele for any and all occasions. We take care of all the details for the engagement so that it is as worry-free for the client as possible."

Becomes:

- "The purpose of the All-Star Talent database is to maintain the data we use in support of the entertainment services we provide to our clientele."

Strategery

- What You *DON'T* Do
  - Try too much, Fail at All
- Amazon.com
  - Specifically decided no volume discounts
  - "Not our market"
- How's the watch biz?
  - Rolex Executive: "Beats me!"

Rolex makes Luxury Goods, not watches

Some Sources:
http://www.missionstatements.com/company_mission_statements.html
http://www.missionstatements.com/technology_mission_statements.html
http://www.missionstatements.com/inc_500_mission_statements.html

Justice, Tom & David W. Jamieson, Ph.D., *The Facilitator's Fieldbook, Second Edition*, New York: AMACOM American Management Association (0-8144-7314-8 978-0-8144-7314-6), 2006, p. 337.

Hernandez, Michael J., *Database Design for More Mortals: A Hands-On Guide to Relational Database Design*, Reading, Massachusetts: Addison-Wesley (0-201-69471-9), 1999 (1997), p9. 84-85.

Mission Nuances

- Which Comes First?
  - The Men or The Mission?
- Whatever!
  - "to engage in any lawful act or activity for which a corporation may be organized under the Law"
- To Refresh the World ... in body, mind, and spirit. To Inspire Moments of Optimism ... through our brands and our actions. To Create Value and Make a Difference ... everywhere we engage.—Coca Cola

"to engage in any lawful act or activity for which a corporation may be organized under the Law". McDermott Computer Decisions, Inc, *Articles of Incorporation*, Sacramento: The California Secretary of State, March 31, 1997.

CSFs: Critical Success Factors

1. No verbs
2. Only objects or objective phrases
3. No "ands", "ors" or slashes "/"
4. Only one subgoal or issue
5. Absolute Consensus
6. Less is More
7. Seven word limit

Drawn from Justice, Tom & David W. Jamieson, Ph.D., *The Facilitator's Fieldbook, Second Edition*, New York: AMACOM American Management Association (0-8144-7314-8 978-0-8144-7314-6), 2006, p. 362.

CSF Examples

For an e-Commerce Site

- ✓ Visually appealing Website
- ✓ Fast, efficient fulfillment process
- ✓ Sufficient cash flow
- ✓ Start up money
- ✓ Profitable customer base
- ✓ Merchandise sources

The Mission Statement

Before we at can decide on our business model and thus our Mission, we need to ask ourselves three questions, then consider them:

- "Which Customers or **Markets** do we – or should we – serve?"
- "Which Products or **Services** do we – or should we – serve them with?"
- "What **Differentiates** us?" or, more clearly, "Why choose us over our competitors?"

Kellogg on Marketing tells us "To **market**, [as opposed to sell] we have to go beyond the product. We must transcend whatever the product is as a physical or objective entity. We must create and convey the meaning of the product". [1] Weiss gives further insight:

> "If we've established that no one buys a drill because he wants a drill, but rather because he needs a hole somewhere, then we can be sure that absolutely no one retains a consultant because she needs a consultant (or even a focus group or a training program). What the buyer needs is improved morale, larger sales per person, a safer plant, and a more competitive compensation system." [2]

And Viardot tells us: Don't define your mission in terms of the product. "Therefore, for instance, a company's mission is not to manufacture computers, resin, or lasers but to offer the possibility of faster calculations, increased fire resistance, or a more precise cut of steel." [3] So we aren't selling a book, we're marketing better computer systems; or computer solutions; or even insight and calmness.

We will also need to decide where to focus, so as not to dissipate our energy. In *The Discipline of Market Leaders*, Treacy and Wiersema [*] identified three disciplines that organizations can focus on: [4]

- Operational Excellence, or "Best Total Cost"—Walmart tries to provide the lowest cost product through efficiency of operation.
- Product Leadership or "Best Product"—Nike wants to provide the best product even though it might cost more.
- Customer Intimacy or "Best Total Solution"—Cable & Wireless wants to understand its customers to provide them with the communication products they might not even know they want.

We're warned that excelling in all three simultaneously is almost impossible, and pursuing even two is dangerous because they are difficult to balance. What do we want to do?

---

[1] Calder, Bobby J. & Steven J. Reagan, "Brand Design" in Dawn Iacobucci, ed., *Kellogg on Marketing*, New York: John Wiley & Sons, 2001, p. 58.

[2] Weiss, Alan, *How to Establish a Unique Brand in the Consulting Profession: Powerful Techniques for the Successful Practitioner*, San Francisco: Jossey-Bass/Pfeifffer, 2002, p. 15.

[3] Viardot, Eric, *Successful Marketing Strategy for High-Tech Firms*, Boston: Artech House, 1998, p. 20.

[*] Treacy and Wiersema present an interesting case study in ethics and marketing schemes. CSX Index, the consulting firm the authors are affiliated with, decided to give every employee a copy of the book and obtain several thousand copies to use as a promotional item over the ensuing years. Instead of placing the usual order for the book with the publisher at a volume and author discount, they had each employee of the company go out and buy several books at each of several retail bookstores. Sound like a waste of money? It depends on how much it's worth to be on bestseller lists: those purchases allegedly caused the book to make the *New York Times* Bestseller List that week, where it remained for some weeks. Would it have made the list anyway, or did the visibility of the contrived appearance provide momentum? In any event, the controversy gave the book a lot of publicity, and although not favorable, probably contributed to the book's success.

[4] Treacy, Michael, and Fred Wiersema, *The Discipline of Market Leaders: Choose Your Customers, Narrow Your Focus, Dominate Your Market*, Reading, Massachusetts: Addison-Wesley, 1995.

5 Generic Strategies

Mintzberg, Henry & James Brian Quinn, *The Strategy Process: Concepts, Context, Cases, Third Edition*, Upper Saddle River, New Jersey: Prentice Hall (0-13-234030-5), 1996.

Although Mintzberg was discussing business strategy generally, note the strategies apply equally well to **Computer Systems.**

5 Generic Strategies

the University of California
Berkeley Extension

pmcdermott@msn.com

Locating the Core Business

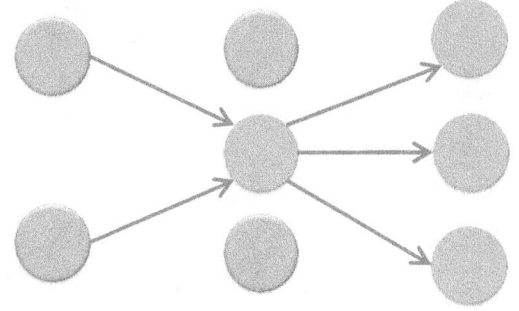

Where your business is located amongst other industries. Where your System is located amongst other systems (both internal & external).

Distinguishing the Core Business

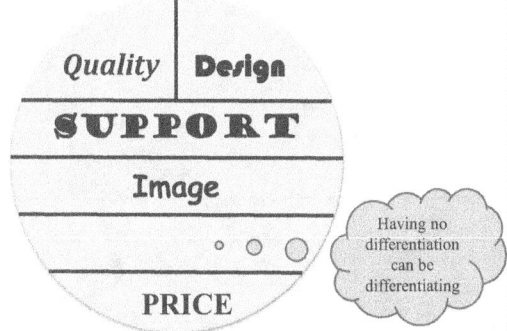

How your business is differentiated from competitors. How your System is differentiated, *or differentiates you*, from competitors.

Elaborating the Core Business

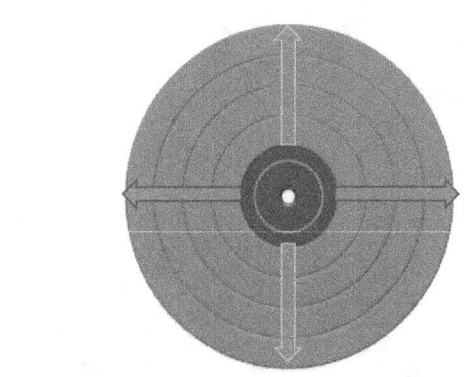

Elaborating your System's Technology.

Extending the Core Business

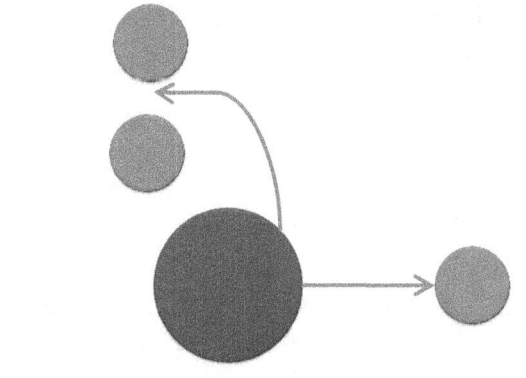

Extending the scope of your System.

Reconceiving the Core Business

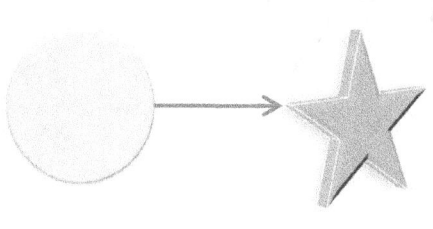

Re-engineering your Systems.

Mintzberg, Henry & James Brian Quinn, *The Strategy Process: Concepts, Context, Cases, Third Edition*, Upper Saddle River, New Jersey: Prentice Hall (0-13-234030-5), 1996, pp. 83, 89, 91, 717 & 719.

Corporate Hierarchy

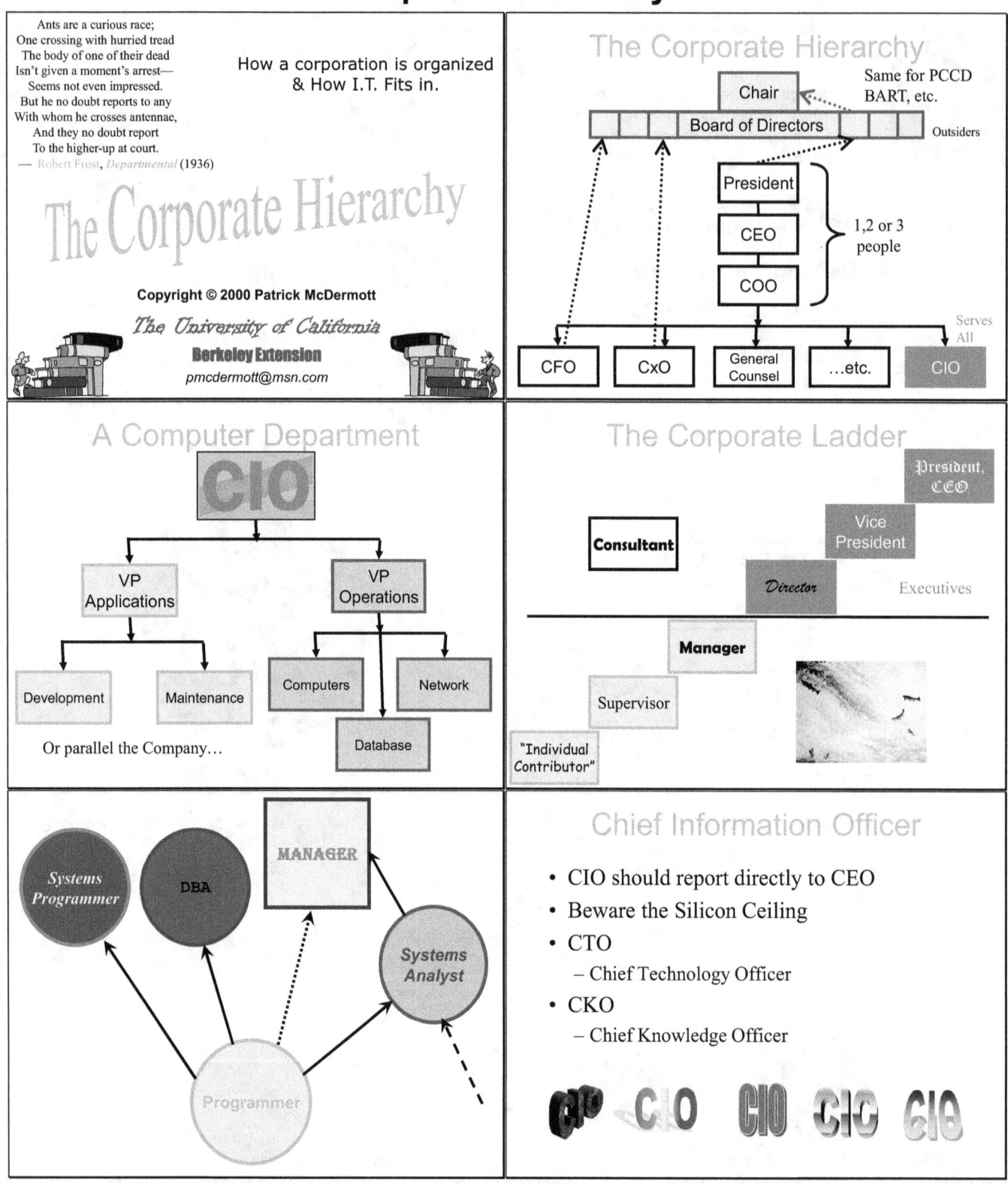

Ants are a curious race;
One crossing with hurried tread
The body of one of their dead
Isn't given a moment's arrest—
Seems not even impressed.
But he no doubt reports to any
With whom he crosses antennae,
And they no doubt report
To the higher-up at court.
— Robert Frost, *Departmental* (1936)

How a corporation is organized
& How I.T. Fits in.

The Corporate Hierarchy

Copyright © 2000 Patrick McDermott
The University of California
Berkeley Extension
pmcdermott@msn.com

The Corporate Hierarchy

Chair — Same for PCCD BART, etc.

Board of Directors — Outsiders

President
CEO
COO } 1,2 or 3 people

Serves All

CFO | CxO | General Counsel | ...etc. | CIO

A Computer Department

CIO

VP Applications | VP Operations

Development | Maintenance | Computers | Network | Database

Or parallel the Company…

The Corporate Ladder

President, CEO

Vice President

Consultant

Director — Executives

Manager

Supervisor

"Individual Contributor"

Systems Programmer | DBA | MANAGER | Systems Analyst

Programmer

Chief Information Officer

- CIO should report directly to CEO
- Beware the Silicon Ceiling
- CTO
  - Chief Technology Officer
- CKO
  - Chief Knowledge Officer

100

The 5 Tiers of Business Systems

The Five Tiers
of Business Systems

1. Business Plan/Model
What the Business does:
its Mission—Products,
Customers and Markets.

2. Business Workflow
The Business is organized into
Processes that accomplish the
work.

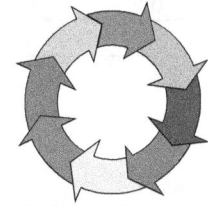

3. User Interface
Information is exchanged
with the User, either a person,
or even another machine.

4. Application Logic
Computer Programs apply
Business Logic and
Process Information .

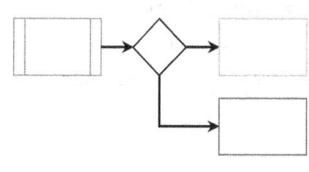

5. Database
Data is stored on disks &
other media and needs to
be retrieved as needed.

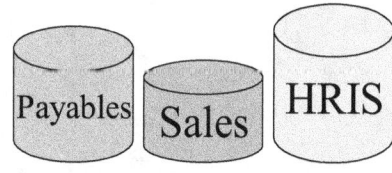

All Five are Essential and Inextricably Interrelated

Computer Systems Goals

The most common axes for computer systems are probably:
- **Cost** efficiency: Everybody always thinks about this one, so consider Veblen Good.
- **Cool**: Innovation. The new, new thing.
- **Customized**: Information. Customer Intimacy, Management Information.

	Cost	Cool	Customized
Goal	Cheaper	Faster	Better
Procedures	Standard	Evolving	Personal
Adjective	Predictable	Innovative	Flexible
Management	Authority	Experiment	Empowerment
Focus	Kaizen	Novelty	Customer Information
Process	Clear	Ad Hoc	Empowered
Motto	One Best Way	The Newest New Thing	Have it Your Way

Arno Penzias, in *Digital Harmony*, offers a perspective based on the "era". [1]

Quantity Era	Quality Era	Harmony Era
Mechanical technology	Programmable control	Direct information access
Economies of scale	Economies of speed	Economies of convenience
Advance-planning emphasis	Customer feedback emphasis	Personalized emphasis
Hierarchical organizations	Team-based organizations	Architectural organizations
Value from volume	Value from performance	Value from coherence
Technology islands	Technology overlap	Technology merger
Environmental exploitation	Environmental concern	Environmental renewal

---

[1] Penzias, Arno, *Digital Harmony: Business, Technology & Life After Paperwork*, New York: HarperBusiness (0-88730-785-X), 1996 (1995), pp. 11 & 13.

Information Systems Ethics

Copyright © 2001 Patrick McDermott

The University of California

Berkeley Extension

pmcdermott@msn.com

Breakfast of Ethical Champions

Ethix in IS

- ACM
  - Association for Computing Machinery
- "At least one class should cover Ethix"

- Don't copy that floppy
- Copyright Infringements

Divinity School

- Computer Overloaded
- He Talk Dirty One Day
- Home is Castle?
- Privy Parties
  - Technician(s)
  - Supervisor
  - Whistle Blower(?)
  - Dean
  - The Press

HARVARD UNIVERSITY

Missing Emails

- Emails to Fired President
- Company Read Them
- Company Said "Burn 'em"
- Technician Erased Them
- Technician Disillusioned

Machiavellian or Lying?

- The Ulterior Motive
- Don't Agree With Orders
  - Act Like you DO to Subordinates
- Let Them Think it's Their Idea
  - Is it Manipulation?
- Layoff Pending
  - Plausible Denial to Avoid Stampede
- Estimate for Bill Gates
  - Is it a Lie if we all know it's not True?
- Monte Cassino Effect

Ethical Questions

- What would be the Limit of Ethics
  - Is there a problem?
  - What is the limit of what you should do?
- How to Teach
  - Lecture
  - Bullet Points
  - Act Out—Skit
  - Whatever
  - Some Combination

You Tell Me!

1. Product that could Harm its User
   - Math is favorable (Pay 'em off)
2. Secret Employee Monitoring
   - Told to keep it confidential
3. Capture Identities of Website Users
4. Find Bad Risks—Illness & Lifestyle (Insurance Company)
   - AIDS
   - Breast Cancer

Reactions

- ✓ Inquiry
- ✓ Refuse
- ✓ Sabotage
- ✓ Blow the Whistle
- ✓ Just Do It
- ✓ Paper Trail
  - Diary
  - Memos

What would You do?

- Quit
- Blow the whistle
- Say your piece, then shut up
  - Stay & try to influence—lose this battle but win the war
- Refuse to do it
- Say you'll do it, but don't
- Avoid doing it yourself—transfer
- Change the Law
- Nazi refusers were not Court-martialed

Would you Quit?

- Would you REALLY quit your $900,000 p/a job over something that is NOT illegal and debatably not even unethical?
  - "Get over it. You have no Privacy."—Scott McNealy of Sun
  - Mike Wallace & Brown & Williamson Tobacco
    - *The Insider* Russell Crow Character
  - Is making someone uncomfortable a crime?
- Is it ethical to impose your ethics on the shareholders? Fiduciary responsibility of corporate officers is to make money.

Make a Business Argument

- It might be arguable that Good Ethics is Good Business, BUT…
- Bad Ethics *is* Bad Business
  - Admittedly an ethical evasion, but realistic
  - Yahoo! drops porn, gets good press
  - Amazon & Price Discrimination

Success Factors for Hi tech

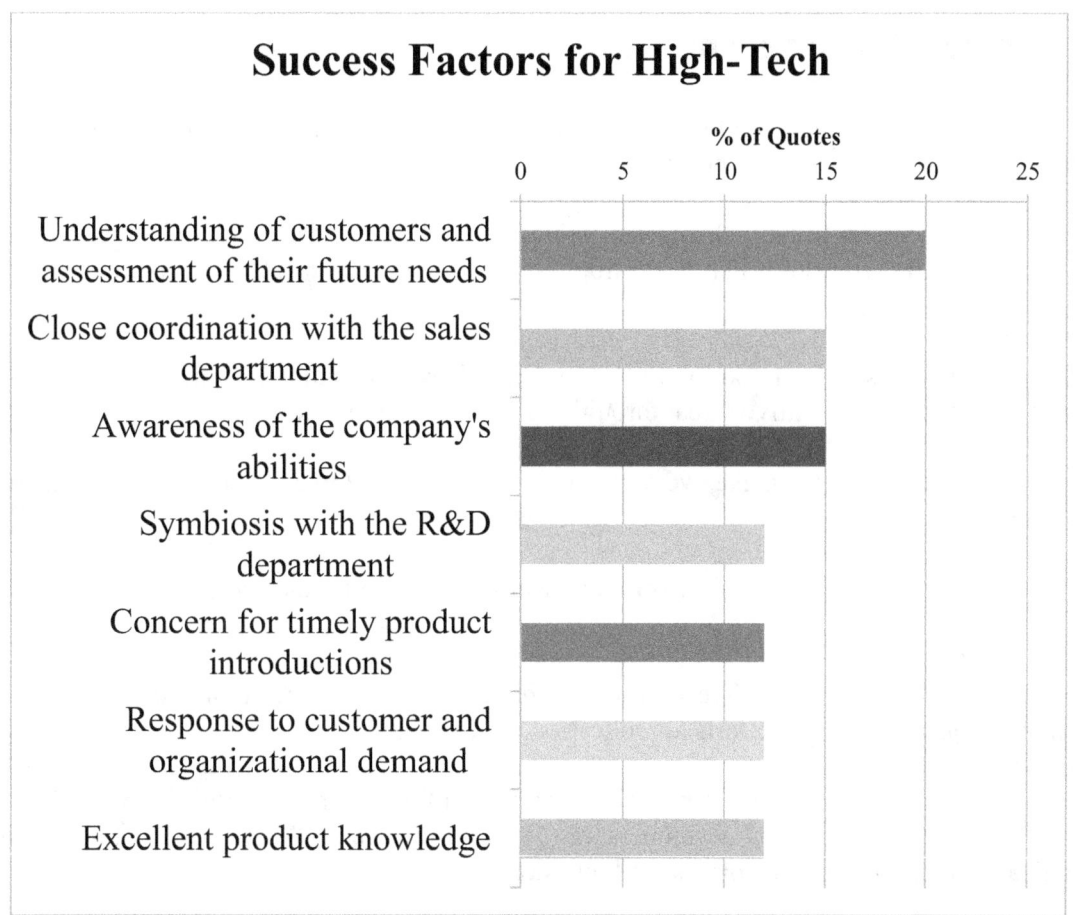

"Key Success Factors of a Marketing Department in a High-Tech Company"

Figure A.1 Success factors of a marketing department in a high-technology company. (Source: Interviews by Eric Viardot.) Viardot, Eric, *Successful Marketing Strategy for High-Tech Firms*, Boston: Artech House (0-89006-854-2), 1998, p. 246.

Shaw's Success Attributes

Modern Strategic Management

1. Embrace Change. Successful firms in their respective sectors do not react to change; they embrace it and seek new avenues to add value to their product.

2. Partner. Successful firms in the newly defined competitive landscape have learned to negotiate affiliations, alliances, and partnerships that either improve their product or create new distribution routes to consumers.

3. Internet. Successful firms exploit the Internet as a new distribution channel to consumers; they do not attempt to supplant this competitive threat through traditional strategic design.

4. Brand. Successful firms make every effort to reinforce brand image and management, now more important than ever.

5. Economies of Scale. Successful firms have learned to exploit scale economies, critical in strengthening profitability.

6. Proprietary Technologies. Successful firms develop proprietary technologies or products, where feasible, such that their competitors' efforts at replication are forestalled.

7. First Philosophy. Successful firms adopt either one of these strategic philosophies: (1) they define themselves as "first-to-market" product developers; or (2) they emphasize a "first-to-market-acceptance" image clearly recognizable to employees, customers, and investors.

8. Out with the old. Successful firms "obsolete" their own product before the competition does it for them.

9. Base & Allegiance. Successful firms have learned the most important lesson of contemporary telecommunications economics: Reach (customer base) loyalty (customer allegiance) rewards providers and content developers, and lays the foundation for future growth.

10. Synergy. Successful firms exploit organizational synergies to enhance value and growth rates by cooperating with any firm, including competitors, that assures this contingency.

Shaw, James, *Telecommunications Deregulation and the Information Economy, 2nd Edition,* Boston: Artech House (1-58053-276-4), 2001, p. 248.

Personalization

Marketing Strategies		**Marketing Attributes**			
		Product	**Target**	**Pricing**	**Techniques**
	Mass Marketing	Simple	All Consumers	One World, One Price	Mass Media
	Direct Marketing	Stratified	Segments	One Price	Targeted Communications (mail/phone)
	Micromarketing	Complex	Micro-Segments	Variable Pricing	Segment Profiles
	1-to-1 Marketing	Highly Complex	Individual	Unique Pricing	Indivdual Profiles

Laudon, Kenneth C. & Carol Guercio Traver, E-commerce: business. technology. society., Fifth Edition, Upper Saddle River, New Jersey: Pearson / Prentice Hall (978-0-13-600711-1 0-13-600711-2), 2008 (2009), p. 397.

Strategic Thinking

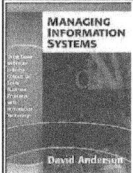

Anderson, David, *Managing Information Systems: Using Cases within an Industry Context to Solve Business Problems with Information Technology*, Upper Saddle River, New Jersey: Prentice Hall (0-201-61176-7), 2000, pp. 1-2.

Strategic Thinking:
Technological Trends

The University of San Francisco
College of Professional Studies
pmcdermott@msn.com

Copyright © 2007 Patrick McDermott

Organizations Have Changed

- Technology is rapidly changing what we do in society, in business, and at work
- Specific skill sets are rewarded rather than broad knowledge about a subject area
- In technology, these skills can be measured and defined
- The goal is to identify those areas where these skills can be specifically applied

"Technology has resulted in the identification and implementation of a number of trends. Understanding the role that these trends play in the industry is important. Recognizing them can assist you in your endeavors to position yourself for career growth and expansion."

Standardization

- Jobs similar, routine, and interchangeable
- Economies saved because the components of the job are the same
- Example: The rule set that McDonald's applies to all of its tasks
  - From making fries to ordering and tracking the inventory

"By measuring everything from hours worked to wasted fries, McDonald's' management information system enforces the rule set required for standardization."

Leverage

- Move the responsibility for all tasks to the lowest possible level
  - Army: "Man on the Ground"
- Tasks carefully evaluated and assigned based on the ability required
- Example: The managerial structure in major consulting firms

"The role and budgetary requirements of the partner, manager, senior, and staff levels force tasks to be accomplished at the level that most closely matches the required expertise. Using technology to direct the billing structure ensures that tasks are accomplished with this approach in mind."

Mass Customization

- The focus of all products and services on a specific customer
- Market products not just to specific market segments, but to specific individuals
- Example: Grocery store coupons specifically printed based on products bought
- Example: A specifically focused mailing from a store based on previous purchases on credit or buyer's card

Amazon.com Pages

Franchise

- Organization into small central office with many autonomous, but identically structured units
- Strict guidelines in terms of cost and output for each location
- Information reported to headquarters in a structured format
- Reduces the need for layers of middle management to evaluate and interpret the information from regional offices
- Examples: Most evident in the fast-food industry

"Franchising has made possible the proliferation of identical restaurants with identical products around the world."

Methodology

- Clear directives to use in the management process
- Step-by-step, almost cookbook-like approach that anyone with a minimum set of skills can pick up and use to deliver a product
- Technology enables this methodology to be available across an organization
- In strategic firms, the methodology defines and reinforces the overall approach used to manage the business
- Example: Systems Development CMM

"Following the methodology provides the programmers with clear directives on what the next steps are, the deliverables from each step, and what to do at each step of the process."

Modularization

- Construct product using sections of code, rather than at the most granular level
- Object orientation enables modules to be constructed and applied
  - If inputs and outputs are standard, objects can be encapsulated & addressed in the same way
- Example: the ability of Word, Excel, Access & PowerPoint to fit together in Microsoft Office suite
- Using the concept of modules, users can apply the components of the suite to their individual needs
- Example: On the World Wide Web, plug-ins inserting a module into your web application

"It is much faster and more straightforward to put objects or modules together than to work with individual lines of code."

Liquid Assets

- Reduce costs by reducing reliance on fixed assets by using liquid assets instead
- Changing costs from fixed to variable enables an organization to more directly link the individual costs of an item to an expenditure
  - Thus, costs can be broken down and only incurred when they are needed rather than purchased as part of a larger package
- Example: Lease rather than purchase of fleet cars and office space.
- Example: Outsourcing of human resources or even technology departments
  - Like a marriage: need to divorce

Client/Servers

- Provides for the decentralization of the technology tools
- Data can be stored at the enterprise-wide, group, and individual levels
- Diversifying the data and the technology enables information to be stored throughout the organization
  - Rather than concentrated in a single place

"Applying a client/server approach enables the technology, applications, and data to be stored and accessed efficiently at the local level while being maintained across the organization."

Knowledge-Driven Workers

- Constantly reassembled to lend expertise to a project not restricted to working in a hierarchy
- Constant reassembly keeps workers fresh and focused
- They must clearly understand that sharpness of expertise keeps them employed and focused
  - Rather their longevity in the organization
- Example: persons are organized into teams to accomplish specific project objectives

"Set with a clear beginning and end, the project is organized to accomplish specific objectives using a cross-section of knowledge-driven skills."

Technology Change Drivers

- The technology innovations that enable technology to be implemented in the organization
  - Point-of-Purchase displays
  - Scanning devices
  - ATM machines
  - Voice-activated data entry
- "The change drivers are the tools that propel the implementation of technology to the next stage."

The Adoption Sequence

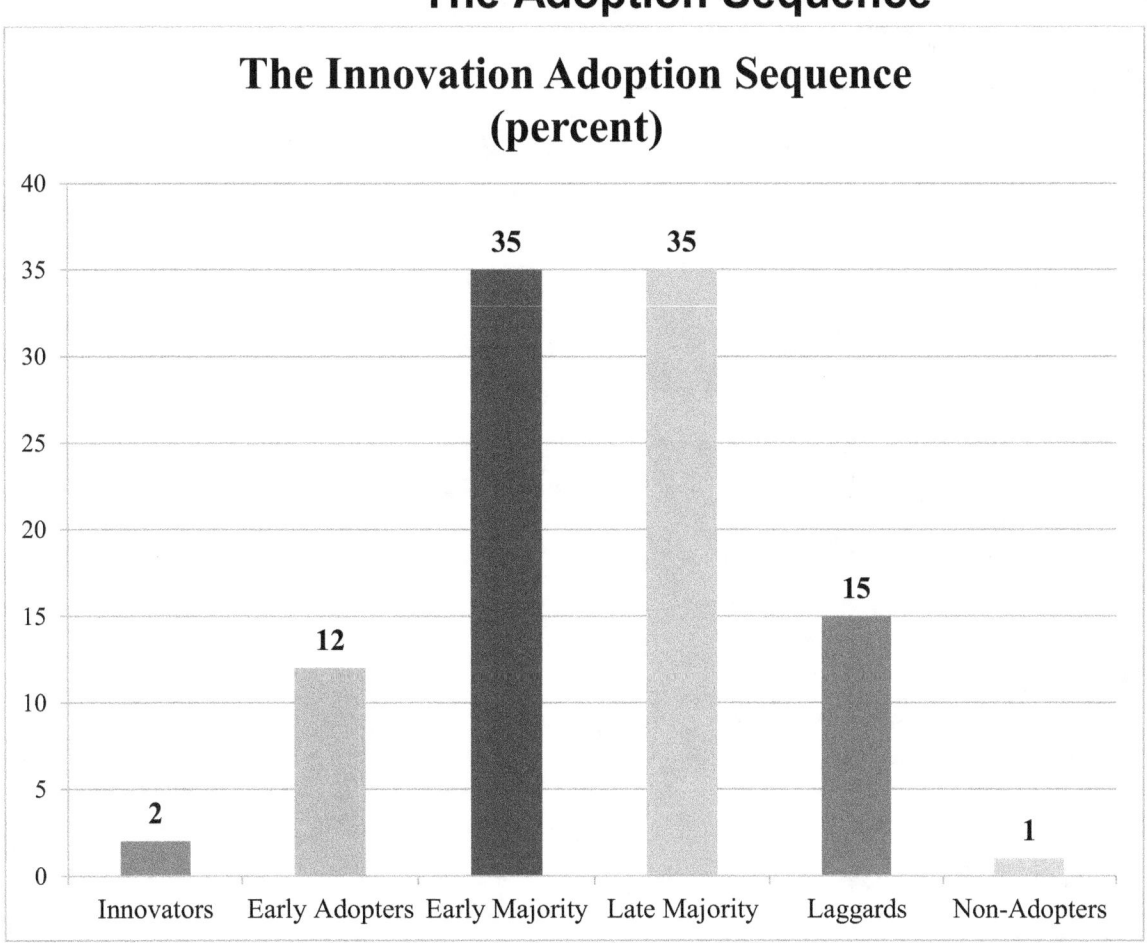

Value Chain

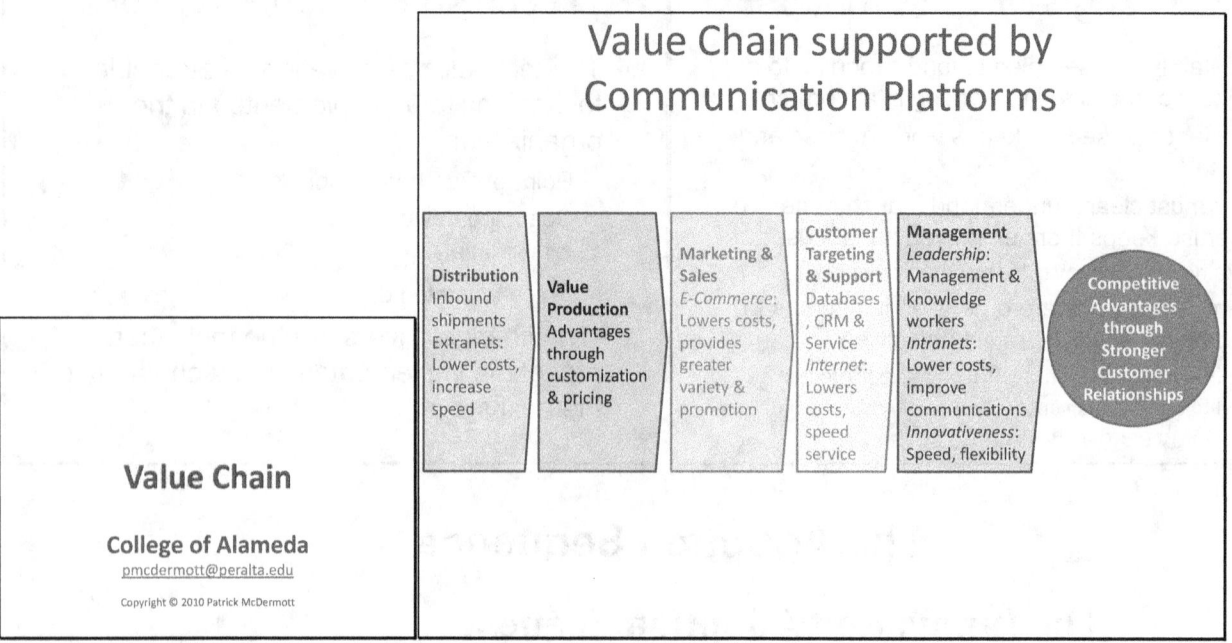

Value Chain supported by Communication Platforms

Distribution
Inbound shipments
Extranets: Lower costs, increase speed

Value Production
Advantages through customization & pricing

Marketing & Sales
E-Commerce: Lowers costs, provides greater variety & promotion

Customer Targeting & Support
Databases, CRM & Service
Internet: Lowers costs, speed service

Management
Leadership: Management & knowledge workers
Intranets: Lower costs, improve communications
Innovativeness: Speed, flexibility

Competitive Advantages through Stronger Customer Relationships

Value Chain

College of Alameda
pmcdermott@peralta.edu

Copyright © 2010 Patrick McDermott

E-Commerce Types

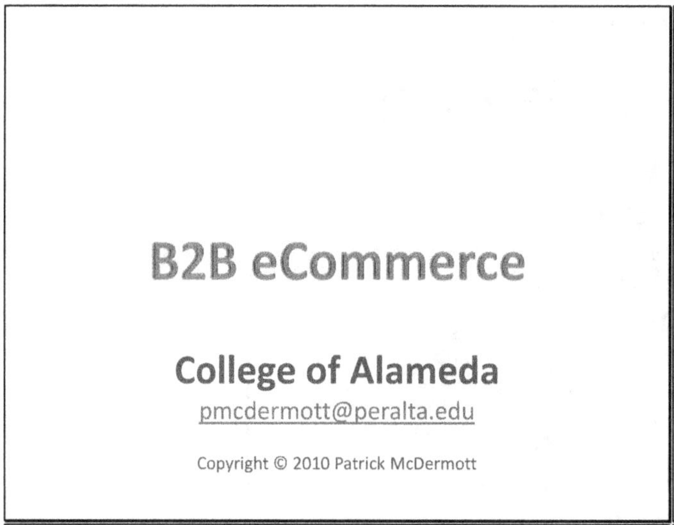

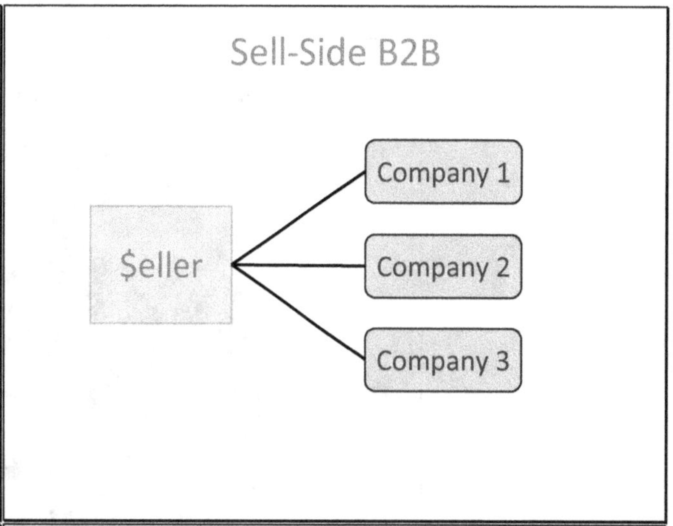

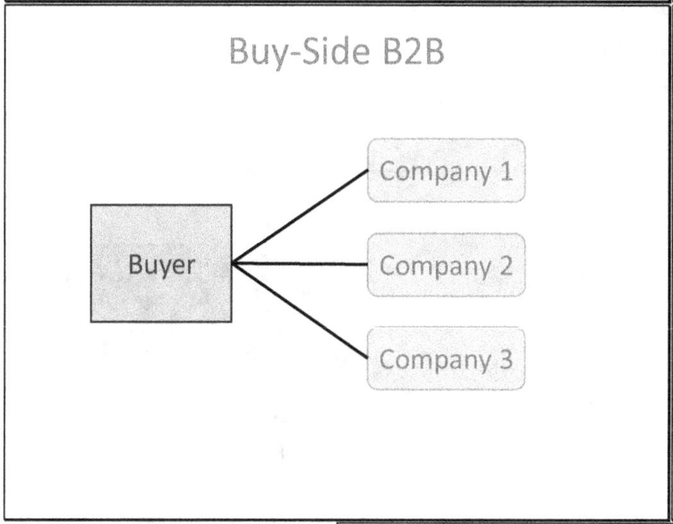

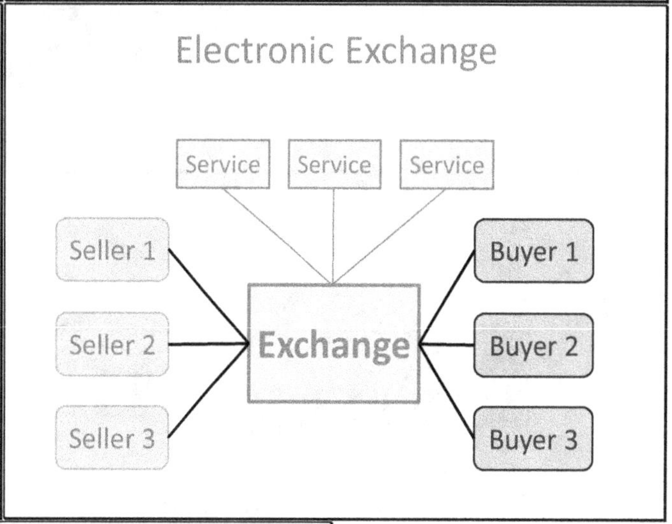

B2B eCommerce **College of Alameda** pmcdermott@peralta.edu Copyright © 2010 Patrick McDermott	Sell-Side B2B $eller → Company 1 $eller → Company 2 $eller → Company 3
Buy-Side B2B Buyer → Company 1 Buyer → Company 2 Buyer → Company 3	Electronic Exchange Service Service Service Seller 1, Seller 2, Seller 3 → Exchange → Buyer 1, Buyer 2, Buyer 3

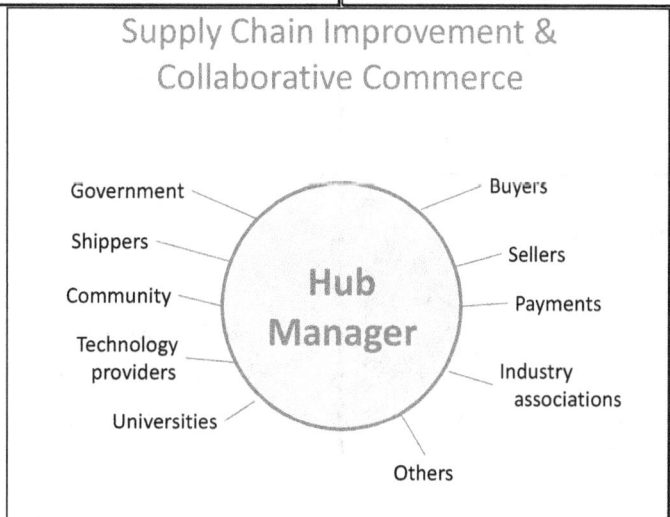

Supply Chain Improvement &
Collaborative Commerce

Government, Shippers, Community, Technology providers, Universities — Hub Manager — Buyers, Sellers, Payments, Industry associations, Others

Marketing

Functions of Marketing

The Functions of Marketing

Selling · Marketing-Information Management · Distribution · Financing · Product / Service Management · Pricing · Promotion

---

**arketing**

The University of California
Berkeley Extension
Copyright © 2007 Patrick McDermott
pmcdermott@msn.com

The 4 P's: Product, Place, Promotion & Price

"Marketing Mix"

✓ Product
✓ Place
✓ Promotion
✓ Price

| **P** Product | **P** Place |
| **P** Promotion | **P** Price |

A 5th P?:
➢ Presence (Web Presence)

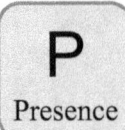
P Presence

---

1. *Product*

✓ Quality
✓ Type of Features
✓ Brand Name
✓ Kind of Packaging
✓ Design Type
✓ Product-Related Services
– Service, Warranties, Maintenance Policies: Website for questions

"Central Agricultural Association of France"
Georges Fay, 1900

---

2. *Place*

➢ Marketing Intermediaries
➢ Market Location
➢ Warehouse Location
➢ Distribution Methods

Hamburg-Amerika Linie
September 1904-January 1905
January 1905-May 1905
Prinzessin Victoria Luise

3. *Promotion*

✓ Developing Promotion Budget
✓ Creating the Advertising Message
✓ Types of Advertising Media
✓ Types of Direct Marketing
✓ Methods of Sales Promotion

Firmin Bouisset
1893
"Menier chocolate"

4. *Price*

✓ Choose Pricing Objective
✓ Estimate Product Demand
✓ Calculate Costs
✓ Maximize Product Mix Pricing
✓ Competitive Factors

Gonzo Marketing

For a completely different point-of-view...

"Gonzo Marketing isn't really about marketing at all. At least not the kind that mutters amnesiacally about the 4 Ps of Product, Place, Price and Promotion. Since the web came along, place no longer matters, the price is often zero, and the first rule of promotion is never talk about the product."

RageBoy Christopher Locke

Christopher Locke, *Gonzo Marketing: Winning through Worst Practices*, Cambridge, Massachusetts: Perseus Publishing (0-7382-0408-0), 2001, p. 103.

Elevator Speech

➢ If you were in an elevator and a potential customer asked: "What is it you could do for me?"
➢ A short description that we can give before the prospect gets off the elevator
➢ To *target* our Brand is *concept* that *point-of-difference*.

	To *target*	MCD, Inc is	*concept*	that	*differentiator*.
1.	To *analysts*	MCD, Inc is	*ideas*	that	*make contradictions useful*.
2.	To *programmers*	MCD, Inc is	*techniques*	that	*improve solutions*.
3.	To *managers*	MCD, Inc is	*understanding*	that	*makes problems productive*.

Evaluate the Storyline

1. If you substitute a competitor's brand, the statement should not make equally good sense.
2. The statement should provide a clear understanding of who should buy, and what would motivate the purchase.
3. It should be clear why the buyer would consider the brand to be a compelling idea.

The Elevator Speech

A major message of RageBoy Christopher Locke's *Gonzo Marketing* is that your marketing should be a story. What is your story?

"Gonzo Marketing isn't really about marketing at all. At least not the kind that mutters amnesiacally about the 4 Ps of Product, Place, Price and Promotion. Since the web came along, place no longer matters, the price is often zero, and the first rule of promotion is never talk about the product." [2]

We need an elevator speech. If you were in an elevator and a potential customer asked: "What is it you could do for me?" we need a short description that we could give before the prospect got off the elevator. Calder & Reagan recommend a sentence paradigm: To *target* our Brand is *concept* that *point-of-difference*. [3] Let's try a few, using my consulting firm, MCD, Inc as an example:

To	**_target_**	Firm is	**_concept_**	that	**_differentiator_**.
1. To *analysts*		MCD, Inc is *ideas*		that *make contradictions useful*.	
2. To *programmers*		MCD, Inc is *techniques*		that *improve solutions*.	
3. To *managers*		MCD, Inc is *understanding*		that *makes problems productive*.	
4. To *students*		MCD, Inc is *skills*		that *lead to good jobs*.	
5. To *people*		MCD, Inc is *insight*		that *shapes policy and understanding*.	

Tybout & Sternthal give us some Questions we can use to evaluate the storyline: [4]

1. If you substitute a competitor's brand, the statement should **not** make equally good sense.

2. The statement should provide a clear understanding of who should buy, and what would motivate the purchase.

3. It should be clear why the buyer would consider the brand to be a compelling idea.

An Agile Elevator Speech

The Speech!	Example
• For [target customer]	• For [construction managers]
• who [statement of need or opportunity]	• who [need to track what work is being done]
• the [product name]	• the [CSWP]
• is a [product category]	• is a [safety work permit system]
• that [key benefit, compelling reason to buy].	• that [tracks and audits safety work permits].
• Unlike [primary competitive alternative]	• Unlike [the current paper-based system]
• our product [statement of primary differentiator].	• our product [is web based and can be accessed any time form anywhere].
— Jonathan Rasmusson, *The Agile Samurai: How Agile Masters Deliver Great Software*, (2010) p. 48.	— Jonathan Rasmusson, *The Agile Samurai: How Agile Masters Deliver Great Software*, (2010) p. 46.

Market Segments

Audience Analysis/Target Audience

Demographics

Characteristics: age, income, education level, gender, race ethnicity, marital status, family size, geographic location, occupation

Gender
Age
Geographic location
Education level
Occupation
Income level

Psychographics

People's interests, activities, lifestyles, values

Risk tolerance
View of money
Political views
Cultural tastes
Comfort with technology

Favorite Internet activities
Feelings about credit card safety online
Types of items commonly purchased online
Likelihood of paying for a service via the internet
Tolerance for receiving promotions through e-mail

Product Usage

ID frequency & quantity of use

Needs & Benefits Segmentation

Divide based on reason or value. e.g. business, entertainment, etc.; convenience, service, price, etc.

Risdahl, Aliza, *Streetwise eCommerce: Establish Your Online Business, Expand Your Reach, and Watch Your Profits Soar!*, Avon Massachusetts: Adams Media (978-1-59869-144-3 1-59869-144-9), 2007, pp. 30-32.

Kleindl, Brad Alan & James L. Burrow, *E-Commerce Marketing*, Mason, Ohio: Thomson / South-Western (0-538-43808-8), 2005, pp. 163-164.

The 4Ps Template

With all our analysis in mind, let's examine and summarize the 4 P's. We'll use the outline from *The Vest-Pocket MBA*. [1]

Product

Quality:
Type of **Features**:
Brand Name:
Kind of Packaging:
Design Type:
Product-Related Services (Service, Warranties, Maintenance Policies):

Place

Number & Type of Marketing **Intermediaries**:
Market Location:
Warehouse Location:
Distribution Methods:

Promotion

Developing **Promotion Budget**:
Creating the **Advertising Message**:
Types of **Advertising Media**:
Types of **Direct Marketing**:
Methods of **Sales Promotion**:

Price

Choose Pricing Objective:
Estimate Product Demand:
Calculate Costs:
Maximize Product Mix Pricing:
Competitive Factors:

---

[1] Shim, Jae K., Joel G. Siegel & Abraham J. Simon, *The Vest-Pocket MBA, Second Edition*, Paramus, New Jersey: Prentice Hall, 1997.

Product Components & Strategies

Product Components
Features
Uses
Brand & Image
Product Quality
Packaging
Guarantees
Customer Service

Strategies

Customer-Based
Market-of-One Strategy
Service Strategy
>> Intangibility
>> Perishability
>> Inseparability
>> Variability

Price-Based
Dynamic Pricing
Auction

Kleindl, Brad Alan & James L. Burrow, *E-Commerce Marketing*, Mason, Ohio: Thomson / South-Western (0-538-43808-8), 2005, pp. 189-190 & 251-254.

---

[2] Locke, Christopher, *Gonzo Marketing: Winning through Worst Practices*, Cambridge, Massachusetts: Perseus Publishing (0-7382-0408-0), 2001, p. 103.

[3] Calder, Bobby J. & Steven J. Reagan, "Brand Design" in Dawn Iacobucci, ed., *Kellogg on Marketing*, New York: John Wiley & Sons, 2001, p. 61.

[4] Tybout, Alice M. & Brian Sternthal, "Brand Positioning" in Dawn Iacobucci, ed., *Kellogg on Marketing*, New York: John Wiley & Sons, 2001, p. 54.

8. Requirements Analysis
Requirements Analysis I

equirements nalysis
Part I

Copyright © 2001 Patrick McDermott
University of California
Berkeley Extension
pmcdermott@msn.com

The most critical phase for Systems Analysis!

A Requirement is…

A Specific Thing your System has to do to Work Correctly.

– Specific: A single thing you can test
– System: The complete app or project
– Correctly: "The <u>customer</u> decides when a system works correctly. So if you leave out a requirement or even if they forget to mention something to you, the system isn't working correctly."

"A requirement is a singular need detailing what a particular produce or service should be or do." —H1OOAD, p. 62.

Domain Analysis

"The process of identifying, collecting, organizing, and representing the relevant information of a domain, based upon the study of existing systems and their development histories, knowledge captured from domain exerts, underlying theory, and emerging technology within a domain."—*H1st OOA&D*

McLaughlin, Brett D., Gary Pollice & David West, *Head First Object-Oriented Analysis & Design*, Sebastopol, California: O'Reilly (0-596-00867-8 978-0-596-00867-3), 2007.

Robert L. Glass

→ Fact 23. One of the two most common causes of runaway projects is unstable requirements.
   (The other is poor estimation)
→ Fact 24. Requirements errors are the most expensive to fix during production.
→ Fact 25. Missing requirements are the hardest requirements errors to correct.
→ Fact 26. Explicit requirements "explode" as implicit (design) requirements for a solution evolve.

Glass, Robert L., *Facts and Fallacies of Software Engineering*, Boston: Addison-Wesley (0-321-11742-5), 2003.

Analyze

- Analyze—Find the details of the situation
- Synthesize—Put together for understanding, communication and improvement
- Investigate
- Data Models
- Use Cases
- Other Models

Béla Uitz
Analysis on a Violet Background
1922

Focus on Requirements

Listen to the Customer: "When it comes to requirements, the best thing you can do is **let the customer talk**. And pay attention to *what* the system needs to do; you can figure out *how* the system will do those things later."—H1OOAD

Don't worry about your code at this stage—just make sure you know what the system should do.

Communicate

✓ Question
✓ Listen
✓ Negotiate
✓ Present
✓ Sell

TALK
LISTEN!

Gause, Donald C. & Gerald M. Weinberg, *Exploring Requirements: Quality Before Design*, New York: Dorset House (0-932633-13-7), 1989.

You Must Ensure

✓ *All* relevant rules within the Scope are
  – Discovered
  – Defined
  – Verified
✓ The Participants ("users", "SMEs", "clients", …) agree that these *are* the Rules
✓ The Rules are documented in such a way that
  – they are unambiguous
  – participants can verify them
✓ They are useful to both audiences
  – IT - analysts, designers, programmers …
  – Business - sponsor, management, subject experts, …

Business Rules

✓ A Purchase Order can specify several Items
✓ A Purchase Order must specify at least one delivery location
✓ Mailing addresses must include a zip code
✓ The format of a zip code is nnnnn-nnnn
✓ An approved vendor must be reviewed every three years
✓ Late fees are calculated by adding 1%
• Exercise: What are the Business Rules for Enrolling in this class?

Process versus Storage

Process vs. Storage
Cognition vs. Memory

Copyright © 2004 Patrick McDermott
UC Berkeley
Extension
pmcdermott@msn.com

Raster or Vector

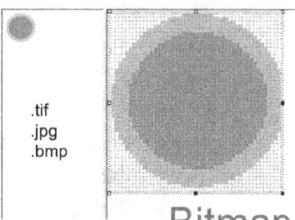
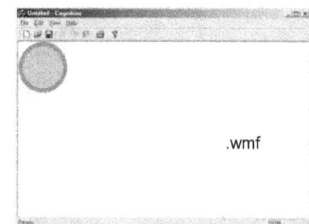

.tif
.jpg
.bmp

800 x 600 Pixels
480,000 pixels
60,000 bytes with 1-Bit Black&White
1,920,000 Bytes with color
Bitmap

1024 x 768 Pixels
786,432 pixels
98,304 bytes 1-Bit Black&White
3,145,728 Bytes with color

.wmf

CPen aPen;
CBrush aBrush;
aPen.CreatePen(1,8,RGB(255,0,0));
aBrush.CreateSolidBrush(RGB(0,255,0));
pDC->SelectObject(aPen);
pDC->SelectObject(aBrush);
pDC->Ellipse(5,5,96,96); // 169 Bytes
Algorithm

Register & Memory

- Mnemonics

- Volatile
  - Phone Number
- Long-Term
- Amnesia
- Autism

The Brain Is a Processor

- Store Highlights, Reconstruct the Rest
- A New Kind of Science?
- Remember Suggestions, Child
- Sgt. Jackson Forgot It was a Story
- Complexity Needs Big Algorithm

Seeing Is Not Believing

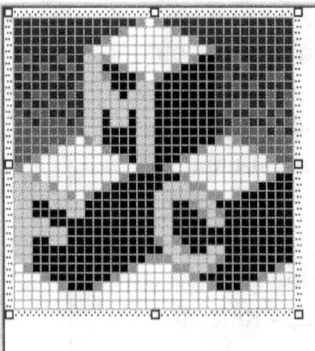

Comix & Pointillism

Un dimanche après-midi à l'Ile de la Grande Jatte

Sunday Afternoon on the Island of La Grande Jatte

Georges Seurat, 1886

"The color is handled in a totally new way, broken down into an infinite series of tiny points, each one separate and detached. Called Pointillism, this technique enhanced the effect of light and shade and provided the model for a "scientific art" Based on a thorough grasp of the principles of optics." [120 in. wide]

COLORS

- (Red + Green) / 2 = Yellow
  - Red 6900Å, Green 4900Å; 5800Å is Yellow
- Where does the averaging take place?
  - In the Eye?
  - In a processor before the sight processors?
    - Like a pre-compiler?
  - By the "seeing" process?
  - By the system
    - Intentional or accidental?
- (Red + Blue) = Purple
  - Wrap Around? 6900Å + 4500Å gives 4000 Å

Requirements Analysis II

Requirements Analysis Part II

Copyright © 2001 Patrick McDermott
University of California
Berkeley Extension
pmcdermott@msn.com

Functions of the Analyst

✓ Help the users identify what is needed to support their business processes

✓ Describe this functionality so the technical staff can build a system to supply it

✓ Translate between business and technicians

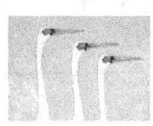 

Suzuki Kiitsu (1796-1858)
Marching Cranes
ca. 1830

Problems

- The existing rules are hidden and tangled
- There are more rules than anyone realizes
- Participants usually operate under similar but *different* rules
  - Multiple participants, multiple points of view
  - Multiple vocabularies and conceptual frameworks
- Many rules are "unconscious"
  - Informal
  - Ad hoc
- Many necessary rules simply don't exist
  - No one knows everything

No Pain, No Gain

- The Acceptability, Usefulness and Integrity of a system is directly proportional to how well business is understood
- The process should be as easy as possible
- But not necessarily easy or painless
  - I never Promised you a Rose Garden
  - No pain, no gain
  - Change ain't easy

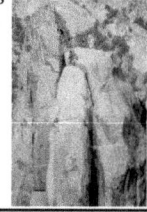

Change to Requirements

- Check your requirements against your Use Cases (Or other list)
- A Change to the Use Cases implies a change to the Requirements
  - and vice versa

The Analyst's Perspective

- But, of course, everyone *thinks* it's all perfectly clear
- You're not just analyzing *what exists;* you're helping define *what will be*
- Some like doing analysis, some hate it
- The All-Seeing I
  - Working outside your area of expertise - you don't know when you don't know
  - At some point, you should know more than any one person

You need to Understand

"You've figured out one of the hardest parts about getting a customer's requirements—sometimes even the *customer* doesn't know what they really want! So you've got to ask the customer questions to figure out what they want before you can determine exactly what the system should do. Then, you can begin to think *beyond* what your customers asked for and anticipate their needs, even before they realize they have a problem."—H1OOAD

What and How

- Separate the "*what*"
- from the "*how*", "*who*" and "*when*"
  ....and "*why*"

- Understanding *business* activities and information so that information systems will support these activities

"Why isn't Anyone Coding yet?"

- "Hey, we all know how this ought to work. Let's get on with it!"

Discuss:
- "The Analysis is Over when the Time Runs Out"

Forms Analysis

Forms Analysis

Copyright © 2007 Patrick McDermott

University of California
Berkeley Extension
pmcdermott@msn.com

Document Analysis

✓ Current Reports
  - *Anything* the Computer Generates
  - And Manually Produced Reports
✓ Forms Analysis
  - Multipart Forms, Rainbow Colors
  - Boxes, Lines
  - The Box Misused: Manila Tax
  - Colored Check Marks
✓ Policy, Procedure, Training manuals

Be Careful—documents could Lie
- Decisions in History

Get a Copy

- The pre-printed stuff is the metadata

The Unformed Form

- The Manila Tax Field
- Diver License # on Checks
- "For Office Use Only"
- Illegal/Embarassing/Shady

Data Flows thru Forms

- Forms & Reports explicitly lay out what data flows in and out
- Get examples of completed forms
- Can become on-line Form
  - Some software calls screens "Forms"
    - Access, dot NET
    - VBA

Things Noticed on a Form

- The company can ship & bill to multiple addresses
- Item # are numeric 5-digits
- Freight is charged to customer
- Tax is calculated

Paper Forms

- On a paper from, you can write in an explanation
  - "Don't Know"
  - "Unknown"
  - "Not Applicable"
  - "None of your Business!"

Use Cases
Use Cases

Use Cases

College of Alameda

pmcdermott@peralta.edu
Copyright © 2007 Patrick McDermott

The Use Case

Use Case Diagrams are a powerful tool to specify and discuss user's roles. They contain Scenarios, which are often used as design or coding specs. Use brainstorming techniques to help come up with Use Cases and Use Case Scenarios to better understand the problem.

The Purpose of Use Case Diagrams
—How users interact with a system

What's a Use Case?

A use case defines discrete system behavior of value to a particular actor (user role). The best use cases are those written in active voice, in present tense, in terms of user action/system response ("the user does this; the system responds by doing that"), and unambiguously using the terms defined in an accompanying glossary or domain model.

A single project may have hundreds of use cases defined. Because the use case defines external system behavior (as observed by the user), it doesn't make inroads into design. In other words, it defines the "what" of a system (as in, what do we want this system to do?) rather than the "how" (as in, how shall it do it?).

Business Level

Use cases are meant to help you understand what a system should do—and often to explain the system to others (like the customer or your boss). If your use case focuses on specific code-level details, it's not going to be useful to anyone but a programmer. As a general rule, your use cases should use simple, everyday language. If you're using lots of programming terms, or technical jargon, your use case is probably getting too detailed to be that useful.—*H1st OOA&D*, p. 77

We are Driven

- ? Procedure Driven
- ? Data Driven
- ? Object Driven
- ? Business Rules Driven
- ? Test-Driven
- ? Workflow Driven
  - ! Sharp & McDermott
- ? Use Case Driven [OOSE]
  - Booch, Rosenberg, Deitels, Agile, etc.
- ☞Real Goal: _____ -Driven

A Use Case…

Describes What your System Does to accomplish a particular Customer Goal:
- What: Use cases are all about the "what"
- System: The complete app or project
- Does: what the system needs to "do".
- Particular: A <u>single</u> UC focus on a <u>single</u> goal
- Customer Goal: "The customer goal is the <u>point</u> of the use case: what do all these steps need to make happen? We're focusing on the customer, remember? The system has to help that customer accomplish their goal."—*H1st OOA&D*, p. 72.

More Formally…

"A use case is a technique for capturing the potential requirements of a new system or software change. Each use case provides one or more *scenarios* that convey how the system should *interact* with the end user or another system to achieve a *specific goal*."—H1st OOA&D, p. 73.

Use Case Benefits

❑ Defines the System Boundary
  ↕ Shows Scope
🐾 IDs Actors
☺ Meaningful to User
➤ Use to Identify/Cross-check classes
📄 Validate the Requirements document

Discovery

Brainstorm
✓ Events
✓ Actors
✓ Document Analysis
✓ CRUD your Classes
✓ CRUD your Relationships
✓ Key Attributes
✓ Methods…

Use Case

✓ A use case will usually define an individual task that is equal to or is less than a business process.
✓ It will usually take place at a single place and time from the user's point-of-view.
✓ It should be logically complete and deliver something of use to the user. It will refer to work done in a process by one actor at one (contiguous) time.

Example

In an activity called Take Order, getting the customer's name is not a good use case, it's part of one, because an order is not logically complete until we know what it is the customer wants to order. The activity is Take an Order, and includes both identifying the customer and recording the items being ordered.

The Book

Rumbaugh, James, Ivar Jacobson & Grady Booch ["The Three Amigos"], *The Unified Modeling Language Reference Manual, Second Edition*, Upper Saddle River, New Jersey: Addison-Wesley (0-321-24562-8), 2006 (2005).

3 Parts to UC Goodness

 Clear Value: Every use case must have a clear value to the system. If the use case doesn't help the customer achieve their goal, then the use case isn't of much use.

 Start & Stop: Every use case must have a definite starting and stopping point. Something must begin the process, and then there must be a condition that indicates the process is complete.

 External Initiator: Every use case is started off by an external initiator, outside of the system. Sometimes that initiator is a person, but it could be anything outside of the system.

Requirements Ripple to UC

✓ Check your requirements against your Use Cases

✓ A Change to the Requirements implies a change to the UCs

✓ Each UC should relate to 1 or more Requirements
   ? Else why is it there?

✓ Each Requirement should be addressed 1 or more UCs

A Use Case has Scenarios

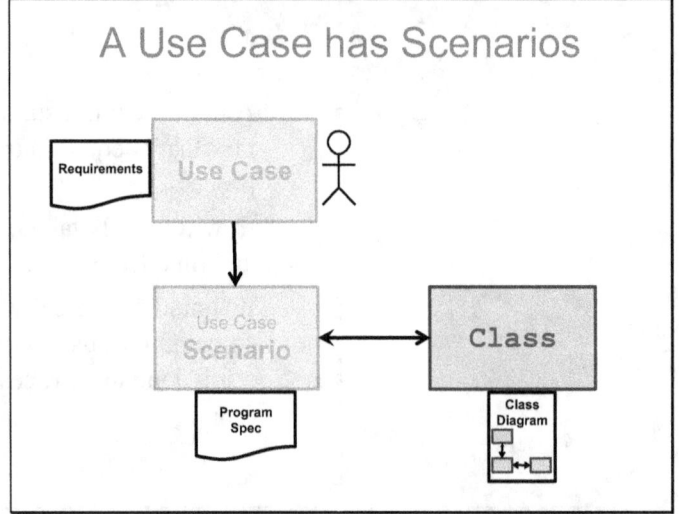

Use Case Diagrams

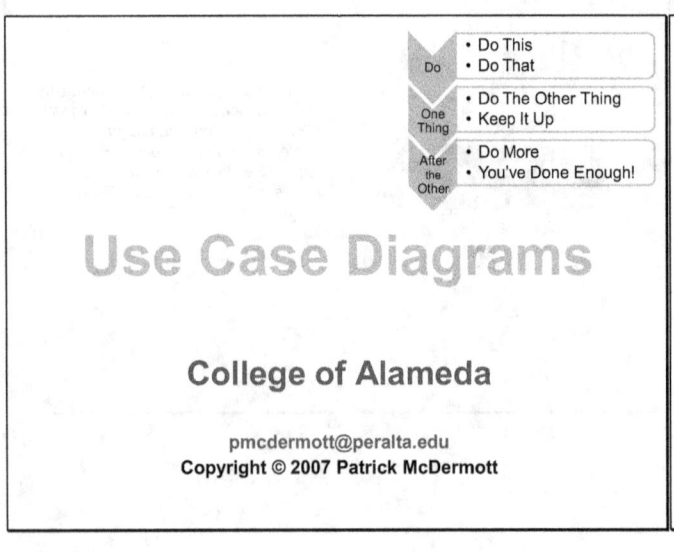

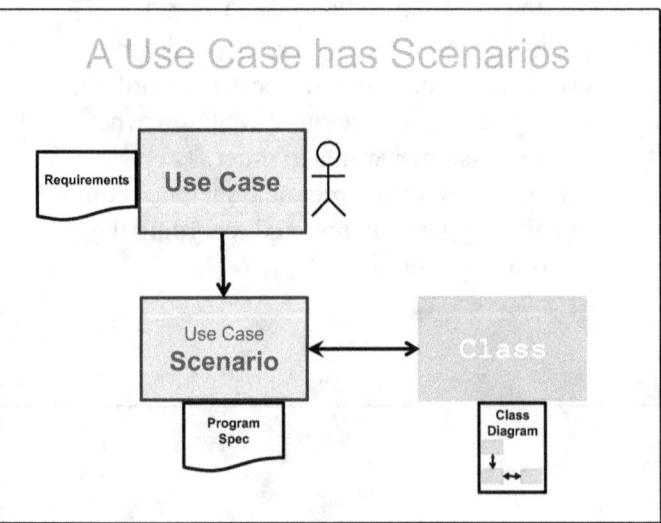

UC Diagrams

"Draw a use case diagram to show what your system <u>IS</u> without getting into unnecessary detail."—*H1st OOA&D*

- The Blueprints for the system
- The Big Picture
- 10,000 foot view

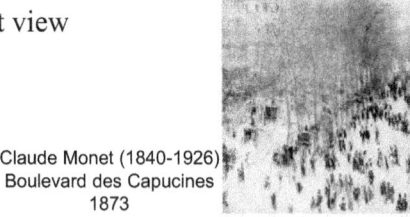

Claude Monet (1840-1926)
Boulevard des Capucines
1873

☐Box☐

- The Box is the System Boundary
- You must provide *everything* inside
- You will NOT provide *anything* outside

- Use it to show Scope

UC Actor

- Outside The System
- Else would be represented inside

Use Cases

- Business "Stories"
- Can become Test Cases
- User Rep: walking use case

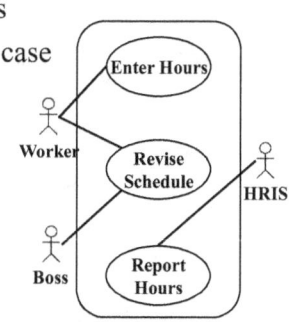

Use Case Diagrams

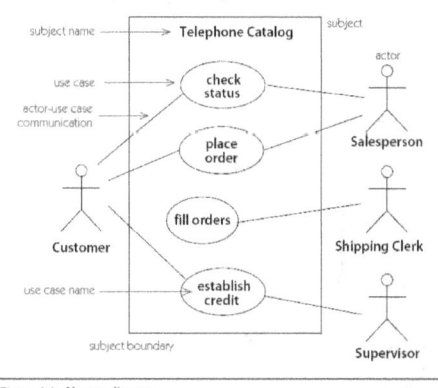

Figure 6-1. *Use case diagram*

A Use Case Diagram

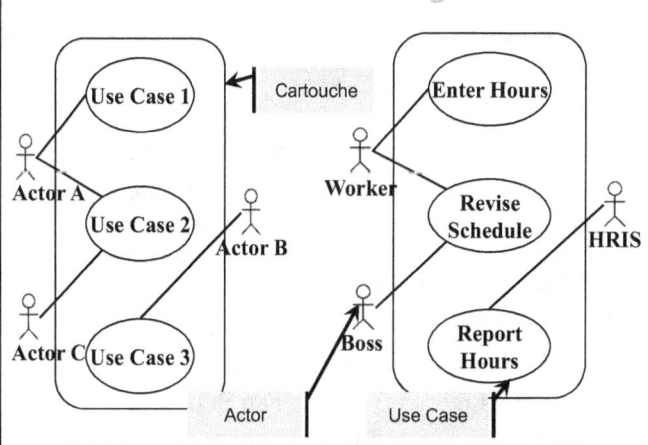

127

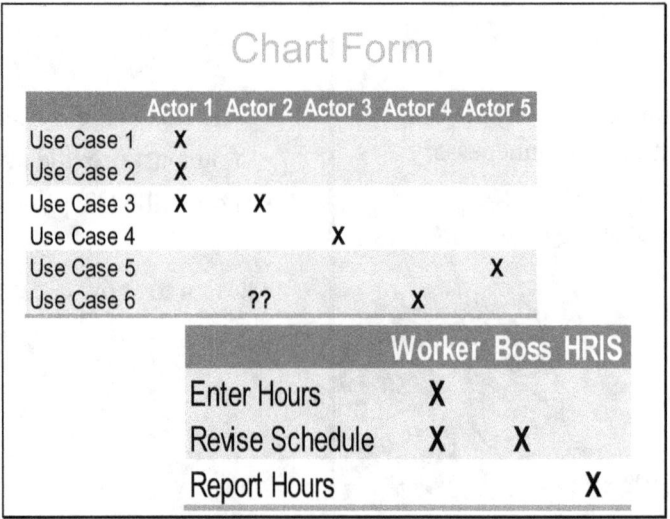

Chart Form

	Actor 1	Actor 2	Actor 3	Actor 4	Actor 5
Use Case 1	X				
Use Case 2	X				
Use Case 3	X	X			
Use Case 4			X		
Use Case 5					X
Use Case 6		??		X	

	Worker	Boss	HRIS
Enter Hours	X		
Revise Schedule	X	X	
Report Hours			X

Use Case Scenarios

The Word

Sometimes a Word is worth a thousand Pictures

The Use of Cases: Use Case Scenarios

College of Alameda

pmcdermott@peralta.edu
Copyright © 2007 Patrick McDermott

Why I Recommend

- Scenario-Driven
- Can become Test Cases
- One Case—user did test cases B4 we started
  - Wonderful!
  - But never worked in another case
- Can become User Manual
- Better yet, can come FROM user Manual:
  - *"Write the user manual, then write the code."*

📖Words & Pictures📖

- Eventually Pictures fail, Words are Needed
- Pictorial diagrams become too complex (e.g., trying to show every decision point and path in an event-driven interface), and don't illustrate desired system functions
- Flowchart is no better than code
  - Once you grasp it, you no longer need it
- Access Query no Better than SQL Code
- Like a storyteller with unnecessary detail
  - It was 5 years ago, Or maybe 6. No, wait, it was 4½ years ago, or was it?

A Use Case has Scenarios

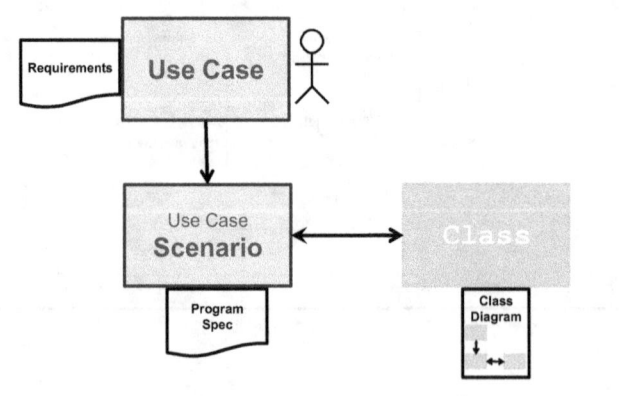

Scenarios

A complete path through a use case, from the first step to the last, is called a **Scenario**.

Most use cases have several scenarios, but they always share the same user goal.

3 Audiences

Write your use cases in a way that makes sense to <u>you</u>, your *boss*, and your <u>customers</u>.—*H1st OOA&D*, p. 151

☞ Check the Weather ☂

⇨ UC Main Path
  ☼ Sunny Day
⇆ Alternate Path
  ☂ Rainy Day
  – Optional Path

UC Formats

- Simple, Step-based format
- Focus on Interaction
- When … Then
- Can be
  ✓ Paragraph
  ✓ Table
  ✓ Steps
    - Numbers/Subnumbers
    - Alternate too

Use Case Scenario

- Note that one use case is a collection of several use case scenarios. A use case might be `Register Vehicle`. Four scenarios: `Register New Vehicle`, `Register Out-of-State Vehicle`, `Re-Register Existing Vehicle`, `Register Stolen Vehicle`.

- We'll use "step" to refer to the lower level items: they are called steps on our diagrams and are portrayed as boxes, but the individual workers often call them tasks, or activities.

A Scenario

Worker Enters Time: Sunny Day Scenario		
When...	**Then...**	**Objects**
Worker logs in	System displays current schedule	Schedule
Worker selects Week	System displays current schedule	Task
Worker selects Task	System displays task	Task
Worker enters hours for task	System edits task entry for reasonableness	Task
Worker indicates "Finished"	System edits schedule for reasonableness	
Worker logs out	System informs Boss of completion	

Instance

Use case behavior for parent Verify Identity:

The parent is abstract, there is no behavior sequence.
A concrete descendant must supply the behavior as shown below.

Use case behavior for child Check Password:

Obtain password from master database
Ask user for password
User supplies password
Check password against user entry

Use case behavior for child Retinal Scan:

Obtain retinal signature from master database
Scan user's retina and obtain signature
Compare master signature against scanned signature

Figure 14-288. *Behavior sequences for parent and child use cases*

Use Case Instance
The execution of a sequence of actions in a specified use case.
An instance of a use case.

Loops in UC

- "Lots of times a use case has a set of steps that need to be repeated, but there's not a standard way to show that in the cases. So we just made one up!"—*H1st OOA&D*
- They put "the system repeats steps a-x until complete."
- In reality, not a problem

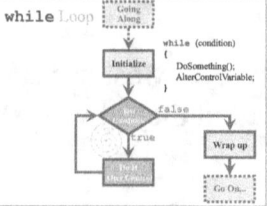

Include & Extend

It's "easy to spend a lot of time arguing over whether a use case extends this use case, or includes that one...but it's really not that big of a deal, and those keywords should <u>never</u> distract from the overall design process."—*H1st OOA&D*

Use Case When/Then's

Worker Enters Time: Sunny Day Scenario		
When...	**Then...**	**Objects**
Worker logs in	System displays current schedule	**Schedule**
Worker selects Week	System displays current schedule	**Task**
Worker selects Task	System displays task	**Task**
Worker enters hours for task	System edits task entry for reasonableness	**Task**
Worker indicates "Finished"	System edits schedule for reasonableness	
Worker logs out	System informs Boss of completion	

9. The Unified Modeling Language
The Notorious 13

UML: Unified Modeling Language
The Notorious 13 (±1)
The 13 Diagrams defined in UML

Structure

Class	Deployment
Component	Object
Composite Structure	Package

CRC

Although not strictly part of UML, CRC (Class-Responsibility-Collaborator) Cards are frequently used in UML projects.

Behavior

Use Case

| Activity | State Machine |

Interaction

| Sequence | Interaction Overview |
| Communication | Timing |

Sequence & Communication are semantically equivalent, with different emphasis.

The Zen of Class

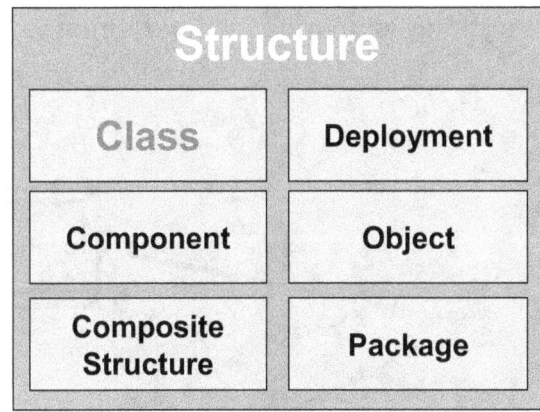

Bathing at Asnières, 1883

A Sunday Afternoon on the Island of La Grande Jatte 1884–86

The Zen of Class

McD, Inc

pmcdermott@msn.com

Georges-Pierre Seurat (1859–91)

Diagram Kinds

1. Fundamental
2. Attributive
   – Multiple attributes
3. Associative
   – Break M2M
   – Employee--Department needs Assignment

Impostors

- Methods
  - Payroll, BOM, Budgeting
- Calculations
  - Average Age
- Reports
- Attributes

Goldilocks

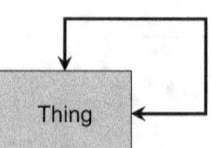

Everything is a Thing   **Everything is Unique**

Apples & Oranges

- Compare Apples and Oranges
- Both fruit, same size, price
- Could substitute in lunches
- Fruit Salad

Henri Fantin-Latour (1836–1904)
Lemon, Apples, and Tulips (Tulips and Fruit)
1865

Captioned "Apples",
but looks like Apple & Orange
or even 2 Oranges!

MVC

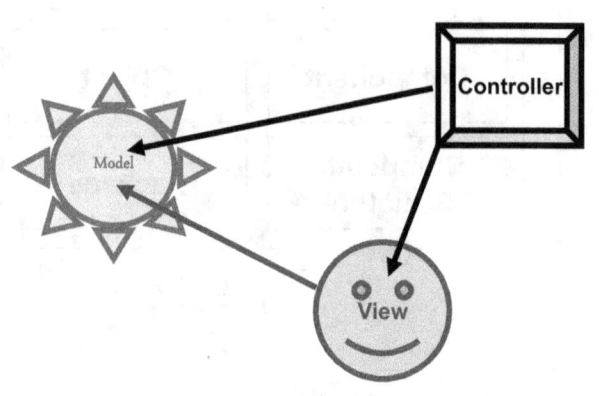

Implemented by Microsoft as Document-View

Who can See

- Public
- Private
- Protected

The Only Thing
known for Certain is:

NOTHING

is known

For Certain

Finding Classes

A Quest:
David, Earl of Huntingdon, 1120
from *A Critical Inquiry into Antient Armour* (1842)

Finding Classes

College of Alameda

pmcdermott@peralta.edu

A Class Tracks…

An Entity: A ***Thing*** the Business needs to know about.

At this stage, a business person should be able to understand every one of them.

"Entity" is best defined by examples…

People

Albrecht Dürer (1471-1528)
Self-Portrait
1498

George Romney (1734-1802)
Emma, Lady Hamilton (1761-1815)
1786

Places

Things

Katsushika Hokusai 葛飾北斎 (1760-1849)
Fuji from beneath Mannen Bridge in Fukagawa
Fukagawa mannenbashi shita
深川万年橋下
36 Views of Mount Fuji
富嶽三十六景 Fugaku Sanjūrokkei
ca. 1831-1834

Gustave Caillebotte (1848–94)
Le pont de l'Europe
1877

Events

Meeting of the Rails
Promontory Point, Utah, 1869
Andrew J. Russell

Organizations

Dorothea Lange (1895-1965)
Richmond shipyards, 1943

Dorothea Lange (1895-1965)
*End of shift 3:30, Richmond, California
September 1943*

Examples of Classes

Tangible
- People
  - Employees
  - Students
- Places
  - Shipping Locations
  - Offices
- Things
  - Equipment
  - Vehicles

Intangible
- Accounts
- Cost Centers
- Departments
- Grades

You need a Class if...

- There's a form
- There's a number
- There's a file
- There are several copies
- It's Important
- NOTE—
  - Sections and boxes on Forms
  - The name might not be obvious

They're Everywhere!

Classes have **Responsibilities**

- Personification Helps
  - What if a person, not a computer, does it?
  - Obligation or Contract

- Know Things
  - Invoice: Know who the Customer is
- Do Things
  - Invoice: Compute Total

Harmon's UML Diagram Relationships

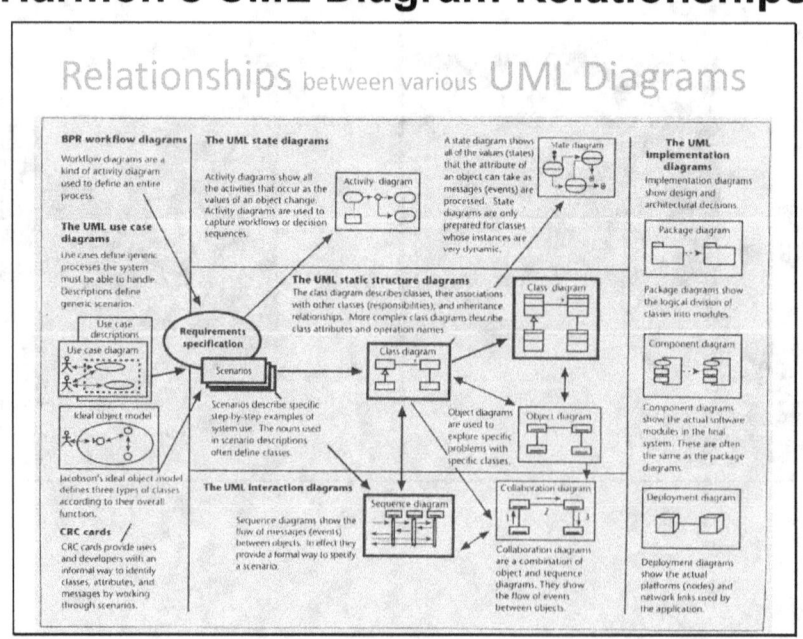

The Tao of Business Modeling

Carlo Carrà (1881-1966)
Rhythms of Objects, 1911

Tao of Business Objects

Copyright © 1999 Patrick McDermott

UC Berkeley

Extension
pmcdermott@msn.com

Precision vs. Clarity

A Well-Designed Computer System requires Precise definitions for all Business Objects

千里の道も一歩から

Even a Journey of a Thousand Miles starts from 0.409332787556283 Step

—OR—

Even a Journey of 2,443.1398 Miles starts from One Step

The Matter of the Dogs in the Park

"A little inaccuracy sometimes saves tons of explanation"—Saki

---

The Sound of One Hand Clapping

Many modeling questions are like Zen koans

☯When is a customer not a customer?

☯When is an attribute not an attribute?

☯How big is big?

☯How Different is Different?

And, yes, even…

"What is the meaning of *is*"?

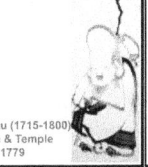

Ito Jakuchu (1715-1800)
Man, Dove & Temple
Detail, ca. 1779

Conundra

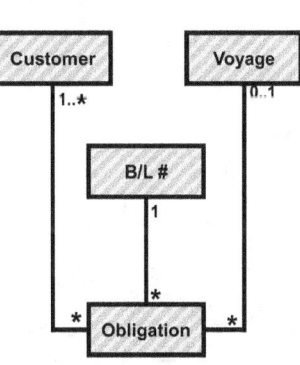

Jackson Pollock
The Moon-Woman Cuts the Circle
1943

Potential vs. Actual
- ✓Is a prospect a customer?
- ✓Is an applicant an employee?
- ✓Is an embryo a person?

Over Time, History
- ✓Is a retiree an employee?
- ✓Is an in-law a relative after a divorce?

There always is one, but you can't know it
- Safeway doesn't know customer
  - Unless Rewards cards

---

1 or Infinite?

- When is it so different it's different?
- A Difference in Degree vs. Kind

- Every thing is a thing
- Each thing is unique in its way

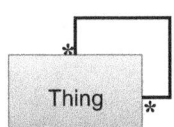

Thing

- Invoice vs. BL at APL…

B/L vs. Invoice

Customer 1..*

Voyage 0..1

B/L # 1

Obligation *

- Customer
  - B/L 2
  - Invoice 1
- Vessel
  - B/L Yes
  - Invoice No
- Multiple #
  - B/L Yes
  - Invoice No

B/L | Invoice

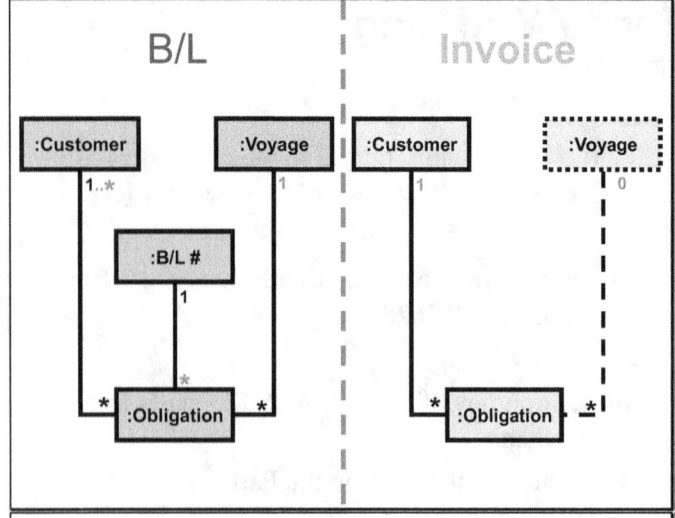

What's a Person?

Moulin de la Galette
Pierre-Auguste Renoir
c. 1876

Peopleness
- "Legal Person"
  – Person
  – Organization
  – Couple (IRS)
- Tracking company subsidiaries
  – If not independent purchaser
- Worker employee, contractor
  – Manager, IRS, HR see differently

Customer

- Do You Know who it is?
  – The Unknown customer at APL (biggest customer)
- Boeing Yes: **Customer <==> Product**
- Safeway NO
  – To Card or Not to Card: That is the Question
  – Reward Cards
- Others maybe
- W/o address

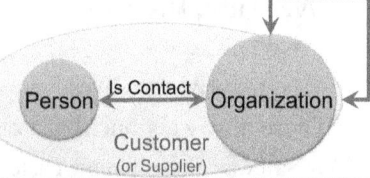

Vendor

Vendor: A supplier of goods or services(?)
  – Government, IRS, Customs
  – Employee for travel expense, bonus, reward
  – Customer—overpay, refund, return
  – Petty Cash—no vendor
  – Anyone you pay
What's a Product???
  – APL
    • Every Commodity on every Port pair?
  – Cadillac
    • With or w/o Options?
  – How Many Vital to Analysis
    • You can't count unless you know what they are

Recursion

- Quaker Oats Box
  – Morton Salt Girl
- Pepsi/Taco Bell
- Employee supervises Employee
- Bill of Materials: BOM

Remember

The **best** modeling technique:

O/O is OK!

O/O Benefits

O/O is OK!
O/O Benefits

Copyright © 2006 Patrick McDermott

UC Berkeley
Extension

pmcdermott@msn.com

Holy Graille

Camille Brven
Machine for Making Objects in my Mind
1938

- Re-Use
  - Instead of re-inventing the wheel, you can build on previous work
- Maintenance
  - Most of the cost of a system is in maintenance. It's claimed O/O reduces maintenance cost.
- The Far-flung Effect
- Bottom-line practical benefit: if a company is using it, they won't hire you if you don't know it.

Deitels[2]

"Using today's object-oriented languages, such as C++, Visual Basic .NET, Java and C#, programmers can program in an object-oriented manner that more naturally reflects the way in which they perceive the world. This has resulted in productivity gains."

Some organizations "indicate that object-oriented programming tends to produce software that is more understandable because it is better organized and has fewer maintenance requirements."

Ontology

Brian Cantwell Smith *Origin of Objects*, the exploding interest in object-oriented languages: "this turn of events had led computer science squarely into the business of doing research into ontology."

"A few years ago, at a workshop on the perception of objects, I raised a question about one of the philosophers' ontological assumptions, which seemed to me altogether too neat. I was concerned about basic issues of object identity—about what makes a newspaper into a single entity as opposed to a large number of separate pieces of paper, what distinguishes the headache that I had this morning from the one I had last night, what it is for Microsoft Word on PCs to be "the same program" as Microsoft Word on the Macintosh."

Kris Jamsa Good Reasons I

1. Ease of design and code reuse—After the code works properly, the use of objects increases your ability to reuse a design or code you created for one application within a second application.
2. Increased reliability—After you have properly tested object libraries, your use of existing (working) code will improve your program's reliability.
3. Ease of understanding—Object use helps programmers focus on and understand key system components. The use of objects lets designers and programmers focus on the smaller pieces of a system and provides a framework within which designers can focus more on the operations programs perform on the objects, the information objects must store, and other key system components.

Jamsa, Kris, PhD, MBA, *Jamsa's C/C++/C# Programmer's Bible: The Ultimate Guide to C/C++/C# Programming, Second Edition*, Albany, New York: Onword Press / Thomson Learning (0-7668-4682-2), 2002, Tip 883, p. 474.

Jamsa Good Reasons II

4. Increased abstraction—Abstraction lets designers and programmers "look at the big picture"—temporarily ignoring underlying details so they can work with system elements they can more easily understand. For example, by focusing only on the word processor objects, the implementation of a word processor can become much less intimidating.
5. Increased encapsulation—*Encapsulation* groups all the pieces of an object into one neat package. For example, a Book class can combine the functions and data fields a program must have to work with a book. The programmers who are working with the Book class do not need to know each piece of the class, only that they need to use the class within their program. The class, in turn, will bring with it all the necessary pieces.
6. Increased information hiding—*Information hiding* is the ability for your program to treat a function, procedure, or an object as a "black box," using the item to perform a specific operation without having to know what goes on inside. For example, your programs can use I/O stream objects for input and output without having to understand how the streams work.

O/O Problems

Hassan Shakir
Objective Contemplations
1986

O/O, Oh No!

Copyright © 2006 Patrick McDermott
College of Alameda
pmcdermott@peralta.edu

Object oriented: Directed toward just about anything you can think of.
–Meilir Page-Jones

What's O/O Good For?

"Some reactionaries would say that object orientation is good for nothing; it's merely a religious cult, or a global conspiracy based somewhere on the West Coast. Some revolutionaries will say that object orientation is the first and only miracle solution to all our software woes." —Meiler Page-Jones

"The revolutionists believe that a group of developers woke up at 3 o'clock one morning and realized that we have been developing software the wrong way all along." —Arthur Riel

Model The World

1. Model the World. Cesar Millan, famed dog trainer, explaining the advice his farmer father gave him that is at the root of his dog-training methods: "Never work against Mother Nature."

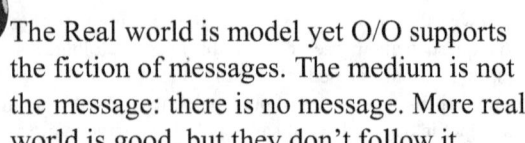

The Real world is model yet O/O supports the fiction of messages. The medium is not the message: there is no message. More real world is good, but they don't follow it.

Do We Think That Way?

2. It's the way we think, but hard to learn. Horstmann: "Books on object-oriented design, such as [Booch] and [Rumbaugh], provide outstanding guidance for object orientation in the development process, but undergraduate students rarely have sufficient experience in large-scale software development to envision the complexities that these methodologies address."

In fact, O/O makes a small program longer, slower, and less understandable.

Can't Be Done Right?

3. It's universally accepted, but no one is doing it right.

"Unfortunately, most OO design books cultivate a priesthood mentality of turgidly written methodologies that are too complex to be actually useful." —Cay S. Horstmann

"The first annoyance you will encounter in learning the object-oriented paradigm is the proliferation of buzzwords that permeates the field." —Arthur Riel

Use Cases & Workflow

4. Use Cases are not Object/Oriented, they're process oriented. So the number 1 O/O technique is not O/O.
- Is *Everything* an Object?
- Jacobsen uses Workflow to describe his own development process.

"The CLR allows types to be marked as *Abstract* or *Sealed* but not both. I think this restriction is unfortunate because a number of types don't allow instances of themselves to be created and can't be used as a base type. For example, it doesn't make sense to construct an instance of the Console or Math type because these types contain only static methods."—Jeffrey Richter

Money & Maintenance

5. It's said to ease maintenance but advocated by people who never maintain, and don't want to.

"Software that is developed with the goal of later reuse can increase costs by as much as 31%. This doesn't say whether the initiative actually succeeds."—Steve McConnell

Is there any proof it IS more maintainable? And maybe maintenance never comes. What percent—if cost, how about a CBA. Net Present Value. % of lines reworked. Lines saved.

In a rapidly changing world, TTM (Time To Market) is more important than reduced maintenance cost.

Business is short-sighted, but so is evolution. Eating is short sighted, but if you die in the short term there will be no long term.

Update Anywhere

6. Predictability is good yet Inheritance-> unpredictability.

7. "Can be updated anywhere" is bad but that's what inheritance does. Inheritance causes Update Anywhere. Update lots of places not that bad; and you have to test it anyway. You're usually looking right at the problem. Why is Update anywhere Bad?—IDE could address. Update anywhere is not a real problem—use pencils, stickies, paper clips. Sorted XRef has been around for a long time. IDE should do it. MFocus, VC++ tools.

Wrong Value, not Object Type

8. The wrong value is usually the problem, not where it happened.

Joel Spolsky: "Types can do only one kind of test, i.e., 'Can I do this thing to that object?' They can't test 'Does this function actually return 2.12 when the input values are 1, 32, and 'aardvark.' "

Standards

9. Standardization can be good—but malls, cars are not standard.
   - One Size Might Not Fit All

10. RAD (Rapid Application Development); XP (eXtreme Programming); AM (Agile Modeling)
    - Versus careful planning implied by Conan the Librarian, function prototypes
    - "Foolish Consistency is the Hobgoblin of Little Minds"—Thoreau(?)

Information Hiding

O/O says Information Hiding is good, but Knowledge is Power. Perhaps you don't need to know the details, but knowing doesn't hurt!

Embraced by academics who think knowledge is good for its own sake

Sometimes the best way to explain the rules is to explain the process. Sometimes the Rules are the process. "How" is easier to explain: O/S startup; Season ticket holders re-issue; File catalog

"Despite the fact that inheriting from a class does not require access to the class's source code, developers often insist on seeing the source code to understand how the class is implemented. They may, for example, want to ensure that they are extending a class that performs well and is implemented securely."—Deitel & Deitel, C#

I Advocate

Hybrids. Cars, Classes, Programs
- Business Objects are Hybrids
- Nature is Hybrid
- Humans are Hybrid
  - People sometimes think procedurally, but sometimes objectify
  - No problem mixing, it's our Universe…
- Life is multi-paradigmatic
- "Why, the best way to explain it is to do it." —*Alice's Adventures in Wonderland*

O/O— Oh, Oh!

In which I collect arguments in favor of and against O/O.

First, I will drink the Kool Aid. Then, I will be a contrarian and point out some problems. You must make up your own mind.

We don't want to get into a deep philosophical discussion, but this will help you understand, and you might be called upon to set standards and choose languages.

Whither objects or wither objects?

Objections to Objects

The Emperor Object is Wearing no Clothes

Lippman: "In C, a data abstraction and the operations that perform on it are declared separately—that is, there is no language-supported relationship between data and functions. We speak of this method of programming as procedural, driven by a set of algorithms divided into task-oriented functions operating on shared, external data." [1]

Riel: "the first annoyance you will encounter in learning the object-oriented paradigm is the proliferation of buzzwords that permeates the field." [2]

"In the last few years, the term object model has been stretched a bit thin through overuse. For a term so heavily used, finding a concrete, generic definition is surprisingly hard." [3]

We Are Driven

"Each analysis technique is driven by a certain perspective. So what's the best perspective? In the beginning, all computer programs were process-driven. Then along came Data Base Management Systems, and we became data-driven—for a time, it was fashionable for Data Administrators to proclaim themselves "data bigots". Just about everyone now agrees that both process and data are essential, in fact we once called our profession data processing, but how to bring both data and process into the equation? The extreme was to bring the procedures and data together into objects, and become object-driven. But even object gurus disagree on whether we should be driven by the objects: the UML object modeling technique as described by the Three Amigos, led by Ivar Jacobson, is use-case-driven, and Peter Coad has become feature-driven. So how about business rules? USoft was business-rule-driven until it was driven out of business. Workflow brought other possibilities. The first workflow tools were document-driven, while current tools like SAP are event-driven. Of course your eventual goal is to be chauffeur-driven, but to get there you need to design the right system." [4]

Metaphysics

Brian Cantwell Smith *Origin of Objects*, the exploding interest in object-oriented languages: "this turn of events had led computer science squarely into the business of doing research into ontology." [5]

"A few years ago, at a workshop on the perception of objects, I raised a question about one of the philosophers' ontological assumptions, which seemed to me altogether too neat. I was concerned about basic issues of object identity—about what makes a newspaper into a single entity as opposed to a large number of separate pieces of paper, what distinguishes the headache that I had this morning from the one I had last night, what it is for Microsoft Word on PCs to be "the same program" as Microsoft Word on the Macintosh." [6]

---

[1] Lippman, Stanley R., *Inside the C++ Object Model*, Reading, Massachusetts: Addison-Wesley (0-201-83454-5), 1996, p. 1.

[2] Riel, Arthur J., *Object-Oriented Design Heuristics*, Reading, Massachusetts: Addison-Wesley (0-201-63385-X), 1996, p. 2.

[3] Stephens, Rod, *Microsoft Office Programming: A Guide for Experienced Developers*, New York: Apress / Springer Verlag (1-59059-121-6), 2003, p. 223.

[4] McDermott, Patrick, *Zen and the Art of Systems Analysis: Meditations on Computer Systems Development*, New York: iUniverse (0-595-25679-1 [Paper], 0-595-75230-6 [eBook] & 0-595-65255-7 [Hardback]), 2003 (2002), p. 49-50.

[5] Smith, Brian Cantwell, *On the Origin of Objects*, Cambridge, Massachusetts: The MIT Press / Bradford Book (0-262-69209-0), 1998 (1996), p. 44.

[6] Smith, Brian Cantwell, *On the Origin of Objects*, Cambridge, Massachusetts: The MIT Press (0-262-69209-0), 1998 (1996), p. vii.

ASSOCIATION: The semantic relationship among two or more classifiers that involves connections among their instances.—Rumbaugh, *Reference*, p. 152.

RELATIONSHIP: A reified semantic connection among model elements. Kinds of relationships include association, generalization, flow, and several kinds of dependency. —Rumbaugh, *Reference*, p. 411.

English

What does the word object mean in English? [1]

1. anything that is visible or tangible and is relatively stable in form.

2. a thing, person, or matter to which thought or action is directed: *an object of medical investigation.*

3. the end toward which effort or action is directed; goal; purpose: *Profit is the object of business.*

4. a person or thing with reference to the impression made on the mind or the feeling or emotion elicited in an observer: *an object of curiosity and pity.*

5. anything that may be apprehended intellectually: *objects of thought.*

Page-Jones "*Object oriented:* Directed toward just about anything you can think of." [2]

Religious War

Riel: "In the process of learning about the object-oriented paradigm and all that it encompasses, you will first become aware of the many divisions within our community. Each division implies two or more camps who are generally very religious about their point of view. One of the first divisions of importance is the revolutionists versus the evolutionists. The revolutionists believe that a group of developers woke up at 3 o'clock one morning and realized that we have been developing software the wrong way all along." [3]

Page-Jones: What's Object Orientation good for? "Some reactionaries would say that object orientation is good for nothing; it's merely a religious cult, or a global conspiracy based somewhere on the West Coast. Some revolutionaries will say that object orientation is the first and only miracle solution to all our software woes." [4]

"Unfortunately, most OO design books cultivate a priesthood mentality of turgidly written methodologies that are too complex to be actually useful." [5] —Cay S. Horstmann, *Practical Object-Oriented Development*

Benefits

Bottom-line practical benefit: if a company is using it, they won't hire you if you don't know it.

Kris Jamsa: "As you will learn, object-oriented programming has many advantages, two of which are object reuse and ease of understanding." [6]

Lee & Tepfenhart: "the object-oriented method allows software developers to manage the complexity of the problem domain and its supporting technology. When developers can manage more aspects of the problem domain, they can produce more flexible and more maintainable software." [7] Is complexity of programs increasing because as machines got better we turned them on harder problems.

---

[1] "object." *Dictionary.com Unabridged (v 1.0.1).* Based on the Random House Unabridged Dictionary, © Random House, Inc. 2006, Retrieved September 03, 2006 from http://dictionary.reference.com/search?q=object.

[2] Page-Jones, Meilir, *Fundamentals of Object-Oriented Design in UML,* Reading, Massachusetts: Addison-Wesley (0-201-69946-X), 2000, p. 1.

[3] Riel, Arthur J., *Object-Oriented Design Heuristics*, Reading, Massachusetts: Addison-Wesley (0-201-63385-X), 1996, p. 1.

[4] Page-Jones, Meilir, *Fundamentals of Object-Oriented Design in UML,* Reading, Massachusetts: Addison-Wesley (0-201-69946-X), 2000, p. 64.

[5] Horstmann, Cay, *Practical Object-Oriented Development in C++ and Java*, New York: John Wiley & Sons (0-471-14767-2), 1997, p. x.

[6] Jamsa, Kris, PHD, MBA, *Jamsa's C/C++/C# Programmer's Bible: The Ultimate Guide to C/C++/C# Programming, Second Edition*, Albany, New York: Onword Press / Thomson Learning (0-7668-4682-2), 2002, Tip 882, p. 473.

[7] Lee, Richard C. & William M. Tepfenhart, *UML and C++: A Practical Guide to Object-Oriented Development*, Upper Saddle River, New Jersey: Prentice Hall (0-13-619719-1), 1997, p. 5.

Pierre-Alain Muller: "The stability of models with respect to real-world entities". [1]

Pierre-Alain Muller: "Iterative construction, which is made easier by the weak coupling between components". [2]

Deitels: "Using today's object-oriented languages, such as C++, Visual Basic .NET, Java and C#, programmers can program in an object-oriented manner that more naturally reflects the way in which they perceive the world. This has resulted in productivity gains." [3]

Deitels: Some organizations "indicate that object-oriented programming tends to produce software that is more understandable because it is better organized and has fewer maintenance requirements." [4]

Pierre-Alain Muller: "it is necessary to decompose—to divide—in order to understand, and it is necessary to compose—to reunite—in order to build. This leads to a paradoxical situation, as it is necessary to divide in order to reunite." [5]

Everything an Object

Farrell: "In C#, every piece of data is an object, providing all data with the functionality of true objects." [6]

Farrell: "Everything is an object, and every object is a member of a more general class." [7] "As a young child, you learned the concept of "animal" long before you knew the word." [8] I don't know if that's true. Induction versus deduction, and language acquisition.

Chocolate is good. Everything chocolate good?

Everything is not an object, any more than "everything is a process", or "everything is an entity". The Scientific method is not an object; gravity is not an object. Hatred is not an object. Rules are not objects. A format is not an object. `cin` and `cout` are not objects.

Jeffrey Richter: "The CLR allows types to be marked as *Abstract* or *Sealed* but not both. I think this restriction is unfortunate because a number of types don't allow instances of themselves to be created and can't be used as a base type. For example, it doesn't make sense to construct an instance of the Console or Math type because these types contain only static methods." [9] The problem is that they aren't objects, so there are no objects created…

Jamsa's Good Reasons

Jamsa's Programmer's Bible, Tip 883:

Kris Jamsa: [10]

1. **Ease of design and code reuse**—After the code works properly, the use of objects increases your ability to reuse a design or code you created for one application within a second application.

---

[1] Muller, Pierre-Alain, Jean-Claude Franchitti (translator from French), *Instant UML*, Olton, Birmingham, UK: Wrox Press (1-861000-87-1), 1997 (*Modélisation objet avec UML*, 1997), p. 15.

[2] Muller, Pierre-Alain, Jean-Claude Franchitti (translator from French), *Instant UML*, Olton, Birmingham, UK: Wrox Press (1-861000-87-1), 1997 (*Modélisation objet avec UML*, 1997), p. 15.

[3] Deitel, H.M., P.J. Deitel, D.R. Choffnes & C.L. Kelsey, *Simply C++: An Application-Driven Tutorial Approach*, Upper Saddle River, New Jersey: Pearson / Prentice-Hall (0-13-142660-5), 2005, p. 9.

[4] Deitel, H.M., P.J. Deitel, D.R. Choffnes & C.L. Kelsey, *Simply C++: An Application-Driven Tutorial Approach*, Upper Saddle River, New Jersey: Pearson / Prentice-Hall (0-13-142660-5), 2005, p. 9.

[5] Muller, Pierre-Alain, Jean-Claude Franchitti (translator from French), *Instant UML*, Olton, Birmingham, UK: Wrox Press (1-861000-87-1), 1997 (*Modélisation objet avec UML*, 1997), p. 15.

[6] Farrell, Joyce, *Microsoft® Visual C# .NET®*, Boston: Thomson / Course Technology (0-619-06273-8), 2002, p. 7.

[7] Farrell, Joyce, *Microsoft® Visual C# .NET®*, Boston: Thomson / Course Technology (0-619-06273-8), 2002, p. 114.

[8] Farrell, Joyce, *Microsoft® Visual C# .NET®*, Boston: Thomson / Course Technology (0-619-06273-8), 2002, p. 113.

[9] Richter, Jeffrey, *Applied Microsoft .NET Framework Programming*, Redmond: Microsoft Press (1-7356-1422-9), 2002, p. 174.

[10] Jamsa, Kris, PhD, MBA, *Jamsa's C/C++/C# Programmer's Bible: The Ultimate Guide to C/C++/C# Programming, Second Edition*, Albany, New York: Onword Press / Thomson Learning (0-7668-4682-2), 2002, Tip 883, p. 474.

2. **Increased reliability**—After you have properly tested object libraries, your use of existing (working) code will improve your program's reliability.

3. **Ease of understanding**—Object use helps programmers focus on and understand key system components. The use of objects lets designers and programmers focus on the smaller pieces of a system and provides a framework within which designers can focus more on the operations programs perform on the objects, the information objects must store, and other key system components.

4. **Increased abstraction**—Abstraction lets designers and programmers "look at the big picture"—temporarily ignoring underlying details so they can work with system elements they can more easily understand. For example, by focusing only on the word processor objects, the implementation of a word processor can become much less intimidating.

5. **Increased encapsulation**—*Encapsulation* groups all the pieces of an object into one neat package. For example, a `Book` class can combine the functions and data fields a program must have to work with a book. The programmers who are working with the `Book` class do not need to know each piece of the class, only that they need to use the class within their program. The class, in turn, will bring with it all the necessary pieces.

6. **Increased information hiding**—*Information hiding* is the ability for your program to treat a function, procedure, or an object as a "black box," using the item to perform a specific operation without having to know what goes on inside. For example, your programs can use I/O stream objects for input and output without having to understand how the streams work.

Information Hiding

O/O says information hiding is good but Knowledge is power. You don't need to know, but knowing is not harmful. Embraced by academics who think knowledge is good for its own sake, but not by secretive business folks. "Black box". But I use `printf` without knowing how it works.

Sometimes the best way to explain the rules is through the process. Sometimes the Rules are IN the process. How is easier to explain: O/S startup. Season ticket holders re-issue. Otherwise you might describe an accidental feature in the documentation, then it becomes an implied contract.

Explaining the implications of the File Catalog: deletion, search, etc.

"Despite the fact that inheriting from a class does not require access to the class's source code, developers often insist on seeing the source code to understand how the class is implemented. They may, for example, want to ensure that they are extending a class that performs well and is implemented securely."— Deitel & Deitel, C# [1]

Maintenance

Any proof it IS more maintainable? Maybe maintenance never comes. What percent—if cost how about a CBA. Time adjusting. % of lines reworked. Lines saved.

In a rapidly changing world, TTM is more important than reduced maintenance cost.

Business is short-sighted, but so is evolution. Eating dinner is short sighted but if you die in the short term there will be no long term.

Model The World

Riel: "One of the biggest reasons for moving to the object-oriented paradigm for developing complex applications is that it allows designers to more closely model the real world." [2] He gives the example that thing in the world are not subject to central control but structured methods are built on the idea of centralized control. Would this mean that if there is central control, O/O is worse?

Structured Analysis Centralized, O/O decentralizes. Event-driven vs. "Procedural" (term?) —*Heuristics, p. 2*

---

[1] Deitel & Deitel, Harvey M. & Paul J., *C# 2005 How to Program, Second Edition*, Upper Saddle River, New Jersey: Prentice-Hall (0-13-152523-9), 2006, Software Engineering Observation 10.7, p. 499.
[2] Riel, Arthur J., *Object-Oriented Design Heuristics*, Reading, Massachusetts: Addison-Wesley (0-201-63385-X), 1996, p. 2.

Coombs: "Object orientation allows programmers to better model the real world in their programs." [1] Because all entities have two things in common: they can be described and they are capable of doing something.

Hackers & Painters: "Good design resembles nature. It's not so much that resembling nature is intrinsically good as that nature has had a long time to work on the problem. So it's a good sign when your answer resembles nature's." [2]

Objections to Objects

We say it puts it all in one place, but we really put it all over the place! Can work for mere mortals? If MSoft guys get in wrong, how can we get it right.

1. Model the World. Cesar Millan, famed dog trainer, explaining the advice his farmer father gave him that is at the root of his dog-training methods: "Never work against Mother Nature." [3]

1.1. Real world is good yet O/O supports the fiction of messages. More real world is good, but they don't follow it. The medium is not the message: there is no message. OO says send message to do something, but it's really you borrow my lawnmower and cut your grass, not you send me a message to cut your grass.

2. It's the way we think, but hard to learn. Horstmann: "Books on object-oriented design, such as [Booch] and [Rumbaugh], provide outstanding guidance for object orientation in the development process, but undergraduate students rarely have sufficient experience in large-scale software development to envision the complexities that these methodologies address." [4] In fact, for a small program, O/O makes it longer, slower, and less understandable.

3. It's universally accepted, but no one is doing it right.

4. Use Cases are not Object/Oriented, they're process oriented. So the number one O/O technique is not O/O. Everything is an object but Jacobsen uses Workflow to describe his own development process.

5. It's all about saving money but the moneygrubbers ignore it.

6. It's about maintenance but supported by people who never maintain.

7. Predictability is good yet Inheritance-> unpredictability.

"Can be updated anywhere" is bad but that's what inheritance does. Inheritance causes Update Anywhere. Update lots of places not that bad; and you have to test it anyway. You're usually looking right at the problem. Why is Update anywhere Bad?—IDE could address. Update anywhere is not a real problem—use pencils, stickies, paper clips. Sorted XRef has been around for a long time. IDE should do it. Mfocus, VC++ tools.

8. The wrong value is usually the problem, not where it happened. Joel Spolsky: "Types can do only one kind of test, i.e., 'Can I do this thing to that object?' They can't test 'Does this function actually return 2.12 when the input values are 1, 32, and 'aardvark.' '" [5]

9. Standardization is good but malls, cars are not standard.

10. RAD versus careful planning implied by Conan the Librarian, function prototypes.

My advocacy: Hybrid it. Business Objects. We're hybrid. People think procedurally, but some objects. Can mix, as in life is multi-paradigmatic.

---

[1] Coombs, Ted, *Programming with C# .NET*, New York: Thomson / Delmar Learning (0-7668-5008-0), 2003, p. 107.

[2] Graham, Paul, *Hackers & Painters: Big Ideas from the Computer Age*, Sebastopol, California: O'Reilly (0-596-00662-4), 2004, pp. 138-193.

[3] Millan, Cesar, interview on *The Charlie Rose Show*, KQED/PBS: August 31, 2006.

[4] Horstmann, Cay S., *Mastering Object-Oriented Design in C++*, New York: John Wiley & Sons (0-471-59484-9), 1995, p. v.

[5] Spolsky, Joel (editor), *The Best Software Writing I*, New York: Apress / Springer-Verlag (1-59059-500-9), 2005, p. 68.

UML Distilled Charts

<table>
<tr>
<td>

Fowler's Charts
UML Distilled 3

Fowler, Martin, *UML Distilled, Third Edition: A Brief Guide to the Standard Object Modeling Language*, Boston: Addison-Wesley (0-321-19368-7), 2006 (2004).

</td>
<td>

Page 1

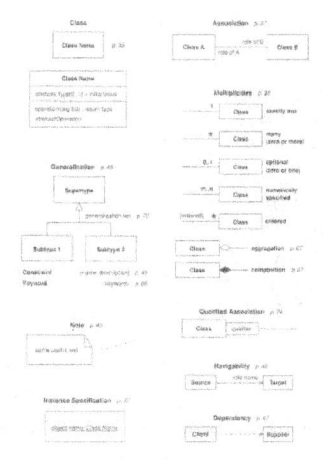

</td>
<td>

Page 2

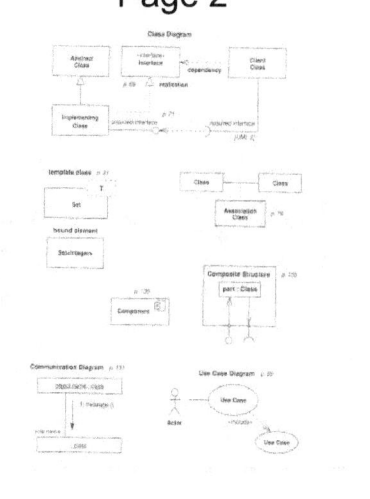

</td>
</tr>
</table>

Page 3

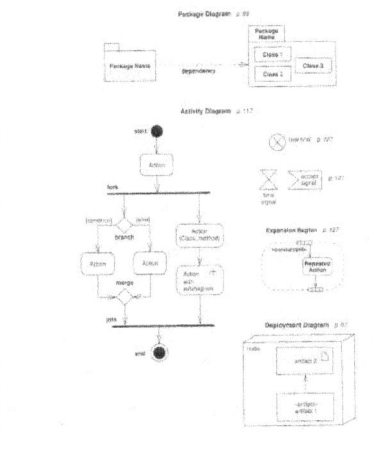

Page 4

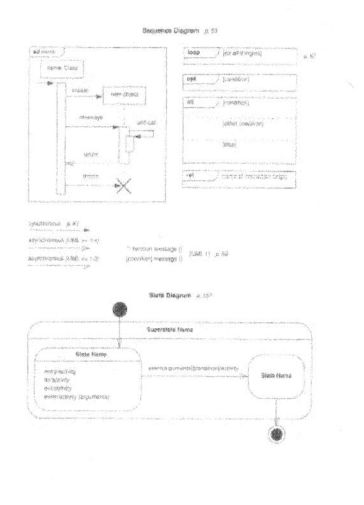

Rumbaugh's UML Schematics

Rumbaugh's Schematics

Rumbaugh, James, Ivar Jacobson & Grady Booch ["The Three Amigos"], *The Unified Modeling Language Reference Manual, Second Edition*, Upper Saddle River, New Jersey: Addison-Wesley (0-321-24562-8), 2006 (2005).

Class Notation

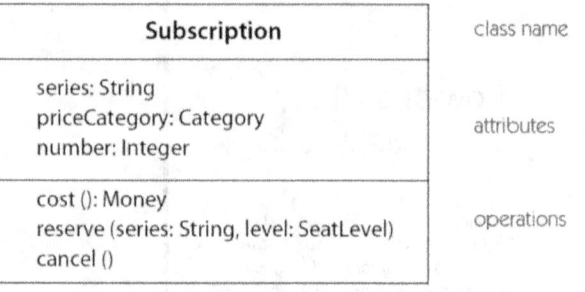

Figure 4-1. *Class notation*

Kinds of Relationships

Table 4-2: *Kinds of Relationships*

Relationship	Function	Notation
association	A description of a connection among instances of classes	
dependency	A relationship between two model elements	
generalization	A relationship between a more specific and a more general description, used for inheritance and polymorphic type declarations	
realization	Relationship between a specification and its implementation	
usage	A situation in which one element requires another for its correct functioning	«kind»

Association Notation

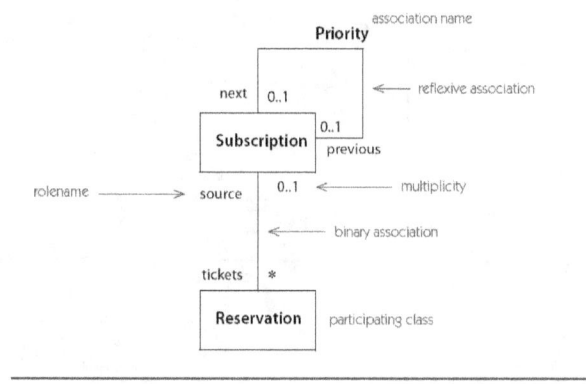

Figure 4-2. *Association notation*

Association Class

Figure 4-2. *Association notation*

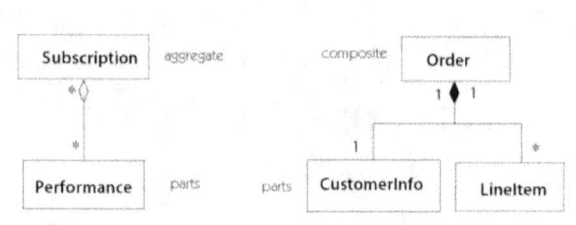

Figure 4-3. *Association class*

Aggregation & Composition

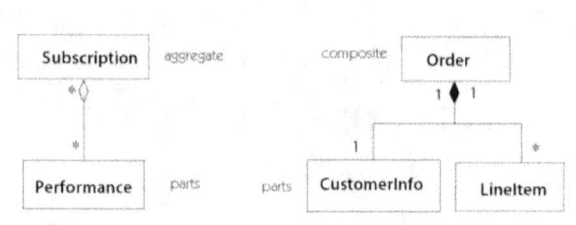

Figure 4-6. *Aggregation and composition*

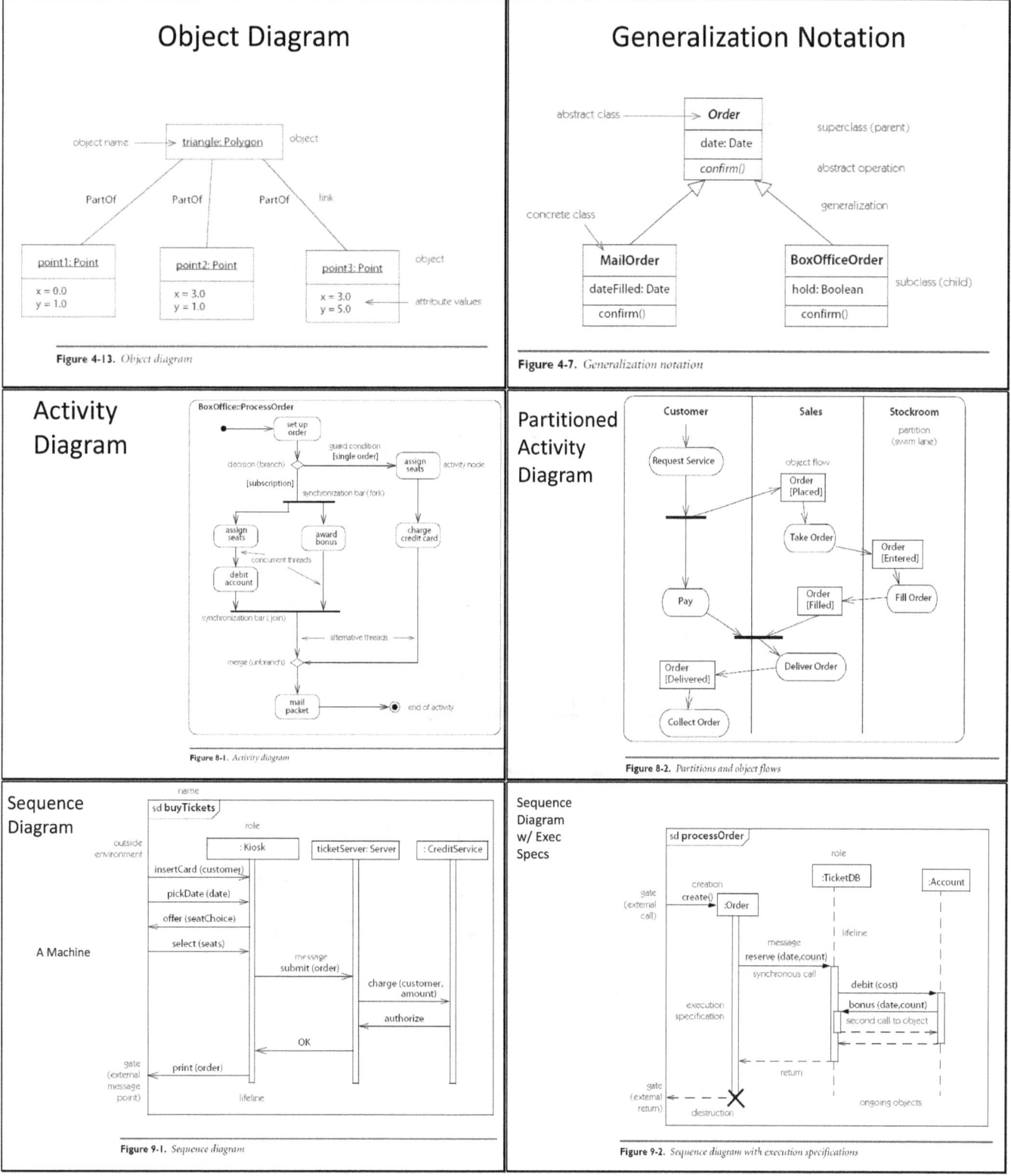

Object Diagram

Figure 4-13. *Object diagram*

Generalization Notation

Figure 4-7. *Generalization notation*

Activity Diagram

Figure 8-1. *Activity diagram*

Partitioned Activity Diagram

Figure 8-2. *Partitions and object flows*

Sequence Diagram

Figure 9-1. *Sequence diagram*

Sequence Diagram w/ Exec Specs

Figure 9-2. *Sequence diagram with execution specifications*

Structured Control Constructs

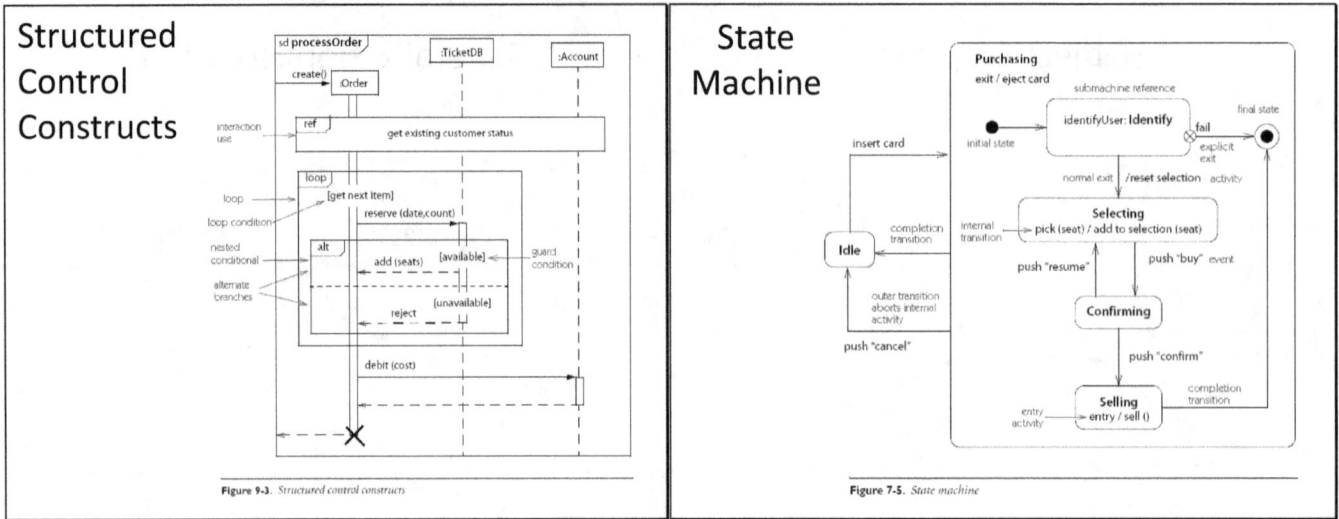

State Machine

Fowler's Notation Comparisons

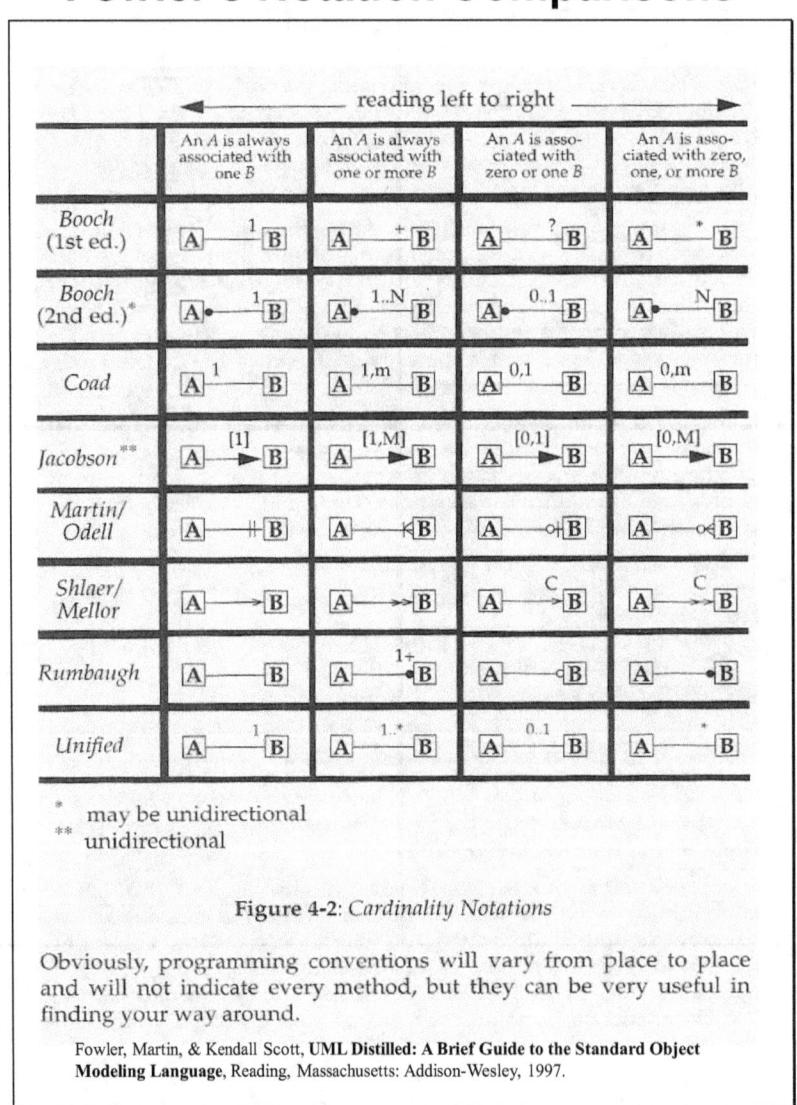

Figure 4-2: *Cardinality Notations*

Obviously, programming conventions will vary from place to place and will not indicate every method, but they can be very useful in finding your way around.

Fowler, Martin, & Kendall Scott, **UML Distilled: A Brief Guide to the Standard Object Modeling Language**, Reading, Massachusetts: Addison-Wesley, 1997.

Banking Example

Banking Example

College of Alameda
pmcdermott@peralta.edu

Copyright © 1998 Patrick McDermott

Bank Qs

- Is Previous Balance an Attribute?
  - Redundant?
  - Balance is also Σ of all History
  - Time Dependent—Missed Run
- Savings, Checking, CD, Credit Card
  - Same `class`?
  - Subtype
  - Different `class`es
- Where's Interest Rate

Procedural Bank

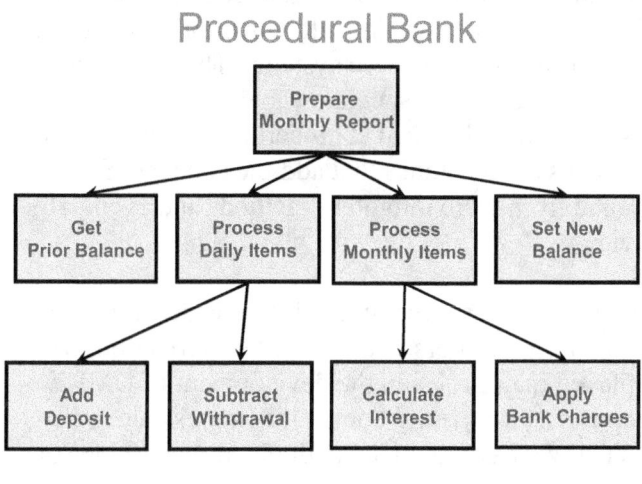

O/O Bank

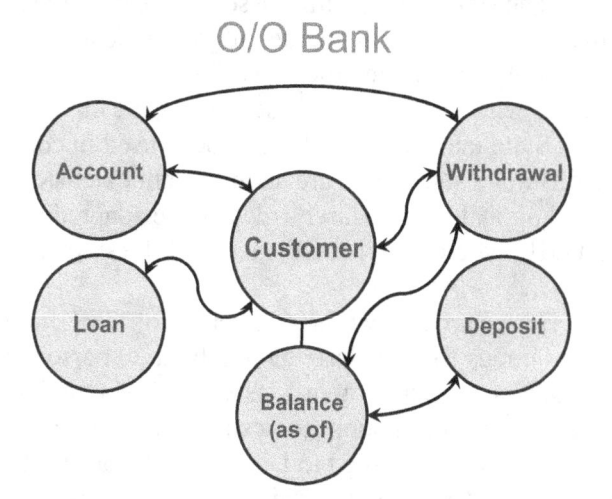

Various Quotes

Some Quotes

Cris Kobryn in Fowler, *UML Distilled 3*: "the UML has matured in expressiveness and precision, but it has also added gratuitous complexity as a result of the standardization process. Regrettably, standardization processes are better known for design-by-committee compromises than parsimonious elegance." [1] My Q: Did Cris get overruled on something he really wanted?

Rumbaugh & Amigos, *UML Reference*, "UML is messy, imprecise, complex, and sprawling. That is both a fault and a virtue. Anything intended for such widespread usage is going to be messy." [2]

Rumbaugh & Amigos, "Other sources": [3]

Quote

In addition to the various development methods cited above and a number of others that came a bit later, certain UML views show strong influences from particular non-object-oriented sources.

The static view, with classes connected by various relationships, is strongly influenced by Peter Chen's Entity-Relationship (ER) model originally developed in 1976. The influence came into UML through most of the early object-oriented methods. The ER model also heavily influenced database systems. The programming language world and the database world have unfortunately mostly gone their separate ways.

State machine models have been used in computer science and electrical engineering for many years. David Harel's statecharts are an important extension to classical state machines that add the concept of nested and orthogonal states. Harel's ideas were adapted by OMT, and from there into other methods and eventually into UML, where they form the basis of the state machine view.

...

There are many other influences of UML, and often the original source of an idea precedes the person who is famous for popularizing it. About 20 persons were major contributors to the UML1 specification, with many others participating in a lesser way. Maybe 30 or so played major roles in the development of UML2, with scores of others submitting suggestions, reviewing proposals, and writing books. It is impossible to list everyone who contributed to UML, and the brief references that we have included undoubtedly overlook some important contributors, for which we ask understanding.

Unquote

Fowler, *UML Distilled 3*: "MDA: Model-Driven Architecture" [4]

Fowler, *UML Distilled 3*: "My code examples are in Java and C#, as I've found that these languages are usually the most widely understood. Don't assume that I prefer those languages; I've done too much Smalltalk for that!" [5]

---

[1] Kobryn, Cris, "Foreword to the Third Edition" in Fowler, Martin, *UML Distilled, Third Edition: A Brief Guide to the Standard Object Modeling Language*, Boston: Addison-Wesley (0-321-19368-7), 2006 (2004), p. xxi.
[2] Rumbaugh, James, Ivar Jacobson & Grady Booch ["The Three Amigos"], *The Unified Modeling Language Reference Manual, Second Edition*, Upper Saddle River, New Jersey: Addison-Wesley (0-321-24562-8), 2006 (2005), p. 12.
[3] Rumbaugh, James, Ivar Jacobson & Grady Booch ["The Three Amigos"], *The Unified Modeling Language Reference Manual, Second Edition*, Upper Saddle River, New Jersey: Addison-Wesley (0-321-24562-8), 2006 (2005), p. 8.
[4] Fowler, Martin, *UML Distilled, Third Edition: A Brief Guide to the Standard Object Modeling Language*, Boston: Addison-Wesley (0-321-19368-7), 2006 (2004), pp. 4-5.
[5] Fowler, Martin, *UML Distilled, Third Edition: A Brief Guide to the Standard Object Modeling Language*, Boston: Addison-Wesley (0-321-19368-7), 2006 (2004), p. xxvi.

Let Me Clarify for You

Object-Oriented design techniques, such as class diagrams and CRC cards, are really useful for the practitioner. Unfortunately, most OO design books cultivate a priesthood mentality of turgidly written methodologies that are too complex to be actually useful. Cay Horstmann, *Practical Object-Oriented Development in C++ and Java.* [1]

Re UML "That notation is a combination of the notations of Booch, Rumbaugh and Jacobson and is far too complex to be used by mere mortals in its entirety." [2]

"Any software implementation method must take into account the organization, interrelationships, and layout of structures in order to obtain the complex macroscopic behavior of the system being created." From *Instant UML.*

"… you form a collaboration diagram by first placing the objects that participate in the interaction as the vertices in a graph. Next, you render the links that connect these objects as the arcs of this graph. Finally, you adorn these links with the messages that objects send and receive." –The Three Amigos

"The order of application of the criteria is often arbitrary, and leads to a covariant decomposition that translates into isomorphic model elements." From *Instant UML.*

---

[1] Horstmann, Cay, *Practical Object-Oriented Development in C++ and Java*, New York: John Wiley & Sons (0-471-14767-2), 1997, p. x.
[2] Horstmann, Cay, *Practical Object-Oriented Development in C++ and Java*, New York: John Wiley & Sons (0-471-14767-2), 1997, p. x.

Rumbaugh's Historical Defense

Rumbaugh, James, Ivar Jacobson & Grady Booch ["The Three Amigos"], *The Unified Modeling Language Reference Manual, Second Edition*, Upper Saddle River, New Jersey: Addison-Wesley (0-321-24562-8), 2006 (2005), p. 11. [1]

Quote:
The complexity of UML must be understood in light of its history:

- UML is a product of consensus of persons with varied goals and interests. It shares the qualities of the product of a democratic process. It is not as dean or coherent as the product of a single will. It contains superfluous features (but different persons might disagree about exactly what is superfluous). It contains overlapping features that are not always well integrated. Most of all, it lacks a consistent viewpoint. Unlike a programming language, which has a fairly narrow usage, it is intended for all kinds of things, from business modeling to graphical programming. Wide breadth of applicability usually comes at the expense of specificity.

- It was originally the merger of four or five leading modeling approaches, and later has been the target for accommodating a number of existing notations, such as SDL (Specification and Description Language, [ITU-T Z.100), various business modeling languages (which themselves had no single standard), action languages, state machine notations, and so on. The desire to preserve previous notation often creates inconsistencies across features and includes redundant notation intended to cater to the familiarities of certain usage groups.

- The official specification documents have been written by teams of uneven ability. There is a wide variation in style, completeness, precision, and consistency among various sections of the documents.

- UML is not a precise specification in the manner of a formal language. Although the computer science community holds formality to be a virtue, few mainstream programming languages are precisely defined, and formal languages are often inaccessible even to experts. It should also be noted that modeling is not the same as coding. In the construction industry, blueprints are written in an informal style using many conventions that depend on the common sense of the craftsperson, but buildings are built from them successfully.

- The semantics sections sometimes contain vague statements without adequate explanation and examples. Terms are introduced in metamodels and not well distinguished from other terms. There are too many fine distinctions that someone thought important but did not explain clearly.

- There is far too much use of generalization at the expense of essential distinctions. The myth that inheritance is always good has been a curse of object-orientation from its earliest days.

- There is a tension between concepts for conceptual modeling and programming language representation, with no consistent guidelines.

Unquote

---

[1] Rumbaugh, James, Ivar Jacobson & Grady Booch ["The Three Amigos"], *The Unified Modeling Language Reference Manual, Second Edition*, Upper Saddle River, New Jersey: Addison-Wesley (0-321-24562-8), 2006 (2005), p. 11.

The Other UML Diagrams
The Other UML Diagrams

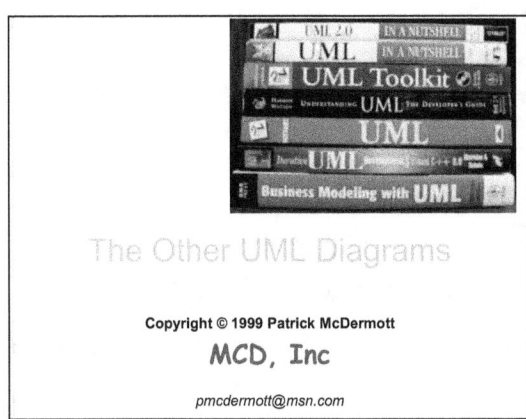

The Other UML Diagrams

Copyright © 1999 Patrick McDermott

MCD, Inc

pmcdermott@msn.com

UML Forever

"There are a lot more symbols and notations in UML, but it's up to you how many of them you use, let alone memorize. Many people just use the basics [Class Diagrams & Use Cases], and are perfectly happy (as are their customers and managers). But other folks like to really get into UML, and use every trick in the UML toolbox. It's really up to you; as long as you can communicate your design, you've used UML the way it's intended."—*HI[st] OOA&D*

From a Table in *UML Distilled 3.* [1]

The Purpose of Activity Diagrams—Procedural and parallel behavior
The Purpose of Class Diagrams —Class, features, and relationships
The Purpose of Communication Diagrams —Interaction between objects; emphasis on links
The Purpose of Component Diagrams —Structure and connections of components
The Purpose of Composite Structure Diagrams —Runtime decomposition of a class
The Purpose of Deployment Diagrams —Deployment of artifacts to nodes
The Purpose of Interaction Overview Diagrams —Mix of sequence and activity diagram
The Purpose of Object Diagrams —Example configurations of instances
The Purpose of Package Diagrams —Compile-time hierarchic structure
The Purpose of Sequence Diagrams —Interaction between objects; emphasis on sequence
The Purpose of State Machine Diagrams —How events change an object over its life
The Purpose of Timing Diagrams —Interaction between objects; emphasis on timing
The Purpose of Use Case Diagrams —How users interact with a system

Activity—Procedural and parallel behavior
Class—Class, features, and relationships
Communication—Interaction between objects; emphasis on links
Component—Structure and connections of components
Composite structure—Runtime decomposition of a class
Deployment—Deployment of artifacts to nodes
Interaction overview—Mix of sequence and activity diagram
Object—Example configurations of instances
Package—Compile-time hierarchic structure
Sequence—Interaction between objects; emphasis on sequence
State machine—How events change an object over its life
Timing—Interaction between objects; emphasis on timing

[1] Fowler, Martin, *UML Distilled, Third Edition: A Brief Guide to the Standard Object Modeling Language*, Boston: Addison-Wesley (0-321-19368-7), 2006 (2004), p. 11.

Use case—How users interact with a system

Object Diagrams

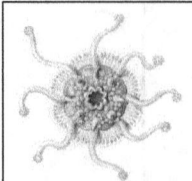

UML
Object Diagrams

Copyright © 1999 Patrick McDermott
MCD, Inc

pmcdermott@msn.com

Thing

~ CRC Cards: N/A
~ ERD: Entity
~ Relational: Tuple
~ Database: Row
~ Programmer: Record
~ UML: Object
~ Etc., etc., etc....: Occurrence, Instance

Classes & Objects

CLASS: The descriptor for a set of objects that share the same attributes, operations, methods, relationships and behavior. A class represents a concept within the system being modeled.—Rumbaugh, *Reference*, p. 185

OBJECT: A discrete entity with a well-defined boundary and identity that encapsulates state and behavior; an instance of a class.—Rumbaugh, *Reference*, p. 360

Types of Objects

1. Entity, Business Object
2. Interface or User
3. Control
4. Database or "Persistence"

5. Attributive
6. Infrastructure

Purpose

The Purpose of Object Diagrams — Show example configurations of instances

Object diagrams can be used to clarify complex relationships. You do not normally need an object diagram unless your relationships are variable or complex.

Object Diagrams

✓Sometimes Object Diagrams are needed to clarify some particular situation.
✓Only use when needed, or for the most critical classes.

154

Patrick's Rule

An object (business object) is a thing the business needs to know about. Classes are groups of objects.

In most discussions, "class", "object" and "entity" can be used interchangeably.

In addition to business objects, there are infrastructure objects. In analysis, you should concentrate on business (entity) objects.

B/L vs Invoice

- Customer
  - B/L 2
  - Invoice 1
- Vessel
  - B/L Yes
  - Invoice No
- Multiple #
  - B/L Yes
  - Invoice No

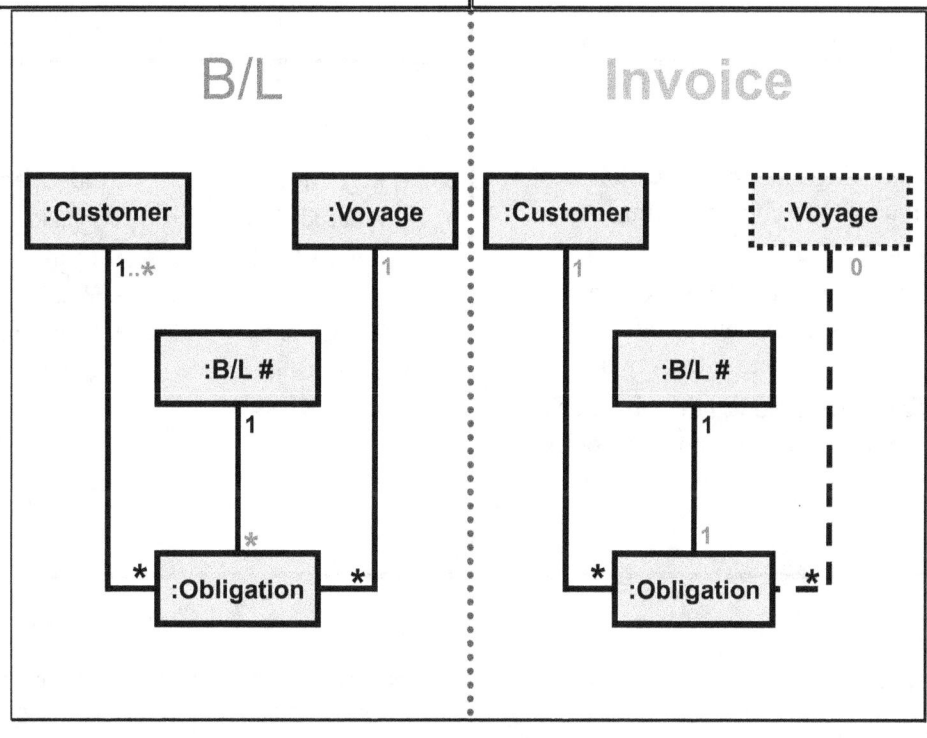

State Diagrams

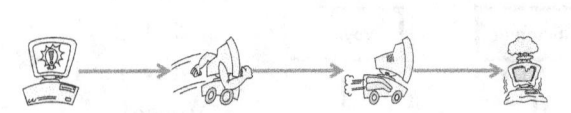

State Machine Diagrams
f.k.a. STD State Transition Diagram

Copyright © 1999 Patrick McDermott

UC Berkeley
Extension
pmcdermott@msn.com

Why STD?

The Purpose of State Machine Diagrams —
✓ To Show How Events change an Object over or during its Life

States or Modes

a.k.a. "Finite State Machines"

State Diagrams

✓ Consider State Diagrams for critical classes that have important or confusing transitions or structural aspects.
✓ State Diagrams show how the state of an object changes based on events, and how each state affects its reaction to events.
✓ Usually Life Cycle, although the trivial case is a switch: on/off and might not have entire life.

Use

- Real Time
- Embedded Systems
- Process Control PLC

- Key Class
- Single Object
  - Not so good for collaboration

Embedded O/S
- Windows CE
- Palm Pilot
- Wind River VxWorks
- Sony Aperios
- Cell Phone

Circles & Arrows

- Circles are States
- Arrows are Transitions
  - From one State to Another

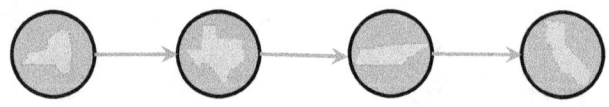

Quotes

❖ "Not everyone finds state diagrams natural. ... It may be that your team does not find state diagrams useful to its way of working."... "If you do use don't try to draw them for every class in the system."
  - Martin Fowler, *UML Distilled*, pp. 114-115
❖ "There is certainly no reason to prepare a state diagram for each class in your system. Indeed, many developers create rather large systems without bothering to create any state diagrams at all."
  - Harmon & Watson, *Understanding UML*, p. 217
❖ "Alert! Don't do state diagrams just because you can."
  - Rosenberg with Scott, *Use Case Driven Object Modeling with UML*, AP alert on p. 114

Transition

- Message / Trigger
- Event
  - [Guard]—t/f test to prevent entry
  - /Action
  - No label means: "Just do it"
- Will be a Function Call

Actions

- **Entry**
  - What to do when entering state
- **Do**
  - What to do while in state
- **On**
  - What to do when a certain event occurs
- **Exit**
  - What to do when leaving state

Coke Machine

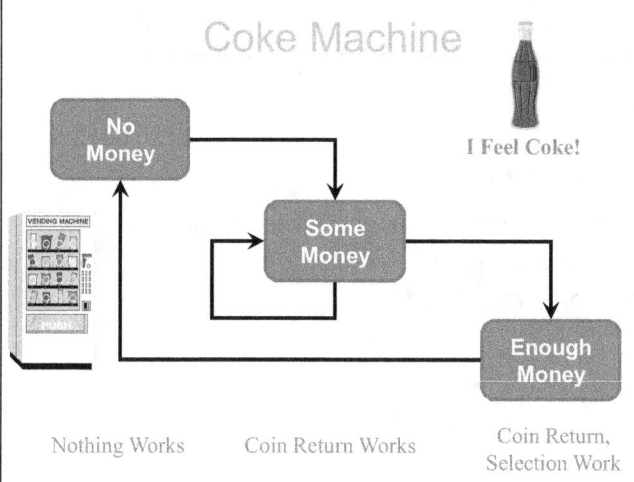

I Feel Coke!

Nothing Works   Coin Return Works   Coin Return,
Selection Work

Life Cycle

- "Life Cycle/Over Time" Problem
  - Unusual Life Path
- "It's there, but we don't know it" Problem
  - Not Omniscient
- Optional vs. Mandatory
  - Have to make logical mandatory optional
  - You don't know

Life Cycles

ORDER
- ✓ Placed
- ✓ Pending
- ✓ Filled
- ✓ Paid
- ✓ Closed

EMPLOYEE
- ➢ Prospect
- ➢ Applicant
- ➢ Candidate
- ➢ Employee
- ➢ Retiree

State Machine

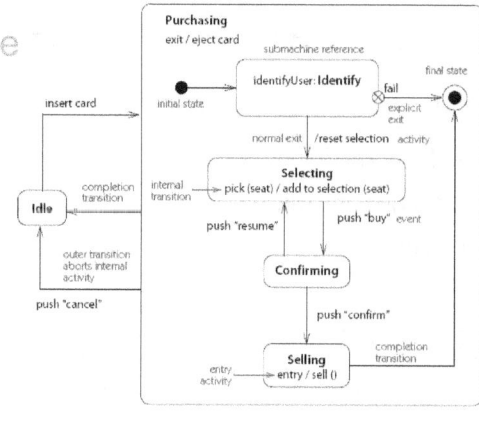

Figure 7-5. *State machine*

Status

The State of Status

UC Berkeley
Extension
pmcdermott@msn.com

Etymology

- State
- Status
- Mode

State vs. Value

- State same as value?
- Bank account with $123,456 different STATE than $123,457?

State

- Coke Machine
- Not for each amount: price changes, so does state diagram; Yen dif from $
- 2do: Graphix

Course

- Tentative
- Under-enrolled
- Open
- Closed
- Cancelled

Order

- Placed
- Pending
- Filled
- Closed

Employee

- Prospect
- Applicant
- Candidate
- Employee
- Retiree

2, not 1

- Paid
- Fulfilled

Task

- Created
- Assigned
- Closed
  - no more hours

Assumed Serial State

- Order of an Order
- DMV

- See Note Page

Questions

- Can they be separate classes?
  - Different Enough?
- Can you swim upstream?
- Can you Re-Open?
  - Re-start
  - Different then?

Employee

- Prospect
- Applicant

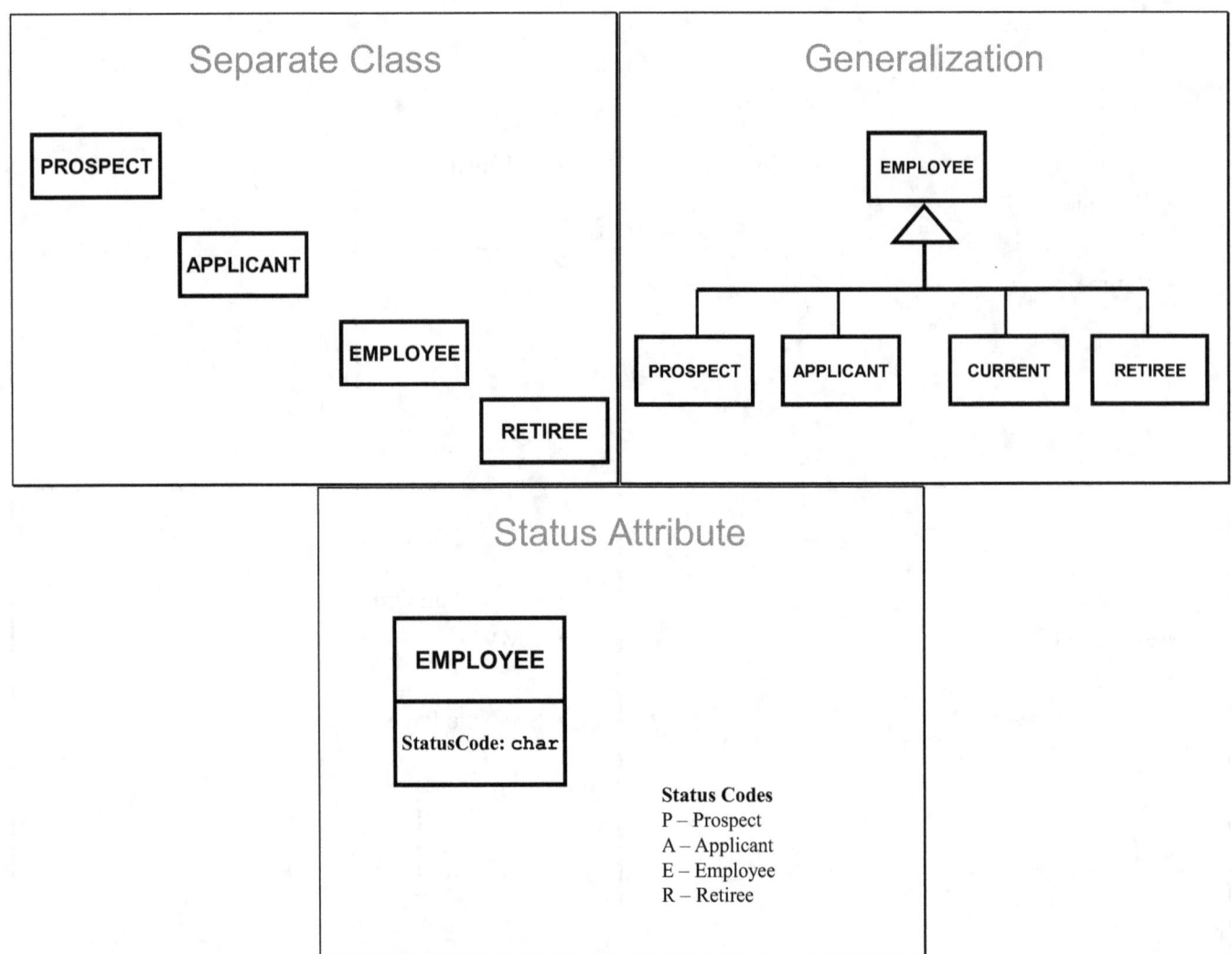

Communication Diagrams

UML Communication Diagrams
formerly known as Interaction: Collaboration

Copyright © 1999 Patrick McDermott

MCD, Inc

pmcdermott@msn.com

Purpose

- The Purpose of Communication Diagrams —Interaction between objects; emphasis on links

Communication

- Consider Interaction Diagrams (sequence and/or communication) if the structural construction of classes is complex or confusing.

Communication

- Use Communication Diagrams to show the communication between objects and their collaboration in completing a task.
- "... you form a collaboration diagram by first placing the objects that participate in the interaction as the vertices in a graph. Next, you render the links that connect these objects as the arcs of this graph. Finally, you adorn these links with the messages that objects send and receive. – The Three Amigos

Recommendations

- Scott, p 78
  - You should use interaction diagrams when you want to look at the behavior of several objects within a single use case.
- Larman
  - *SYSTEM* Sequence, Object Collaboration.

Semantic Equivalence

- One can become the other.
- Sequence emphasizes Action.
- Communication emphasizes Object.

Sequence Diagrams

UML Sequence Diagrams

formerly known as Interaction: Sequence

Copyright © 1999 Patrick McDermott

MCD, Inc

pmcdermott@msn.com

Purpose

- The Purpose of Sequence Diagrams — Interaction between objects; emphasis on sequence

Sequence

- Consider Interaction Diagrams (sequence and/or Communication) if the structural construction of classes is complex or confusing.
- Using Sequence Diagrams to graphically illustrate scenarios.

Recommendations

- Rosenberg, p. 84
  - Within our approach, *sequence diagrams represent the major work product of design*.
- Scott, p 78
  - You should use interaction diagrams when you want to look at the behavior of several objects within a single use case.
- Larman
  - *SYSTEM* Sequence, Object Collaboration.

Semantic Equivalence

- One can become the other.
- Sequence emphasizes Action.
- Communication emphasizes Object.

10. Methodologies
We Are Driven!!!

"Each analysis technique is driven by a certain perspective. So what's the best perspective? In the beginning, all computer programs were process-driven. Then along came Data Base Management Systems, and we became data-driven—for a time, it was fashionable for Data Administrators to proclaim themselves "data bigots". Just about everyone now agrees that both process and data are essential, in fact we once called our profession data processing, but how to bring both data and process into the equation? The extreme was to bring the procedures and data together into objects, and become object-driven. But even object gurus disagree on whether we should be driven by the objects: the UML object modeling technique as described by the Three Amigos, led by Ivar Jacobson, is use-case-driven, and Peter Coad has become feature-driven. So how about business rules? USoft was business-rule-driven until it was driven out of business. Workflow brought other possibilities. The first workflow tools were document-driven, while current tools like SAP are event-driven. Of course your eventual goal is to be chauffeur-driven, but to get there you need to design the right system." [5]

The Universal Data Model

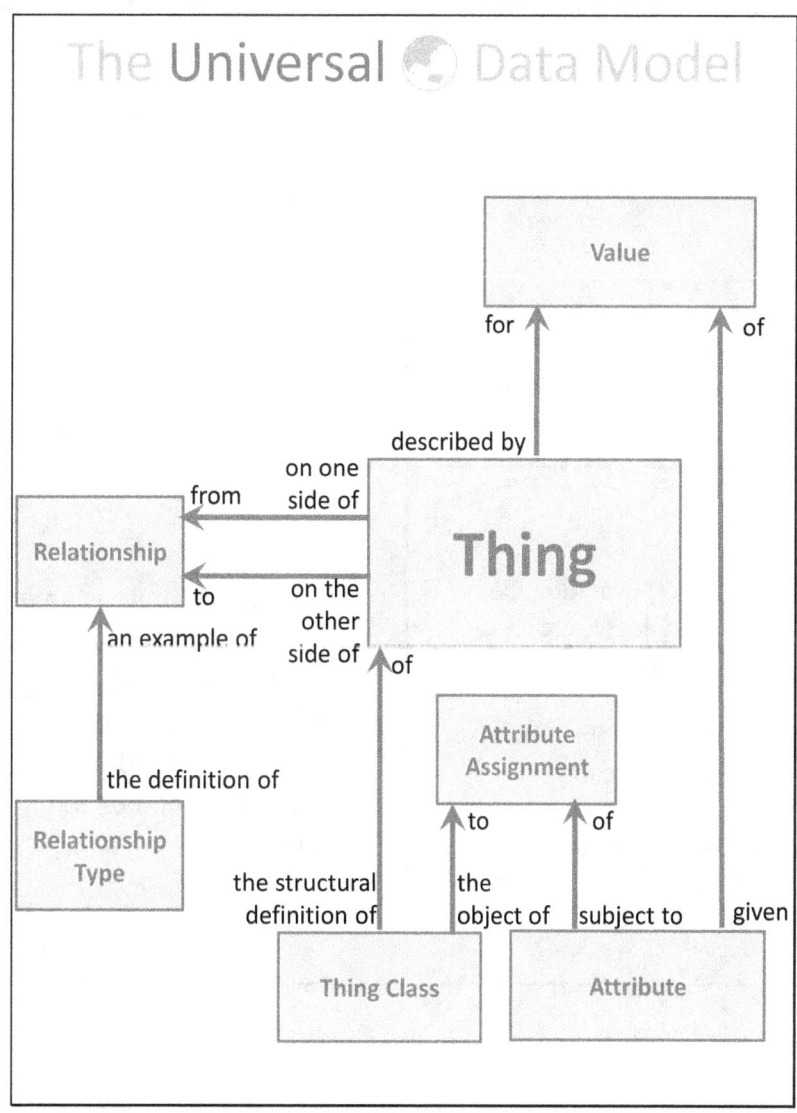

Which CRAM?

Class
Relationship
Attribute
Method

Which CRAM?

College of Alameda

pmcdermott@peralta.edu
Copyright © 1999 Patrick McDermott

The Meta-Objects

Object C.R.A.M.

Objects
➤ Classes
➤ Relationships
➤ Attributes
➤ Methods

Relationship

CLASS
Attribute1
Attribute2
Attribute3
Method1()
Method2()

CLASS

UML

Which C.R.A.M?

- Relationship/Attribute can be a class if Data, a Method if behavior
  - Marriage
  - Color to artist, painter
  - Eskimo Snow
- Telephone Number
  - Phone Number at Ma Bell
  - Japanese phone number: it's an asset
  - Area code, exchange, number
- Whose Attribute? License Plate #
  - Car
  - Driver

Purpose of Objects

- Entity
- Business Object

- Infrastructure
  - User Interface
  - Data
    - Persistence
  - Control
  - Static
    - For things that aren't really objects

Object

An object (business object) is a thing the business needs to know about. Classes are groups (classifications) of objects.

In most discussions, "class", "object" and "entity" can be used interchangeably.

In addition to business objects, there are infrastructure objects. During analysis, you should only discuss business (entity) objects.

Attribute

An attribute is a piece of information about an object needed in your business. Often objects, attributes and/or relationships are established or modified by methods. In fact, there should be methods to CRUD all the meta-objects.

CRUD: Create, Read, Update, Delete

Attribute or Class?

Attributes Don't have Attributes

Attributes are "OF" a Class

Method

A *method* or *function* is an action needed in your business. Often objects, attributes and/or relationships are established or modified by methods. In fact, there should be methods to CRUD all the meta-objects.

CRUD: Create, Read/Retrieve, Update, Delete

Grammatical Analysis

✓ Classes are Nouns
✓ Relationships are Verbs
✓ Attributes are Adjectives
✓ Methods are Phrases
  – Including an action and
  – a Class, Relationship or Attribute

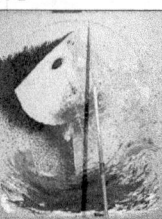

Joel Kermarrec
*In Principle
the Ghost
is the Verb
of the Form*
1987

The Twenty Guiding Principles

#	Principle of Computing	Explanation
1	Brooks' Law	Adding Staff to a Late Software Project makes it *LATER*
2	Conservation of Complexity	Simplicity is Complicated
3	Cranes & Spandrels	Things are the Way They are because They got that Way
4	Embrace Contradiction	True Lies & Other Oxymorons
5	Hofstadter's Law	Mis-under-estimating
6	K.I.S.S.	Occam's Razor—Keep it Simple, Stupid
7	Laziness Unleashed	A Good Programmer is a Lazy Programmer
8	Lubarsky's Entomology Law	There's Always One More Bug
9	The Middle Way	Goldilocks, the Super Systems Analyst
10	Moore's Law	Computing Power Doubles every 18 Months
11	Murphy's Law	Anything that can Go Wrong, will Go Wrong
12	No Silver Bullet	Software is Hard
13	Pareto Principle	The 80%-20% Rule [Or even 90-10]
14	Parkinson's Law	Work Expands to Fill the Time Allotted
15	Populations aren't People	Veblen's Principle: Change that Helps One usually Hurts Another
16	Shapiro's Observation	Technology Changes. Economic Laws do not
17	Slingerland's Rule of Fools	No System's Foolproof, because there's Always a Bigger Fool
18	TINSTAAFL	There is No Such Thing as a Free Lunch
19	Unintended Consequences	1st Law of Ecology: Everything is Connected to Everything Else
20	Ways to the Mountaintop	All the One True Ways: T>1W2DI

With A Deep Bow to Funakoshi Gichin & Nakasone Genwa

The Twenty Guiding Principles of Karate

Karate-dō Nijukkajo to sono kaishaku, 1938

Funakoshi Gichin & Genwa Nakasone, John Teramoto (translator from Japanese), *The Twenty Guiding Principles of Karate: The Spiritual Legacy of the Master*, Tokyo: Kodansha International (4-7700-2796-6), 2003 (*Karate-dō Nijukkajo to sono kaishaku*, 1938).

20 Guiding Principles I

The **Guiding Principles** of **Computing I**

Copyright © 2004 Patrick McDermott

UC Berkeley

Extension

pmcdermott@msn.com

1. Brooks' Law

- Adding Staff to a Late Software Project will make it Later.
- Chicken's Pecking Order
- FSNP

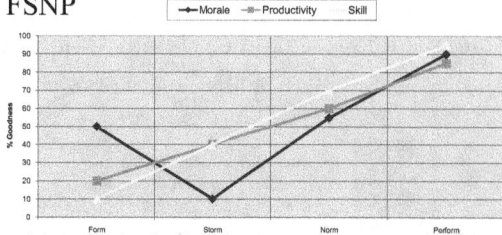

Brooks, Frederick P., Jr., *The Mythical Man-Month: Essays on Software Engineering, 20th Anniversary Edition*, Reading, Massachusetts: Addison-Wesley (0-201-83595-9), 1995 (1975), p. 25.

2. Conservation of Complexity

- Simplicity is Complicated
  - John Naisbitt has observed that the computer is a tool that manages complexity, and as such, just as highways encourage more cars, the computer invites more complexity into society.
- Human Languages
  - 日本語 Japanese: No tense, number, gender
  - but Honorifics, Kanji 漢字
- IRS
  - The Tax Code as we know it could not exist without computers
  - Technology was supposed to simplify our lives?!?

3. Cranes & Spandrels

- A Good Reason, a Bad Reason…
  - or No Reason At All
- Things are the Way They are because They got that Way: Vestigial Organs
- Hume's Fallacy
  - Ought not Deducible from Is

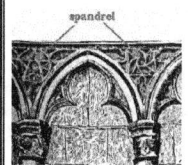

spandrel

Stephen J. Gould
Spandrels

Patrick McDermott
Cranes

4. Embrace Contradiction

- **The First Law of Logic for Analysts:**
  Logic doesn't always Work!
- You can hide in plain sight.
- If Everybody agrees, Somebody is Wrong!
- There is no such thing as Nothing.
- The greatest Truths are told in fiction.
- To remember something, stop trying to remember it.
- If you want something done, assign it to someone who is busy.
- Dickens was right: This *is* the best of times, and the worst of times.

5. Hofstadter's Law

- Mis-under-estimating
- It always takes longer than you expect, even when taking into account Hofstadter's Law
- Douglas Hofstadter, Author of:
  - *I Am a Strange Loop*
  - *Gödel, Escher, Bach: An Eternal Golden Braid*
  - *The Mind's I: Fantasies and Reflections on Self and Soul*
  - *Fluid Concepts and Creative Analogies: Computer Models of the Fundamental Mechanisms of Thought*
  - *Le Ton beau de Marot: In Praise of the Music of Language*

6. K.I.S.S.

- Keep it Simple, Stupid!
- Occam's Razor—
  - Given 2 equally likely alternatives
  - Choose the one with the fewest assumptions
  - i.e. the simplest.
- "Simple things should be simple. Complex things should be possible."—Widely attributed to Alan Kay

Newton, Harry, *Newton's Telecom Dictionary, 22nd Edition*, San Francisco: CMP Books (1-57820-319-8), 2006.

7. Laziness Unleashed

- A Good Programmer is a Lazy Programmer
- Eric S. Raymond:
  - "An important trait of the great ones is constructive laziness."
  - "Good programmers know what to write. Great ones know what to rewrite (and reuse)"
- Don't do anything twice

- How do you avoid an accident while backing?

8. Lubarsky's Law

- Lubarsky's Law of Cybernetic Entomology
- There's Always Another Bug
- Amelia Earhardt
- Typos in riting
- No perfect Kata
- Linus's Law
  - Given Enough Eyeballs, All Bugs Are Shallow
    - Linus Torvalds (Linus of Linux)

9. The Middle Way

- Best of Both Worlds
- Goldilocks, Super Systems Analyst

- Bad Ideas are just Good Ideas carried to Extreme
- Use it to Your Advantage
  - Too much, What you want, Too little

10. Moore's Law

- Gordon Moore, Intel co-founder
- Computing Power doubles every 18 Months
- Trend has held for three decades
- Will we Hit the Wall??

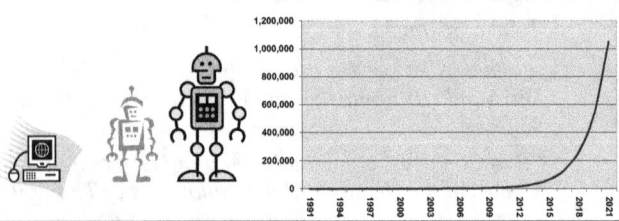

The Exponential Growth of Computing Power

Human Smartest?

"Before [the 21st] century is over "human beings will no longer be the most intelligent or capable type of entity on the planet."

"Once a computer achieves a human level of intelligence, it will necessarily soar past it."

"There are more than enough new computing technologies now being researched, including three-dimensional chips, optical computing, crystalline computing, DNA computing, and quantum computing, to keep the law of accelerating returns [Moore's Law] going for a long time."

Kurzweil, Ray, *The Age of Spiritual Machines: When Computers Exceed Human Intelligence*, New York: Viking (0-670-88217-8), 1999.

20 Guiding Principles II

The **Guiding Principles** of Computing **II**

UC Berkeley
Extension

pmcdermott@msn.com

11. Murphy's Law

Anything that Can Go Wrong
Will Go Wrong

- Captain Edward A. Murphy, Jr.
  - U.S. Air Force, 1949
- The Bread Always falls Butter side Down
- Files are Always lost just before Backup
- The bad news:
  - Many I.T. people know O'Niel's Law: "Murphy was an optimist."

12. No Silver Bullet

Software is Hard!

Brooks, Frederick P., Jr., "No Silver Bullet: Essence and Accident in Software Engineering" (1986) reprinted in Brooks, Frederick P., Jr., *The Mythical Man-Month: Essays on Software Engineering, Anniversary Edition*, Reading, Massachusetts: Addison-Wesley (0-201-83595-9), 1995 (1975)

13. Pareto Principle

- The 80%-20% Rule
- Vilfredo Pareto (1848-1923)
  - Italian Economist
- Income, Employment
- Bugs, Problems

- Maybe Even 90/10!

BUT: Joel Spolsky's Modification:
Each wants only 20%
But a different 20%

Pareto Distribution

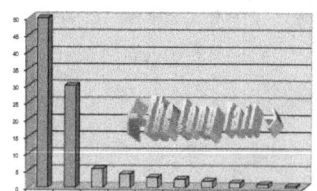

The Red bars are
20% of the Entities
But account for
80% of the Items

14. Parkinson's Law

- "Work Expands to Fill the Time Allotted"
- C Northcote Parkinson, 1954
- Sometimes you Need an Arbitrary Deadline
  - Due on Tuesday, even if I'm not here
  - The work at home problem

15. Populations aren't People

- Seemingly against own interest
  - The individual's and organization's interests do not always align
- Manager's project vs. Good of Company
  - "Have a Lousy Day!"
- Veblen's Principle
  - A Change that Benefits Somebody
  - ...usually Hurts Somebody Else
- Communities are
  - A super-organism
  - Or a bunch of Individuals
  - Or a Swarm

Crichton, Michael, *Prey*, New York: HarperCollins (0-06-621412-2), 2002.

16. Shapiro's Observation

- Technology changes—Economic Laws do not.
- Silicon Circuits evolve much more quickly than Human Genes.
- Social systems change incrementally, Technology exponentially.

Shapiro, Carl & Hal Varian, *Information Rules: a Strategic Guide to the Network Economy*, Boston: Harvard Business Review Press (0-87584-863-X), 1999, p. 2.

Shenk, David, *Data Smog: Surviving the Information Glut*, New York: HarperEdge (0-06-251551-9), 1997, p. 42.

17. Slingerland's Rule of Fools

No System is Foolproof,

　　… because there's Always a Bigger Fool

　－ The General's Landing

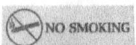

18. TINSTAAFL

- There is No Such Thing as a Free Lunch
- There is always a Trade Off
- Processing vs. Memory
  - Compression versus Storage
  - Save versus re-compute

	Computer says "Right"	Computer says "Wrong"
Right in the World	GOOD	Type II: **False Positive**
Wrong in the World	Type I: **Miss**	GOOD

19. Unintended Consequences

- All Changes Have Effects that weren't Intended and not Expected
- Culture + New Technology ➔ New Culture
- 1st Law of Ecology
  - Everything is Connected to Everything Else
  - You can Never Do Just One Thing.
    - Barry Commoner, *The Closing Circle*

Unintended Consequences

- Emergence's Evil Twin
  - Freeway Fliers & Contract Programmers
  - Email & Spam: Productivity Paradox
  - Labor Saving Devices and Long Hours
  - Environmental Damages
  - Peltzman Effect & Seatbelts

Tenner, Edward, *Why Things Bite Back: Technology and the Revenge of Unintended Consequences*, New York: Vintage Books (0-679-74756-7), 1996.

- The Only Defense: Expect the Unexpected

20. Many Ways to Mountaintop

- T>1W2DI: There's more than 1 Way to Do It
- We've found the One Best Way
  - About 100 of them
- If you fail, try something different

Hokusai Katsushika 1760-1849

If life is a climb to the summit, you and I might take a different route, but we can both reach the top, and enjoy the view together. PMcD

Steps for Use Case Diagrams

1. Get a first list of Use Cases, using Brainstorming, Grammatical Analysis, Prototyping or derivation from class or activity (workflow) diagrams.

2. Get a list of Actors using Brainstorming, Org Charts, or derivation from activity (workflow) diagrams.

3. If needed, use **Workflow diagrams** to detail complex or involved decisions.

4. Draw the UC Diagram with stick-figure actors and major responsibilities.

5. Review with SME's (subject matter experts), users, etc.

6. Prepare Sunny Day Scenarios for the most common paths without worrying about exceptions.

7. Prototype User Interfaces.

8. Detail Use Case **alternate cases.**

9. If necessary, do **Interaction (sequence and/or collaboration) Diagrams** if the use case sequence is complex or confusing.

10. Detail Use Case Scenarios by **add exceptional paths.**

11. If needed, use **Activity diagrams** to detail complex or involved decisions.

12. Review with SME's (subject matter experts), users, etc.

13. Get Test Cases from the users. The sooner the users do this the better—it could even be step 1, but realistically you probably won't get it until late.

14. Code functions.

15. Test.

16. Party!

COnstructive COst MOdel
CoCoMo II

It's a Name Game,
Don't Blame Boehm!
(rhymes)

COCOMO
COnstructive COst MOdel II

Copyright © 2007 Patrick McDermott
UC Berkeley
Extension
pmcdermott@msn.com

Even if the numbers are not truly predictive, qualitative
assessments are useful, and just pondering is a benefit.

Made up numbers can be surprisingly good!

Boehm
& Friends

Boehm, Barry W., Chris Abts, A.
Winsor Brown, Sunita Chulani,
Bradford K. Clark, Ellis Horowitz, Ray
Madachy, Donald J. Reifer & Bert
Steece,
*Software Cost Estimation with
COCOMO II,*
Upper Saddle River, New Jersey:
Prentice Hall PTR
(0-13-026692-2), 2000.

**SOFTWARE COST
ESTIMATION
WITH COCOMO II**

Barry W. Boehm · Chris Abts · A. Winsor Brown
Sunita Chulani · Bradford K. Clark · Ellis Horowitz
Ray Madachy · Donald Reifer · Bert Steece

Center for Software Engineering
University of Southern California

Simplified Formula

Multipliers × Size Factors

Multipliers × Size $^{0.91 + 0.01 \times \Sigma\text{Factors}}$

The Scale **Factors**

Driver	Symbol	VL	Low	Nominal	High	VH	XH
PREC	Precedentedness	6.20	4.96	3.72	2.48	1.24	0.00
FLEX	Development flexibility	5.07	4.05	3.04	2.03	1.01	0.00
RESL	Architecture & risk	7.07	5.65	4.24	2.83	1.41	0.00
TEAM	Team cohesion	5.48	4.38	3.29	2.19	1.10	0.00
PMAT	Process maturity	7.80	6.24	4.68	3.12	1.56	0.00

Driver	Factor	Low	Nominal	High
PREC	Precedentedness	Largely Unprecedented	Somewhat Unprecedented	Generally Familiar
FLEX	Development flexibility	Occassional Relaxation	Some Relaxation	General Conformity
RESL	Architecture & risk	Some	Often	Generally
TEAM	Team cohesion	Some Difficult Interactions	Basically Cooperative	Largely Cooperative
PMAT	Process maturity	CMM1	CMM 2	CMM 3

COCOMO II Scale Factors & Co$t Driver$

COCOMO (COnstructive COst MOdel) is a methodology/tool set for making software estimates http://sunset.usc.edu/research/COCOMOII/ ans says these factors affect systems development costs Factors & Drivers from Boehm & Friends, *COCOMO II*, [*] questions from Reifer: [†]

Scale Factors

PREC – Precedentedness: Has the system ever been built before?
FLEX - Development flexibility: Must you strictly conform to requirements?
RESL - Architecture & risk resolution: Is the architecture stable and have the risks been mitigated?
TEAM - Team cohesion: How complicated are stakeholder interactions?
PMAT - Process maturity: How mature are the processes used?

Cost Drivers

RELY - Required software reliability: How risky is the software to people and property?
DATA - Database size: How big are the databases relative to norms?
CPLX - Product complexity: How complex is the product to be built?
RUSE - Developed for reusability: How much design for reuse is planned?
DOCU - Documentation match to life cycle needs: Is the documentation the right size for the project's needs?
TIME - Execution time constraint: Is timing a constraint?
STOR - Main storage constraint: Is memory a constraint?
PVOL - Platform volatility: How volatile is the development platform?
ACAP - Analyst capability: How capable are the analysts?
PCAP - Programmer capability: How capable are the programmers?
PCON - Personnel continuity: How stable is the workforce?
APEX - Applications experience: What's the team's average application experience? [6]
PLEX - Platform experience: What's the team's average platform experience? [7]
LTEX - Language and tool experience: What's the team's language and/or tool experience?
TOOL - Use of software tools: How sophisticated is toolset to be used?
SITE [8] - Multisite development: Will the team use multiple development sites?
SCED - Required development schedule: Will the development schedule be constrained?

---

[*] Boehm, Barry W., Chris Abts, A. Winsor Brown, Sunita Chulani, Bradford K. Clark, Ellis Horowitz, Ray Madachy, Donald J. Reifer & Bert Steece, *Software Cost Estimation with COCOMO II*, Upper Saddle River, New Jersey: Prentice Hall PTR (0-13-026692-2), 2000.
[†] Reifer, Donald J., *Making the Software Business Case: Improvement by the Numbers*, Boston: Addison-Wesley (0-201-72887-7), 2002, p. 69.

Capability Maturity Model Levels

Based on Hamlet & Maybee, *The Engineering of Software.* [9]

Level 1- **Initial**. Pays no particular attention to the development process.

Level 2- **Repeatable**. Can track crucial development parameters of cost, schedule and functionality, and can repeat past successes on new projects.

Level 3- **Defined**. Management practices formally defined and recorded. Followed throughout the organization dependably, even when things go wrong. There is a Software Engineering Process Group.

Level 4- **Managed**. The central concept is "measurement" of the development process. Quantitative analysis for management understanding and for control of development.

Level 5- **Optimizing**. Process measurements used as feedback. Defect analysis identifies problems, discover the root cause and correct them, and change the process to prevent similar problems in the future.

Agile Modeling & eXtreme Programming

XP & AM

eXtreme Programming
&
Agile Modeling
Copyright © 2003 Patrick McDermott
UC Berkeley
Extension

pmcdermott@msn.com

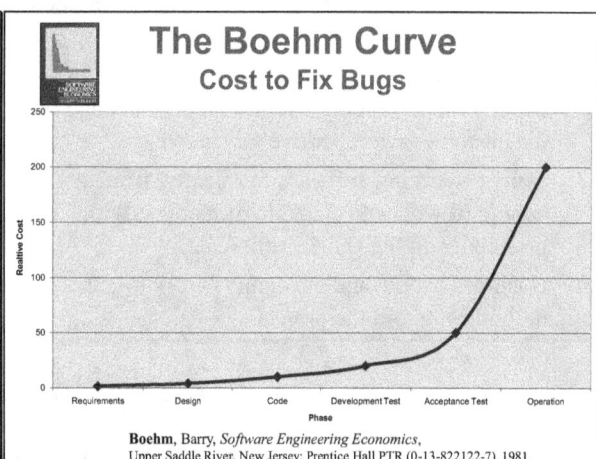

The Boehm Curve
Cost to Fix Bugs

Boehm, Barry, *Software Engineering Economics*,
Upper Saddle River, New Jersey: Prentice Hall PTR (0-13-822122-7), 1981.

XP Thesis

Under certain circumstances, the exponential rise in the cost of changing software over time can be flattened. If we can flatten the curve, old assumptions about the best way to develop software no longer hold.

Beck, Kent, ***Extreme Programming Explained***: *Embrace Change*, 2000, p. 21-22.

...

XP Thesis

One of the universal assumptions of software engineering is that the cost of changing a program rises exponentially over time. I can remember sitting in a big linoleum-floored classroom as a college junior and seeing the professor draw on the board the curve found in Figure 1. [Figure 1 is A Boehm Curve]

"The cost to fix a problem in a piece of software rises exponential over time. A problem that might take a dollar to fix if you found it during requirements analysis might costs thousands to fix once the software is in production.""

I resolved then and there that I would never let a problem get through to production. No sirree, I was going to catch problems soon as possible. I would work out every possible problem in advance. I would review and crosscheck my code. No way was I going to cost employer $100,000.

The problem is that this curve is no longer valid. Or rather, with combination of technology and programming practices, it is possible to experience a curve that is really quite the opposite.

XP Programmers

1. 40-hour week ("Sustainable Pace")
2. Pair Programming (Scrum)
3. Collective Ownership
4. Continuous Integration
5. Simple Design (No BDUF)
6. Coding Standards
7. Test-Driven
8. Refactoring

Fowler, Martin, ***Refactoring***: *Improving the Design of Existing Code*,
Reading, Massachusetts: Addison-Wesley (0-201-48567-2), 2000.

Agile Modeling

Favor *Left* over Right (but both important)

A *Individuals and interactions* over Processes and tools.

B *Working software* over Comprehensive documentation.

C *Customer collaboration* over Contract negotiation.

D *Responding to change* over Following a plan.

Ambler, Scott W., *Agile Modeling*:
Effective Practices for eXtreme Programming and the Unified Process,
New York: Wiley Computer Publishing (0-471-20282-7), 2002.

 **AM Principles**

1. Our highest priority is to satisfy the customer through early and continuous delivery of valuable software.
2. Welcome changing requirements, even late in development. Agile processes harness change for the customer's competitive advantage.
3. Deliver working software frequently, from a couple of weeks to a couple of months, with a preference to the shorter timescale.
4. Business people and developers work together daily throughout the project. ...

AM Principles, Continued

5. Build projects around motivated individuals. Give them the environment and support they need, and trust them to get the job done.
6. The most efficient and effective method of conveying information to and within a development team is face-to-face conversation.
7. Working software is the primary measure of progress.
8. Agile processes promote sustainable development. The sponsors, developers and users should be able to maintain a constant pace indefinitely. ...

AM Principles, Continued

9. Continuous attention to technical excellence and good design enhances agility.
10. Simplicity—the art of maximizing the amount of work not done—is essential.
11. The best architectures, requirements and designs emerge from self-organizing teams.
12. At regular intervals, the team reflects on how to become more effective, then tunes and adjusts its behavior accordingly.

H_2OFall vs. Spiral Progress

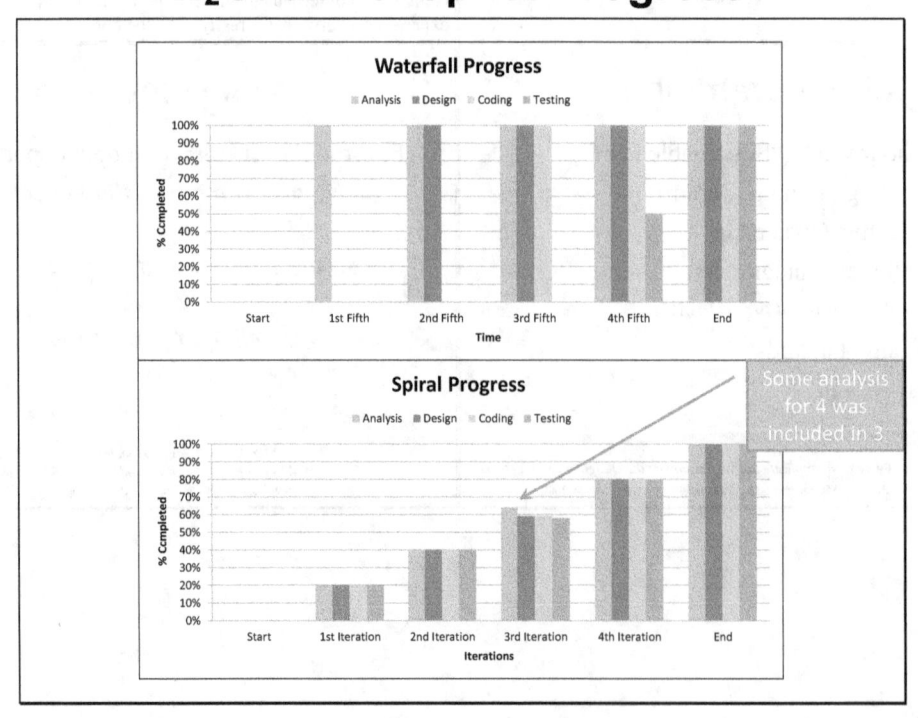

XP Practices

XP Practices

The University of California

Chaordic

- = Chaos + Order
- Small Releases
- Simple Design
- Change from *fixed scope, variable date* to *variable scope, fixed date.*
- Continuous Integration

- Embrace Change

Documentation

- Test First Development
  - Automated Tests

- The Source Code is the Design
  - Emergence
  - No BDUF
    - Big Design Up Front

DTSTTCPW

- Do The Simplest Thing That Could Possibly Work
- Go with Instincts

- Cf. K.I.S.S.

YAGNI

- "You Ain't Gonna Need It"
- Not in this Release
- Plan for the Battle, not the War
- Change is inevitable, Planning a Waste

Organize

- On-Site Customer
- Co-Locate the Team
- Stand-Up Meetings
- Sustainable Pace
  - Aka 40-Hour Week, No Overtime

Pair Programming

- Some things: Definitely
- Other: Maybe Not

- Is pair programming like the pilot/copilot question
  - Obviously, there are single seat aircraft, so the plane can be flown without a copilot
- Is the number of copilots killed less than the number of crewmembers saved by copilots who took over an airplane?

Spike

- Drive a Spike into the Technology
- Experimentation & Research
- No need for Test First

No Acceptable Bug

- There is no such thing as an acceptable bug
- Cf Good enough Yourdon

---

[5] McDermott, Patrick, *Zen and the Art of Systems Analysis: Meditations on Computer Systems Development*, New York: iUniverse (0-595-25679-1 [Paper], 0-595-75230-6 [eBook] & 0-595-65255-7 [Hardback]), 2003 (2002), p. 49-50.
[6] Reifer uses "AEXP" for APEX.
[7] Reifer uses "PEXP" for PLEX.
[8] SITE has 2 aspects: Collocation & Communication
[9] Hamlet, Dick & Joe Maybee, *The Engineering of Software: Technical Foundations for the Individual*, Boston: Addison Wesley (0-201-70103-0), 2001, pp. 70-72.

11. People Problems

The Bad News

The Worst problems you will encounter as a Systems Analyst are

People Problems

The Worse News

In the final analysis,

ALL PROBLEMS

are People Problems.

Agendae

	Public	Private
Official	Open	Closed
Personal	Open	Hidden Agenda

Computer Calamities

Field, Tom, "When Bad Things Happen to Good Projects", in Glass, Robert L., *Computing Calamities: Lessons Learned from Products, Projects, and Companies that Failed*, Upper Saddle River, New Jersey: Prentice Hall PTR (0-13-082862-9), 1999.

Computer Calamities

The University of California

Berkeley Extension

pmcdermott@msn.com

Copyright © 2007 Patrick McDermott

Bad Things & Good Projects

- Tom Field's article "When Bad Things Happen to Good Projects" lists

- The 7 Deadly Sins of Project Management
  - The ones most likely to help cause a failure
- 10 signs of an onrushing IS project failure
- 4 Ways to spot impending doom
- 3 criteria for canceling a project

The 7 Deadly Sins

1. Mistaking half-baked ideas for viable projects
2. Dictating unrealistic project deadlines
3. Assigning underskilled project managers to high-complexity projects
4. Not ensuring solid business sponsorship
5. Failing to break projects into manageable "chunks"
6. Failing to institute a robust project process architecture
7. Not establishing a comprehensive project portfolio to track progress of ongoing projects

10 Signs of IS Failure

1. Project managers don't understand users' needs
2. Scope is ill-defined
3. Project changes are managed poorly
4. Chosen technology changes
5. Business needs change
6. Deadlines are unrealistic
7. Users are resistant
8. Sponsorship is lost
9. Project lacks people with appropriate skills
10. Best practices and lessons are ignored

How to Spot Impending Doom

"Warning! Warning!"

1. Benchmark goals aren't met
2. Unresolved issues outnumber deliverables
3. Communication breaks down within project team and with customers
4. Project costs escalate

When to Call IT Quits

"Let's Call the Whole Thing Off"

1. When costs exceed business benefits
2. When deadlines continue to be missed
3. When technology and/or business needs evolve beyond project's scope

Conflict

Tyrannosaurus Rex and Triceratops
Tyrannosaurus (meaning 'tyrant lizard')
The term Triceratops, which literally means "three-horned face", is derived from the Greek tri/τρι- meaning "three", ceras/κέρας meaning "horn", and -ops/ωψ meaning "face".

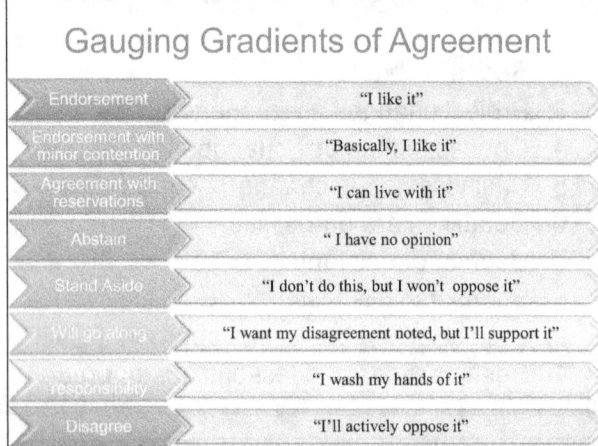

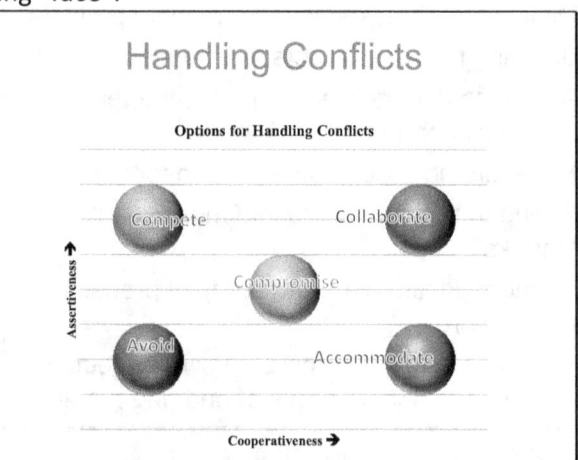

Justice, Tom & David W. Jamieson, Ph.D., *The Facilitator's Fieldbook, Second Edition*, New York: AMACOM American Management Association (0-8144-7314-8 978-0-8144-7314-6), 2006, pp . 203 & 241.

Conflict introduces life in the laboratory. When there's no conflict, a lab is no good.

E.R. Piore
U.S. Navy Chief Scientist

Conflict in Technical Culture

Conflicts over ideals and style may loom large
  – But they are the lifeblood of innovation
Code writers rely on logic and mathematics so they
  – Downplay the personality in technical decisions.
But the sense of inevitability, ascribed to all seminal inventions, is an illusion.
  – There are invariably many ways to achieve roughly the same technological ends.
  – Technical choices are often highly personal.
While shaped by commercial considerations, technical decisions also reflect human values & psychology.

Zachary, G. Pascal, *Showstopper: The Breakneck Race to Create Windows NT and the Next Generation at Microsoft*, New York: The Free Press, 1994. p. 224.

Consensus

Edward Hicks (1780-1849)
The Peaceable Kingdom
c. 1837

Consensus

Copyright © 2004 Patrick McDermott

UC Berkeley

Extension

pmcdermott@msn.com

Consensus

1. Everyone agrees: **I have been heard**
2. Everyone agrees: **I will support the decision, even if it is not my first choice.**
3. Silence is Assent.

- Consent, not Census
- Not Theory X or Y, *Theory Z*

Ouchi, William, *Theory Z: How American Business can Meet the Japanese Challenge*, New York: Avon Books (0-380-71944-4), 1993 (1981), p. 37.

Consensus

Each & Every can say:

1. I believe that you understand my point of view.
2. I believe that I understand your point of view.
3. Whether or not I prefer this decision, I will support it, because it was arrived at in an open and fair manner.

Ouchi, William, *Theory Z: How American Business can meet the Japanese Challenge*, Reading, Massachusetts: Addison-Wesley (0-201-05524-4), 1981, p. 43.

Consensus or Not?

Consensus Good	NOT so Good
• Lots of Input, Many Options	• Need Expert Opinion
• Need Commitment	• When there is One True Answer
• Want a Sense of Involvement	• Science
	– But Climate Change is a consensus issue(?)

- Beware of Groupthink!

Groupthink

- It's possible for the majority, or even the entire group, to be wrong
- "If everybody agrees, somebody is wrong!"
- 12 Angry Men
- Folie à deux
- Fighter Formation

Round Robin Brainstorming

- Take 2-5 minutes to think silently
- Take turns going around the group
- Okay to "Pass"
- "No one speaks twice until everyone has spoken once."

- Gets all involved, BUT
- Not as spontaneous

John James Audubon (1785-1851)
American Robin
The Birds of America, 1840-1844

Drucker's 2 Tales

- Secret
  - "They'll Love It"
  - They hated it
- Consultative
  - Don't like Surprises
  - Missed good input
- Best meeting confirms, not reveals
  - Rubber Stamps are good!
  - Surprises are Bad

日米 NichiBei Management

The generalization:

- Japanese management is consensus-driven, Western management is command-driven.
- Japanese take a long time to decide, but then implement quickly and seamlessly.
- Americans decide fast, but sometimes find that they missed something, or everyone isn't on board.

Developing Consensus

Model (for major decisions)

1. Ensure that all ideas are **thoroughly discussed.**
2. **Solicit reactions** to ideas, particularly from previous critics and quiet members, to determine what most people seem to want.
3. **Summarize** the group's feeling and **check for acceptance**.
4. **Do not** take a vote to determine the appropriate action.

Behaviors that facilitate consensus

1. Avoid arguing for your own position. Present it as clearly and logically as possible, but be sensitive to and consider seriously the reaction of the group in any subsequent presentations of the same point.

2. Avoid "win-lose" statements in the discussion of opinions. Discard the notion that someone must win and someone must lose in the discussion. When impasses occur, look for the next most acceptable alternative for all the parties involved.

3. Avoid changing your mind only in order to avoid conflict and to reach agreement and harmony. Withstand pressures to yield which have no objective or logically sound foundation. Strive for enlightened flexibility, but avoid outright capitulation.

4. Avoid conflict-reducing techniques such as the majority vote, averaging, bargaining, coin-flipping, trading out, and the like. Treat differences of opinion as indicative of an incomplete sharing of relevant information on someone's part, either about task issues, emotional data, or 'gut level' intuitions.

5. View differences of opinion as both natural and helpful, rather than as a hindrance in decision making. Generally, the more ideas that are expressed, the greater the likelihood of conflict will be, but the richer the array of resources will be as well.

6. View initial agreement as suspect. Explore the reasons underlying apparent agreements; make sure people have arrived at the same conclusions for either the same basic reasons or for complementary reasons before incorporating such opinions into the group decision.

7. Avoid subtle forms of influence and decision modification. For example, when a dissenting member finally agrees, don't feel that he/she must be 'rewarded' by having his/her own way on some subsequent point.

8. Be willing to entertain the possibility that your team can achieve all the foregoing and actually excel at its task; avoid dismaying and negative predictions for group potential.

The Iceberg Secret

"The Iceberg Secret, Revealed", February 13, 2002, in Spolsky, Joel, *Joel on Software: And on Diverse and Occasionally Related Matters That Will Prove of Interest to Software Developers, Designers, and Managers, and to Those Who, Whether by Good Fortune or Ill Luck, Work with Them in Some Capacity*, New York: Apress / Springer-Verlag (1-59059-389-8), 2004, pp. 189-195.

"The Iceberg Secret, Revealed", February 13, 2002, in Spolsky, Joel, *Joel on Software: And on Diverse and Occasionally Related Matters That Will Prove of Interest to Software Developers, Designers, and Managers, and to Those Who, Whether by Good Fortune or Ill Luck, Work with Them in Some Capacity*, New York: Apress / Springer-Verlag (1-59059-389-8), 2004, pp. 189-195.

The Iceberg Secret

The University of California

Berkeley Extension
pmcdermott@msn.com

The Iceberg Secret

"It's pretty clear that programmers think in one language, and MBAs think in another. I've been thinking about the problem of communication in software management for a while, because it's pretty clear to me that the power and rewards accrue to those are individuals who know how to translate between Programmerese and MBAese." —Joel Spolsky

Like an iceberg, software is 90% underwater. The UI takes 10% of the work, and 90% of the programming work is under the covers.

The Iceberg Secret:
"People who are not programmers don't understand this."

Get Real

Customers don't know what they want.

Stop expecting customers to know what they want.

The Polar Sea
Casper David Friedrich
c. 1824

"It's just never going to happen.
Get over it."

"Important Corollaries"

1. If you show a nonprogrammer a screen that has a user interface that is 90 percent worse, they will think that the program is 90 percent worse.

2. If you show a nonprogrammer a screen that is 100 percent beautiful, they will think that the program is almost done.

3. The dotcom that has the cool polished-looking website and about four webpages will get a higher valuation than the highly functional dotcom with 3,700 years of archives and a default gray background.

...

"Important Corollaries"

4. When politics demands that various nontechnical managers or customers "sign off" on a project, give them several versions of the graphic design to choose from.

5. When you're showing off, the only thing that matters is the screen shot. Make it 100 percent beautiful.

What 2 Do

✓ Don't, for a minute, think you can get away with asking *anybody* to *imagine how cool this would be*.

✓ Build your UI in such a way that unfinished parts *look* unfinished.

✓ Make sure you control what people think about the schedule.

✓ Make sure that the actual facts dominate any thinking about whether the project is moving forward at the right speed.

Individuals
Personality Traits

There are Two Types of People in the World:
1. Those who divide people into 2 categories
2. Those who do not

Personality Traits

Copyright © 2004 Patrick McDermott
UC Berkeley
Extension
pmcdermott@msn.com

Science

- *Scientific American* objection
  - Specialization of brain not that clear
  - No Experimental Testing of Hypotheses
  Id|Ego|Superego ≠ Cerebrum|Cerebellum|Medula
- Not Science, but maybe, like Literature
  - "The truest truths are told in Fiction"
  - Scientific or not, Many People use them
  - Self Fulfilling
  - Seem to offer insight
- This very debate illustrates the differences

Types A & B

- Meyer Friedman & R.H. Rosenman
  - 1950s
  - Evaluating Coronary Risk
- Type A: impatient, excessively time-conscious, insecure about one's status, highly competitive, hostile and aggressive, and incapable of relaxation
- Type B: patient, relaxed, and easy-going
- Type AB

Intelligences

1. Verbal-Linguistic
2. Logical/Mathematical
3. Visual/Spatial
4. Bodily/Kinesthetic
5. Musical/Rhythmic
6. Intrapersonal
7. Interpersonal
8. Naturalist
9. Existentialist

Intelligence, Skill, or Talent?

Can also be Learning Preferences

Howard Gardner
Harvard psychologist

Teaching Styles

✓ Lecture
✓ Read
✓ Write
✓ Modeling
✓ Try then Teach
✓ Apply
✓ Group Work
✓ To Learn, Teach

Maslow's Hierarchy of Needs

- Self-Actualization
- Esteem
  - R-e-s-p-e-c-t
- Love & Belonging
  - Family & Friends
- Safety & Security
  - (Job Security)
- Physiological
  - Air, Food, H_2O

Esteem
Love
Safety
Physical Needs

Abraham Maslow, 1908-1970.

Self-Actualization

1. **Awareness**
   - Efficient perception of reality
   - Freshness of appreciation
   - Peak experiences
   - Ethical awareness
2. **Honesty**
   - Philosophical sense of humor
   - Social interest
   - Deep interpersonal relationships
   - Democratic character structure
3. **Freedom**
   - Need for solitude
   - Autonomous, independent
   - Creativity, originality
   - Spontaneous
4. **Trust**
   - Problem centered
   - Acceptance of self, others, nature
   - Resistance to enculturation - identity with humanity

Personality Traits

TRAITS	*Clever*	*Stupid*
Industrious	Great!!!	Danger!!
Lazy	Efficient	Useable

Hackworth, Colonel David H. & Eilhys England, *Steel my Soldiers' Hearts: The Hopeless to Hardcore Transformation of 4th Battalion, 39th Infantry, United Sates Army, Vietnam*, New York: Rugged Land (1-59071-002-9), 2002, p. 347.

4 Personality Types

2 Cultures

2 [or 3?] Cultures

The University of California
Berkeley Extension
pmcdermott@msn.com

Copyright © 2007 Patrick McDermott

If I had my life to live over again, I would have made a rule to read some poetry and listen to some music at least once a week; for perhaps the parts of my brain now atrophied would have thus been kept active through use. The loss of these tastes is a loss of happiness, and may possibly be injurious to the intellect, and more probably to the moral character, by enfeebling the emotional part of our nature.—Charles Darwin

C.P. Snow

C.P. Snow delivered his famous lecture on *The Two Cultures* in 1959. He suggested that intellectual life divided into two isolated cultures, with Science on one side, versus the Arts and Humanities, 'the literary Intellectuals', on the other. We are likewise faced with two cultures in developing a computer system. Guy Kawasaki in *The Macintosh Way* calls them **T-Shirts** and **Ties** for their sartorial preferences: T-Shirts are commonly worn by Technologists such as programmers; Ties are de rigueur in the business departments in typical companies and in marketing departments in high-tech firms.

Two Cultures

- Creative
  - Arts & Humanities, 'the literary Intellectuals'
- Logical
  - Science & Mathematics

Snow, C.P., *The Two Cultures*, Cambridge, United Kingdom: Cambridge University Press (0-521-45730-0), 1998 (1959).

YIN	YANG
Bun : Cultural	*Bu* : Martial
Scholar	Warrior
Mental	Physical
Creative	Logical
Introspection	Teamwork
Contracting	Expanding
Dark	Light
Shaded	Sunny
Cool	Warm
Wet	Dry
Gentle	Strong
Sweet	Sour
Receptive	Active
Moon	Sun
Earth	Heaven
Feminine	Masculine
Process-Oriented	Results-Oriented
Retreating Hand	Punching Hand
Negative Electricity	Positive Electricity
Eastern Philosophy	Western Philosophy

Complements:
Yin & Yang

陰陽
いんよう

In'yō

Neither is "Better"

Digital or Analog?

- SAT Math versus Verbal
- Guy Kawasaki: T-Shirts & Ties
  - Technology & Business
  - Science & Art
- "Left Brain"
  - Logic
  - Digital
- "Right Brain"
  - Creativity
  - Analog

It is easy to imagine a world full of poets who do not build radio telescopes.—Carl Sagan

Andrew Lloyd Weber certainly understands Business!

Science vs. Engineering

- The Scientist builds in order to study.
- The Engineer studies in order to build.

  The difference between Theory & Practice is that in theory, there is no difference between Theory & Practice.

  - Software Engineering falls between CS & CIS, but leans toward the pragmatic
    - Computer Science: Know Things
    - Software Engineering: Build Things
    - Computer Information Systems: Build Things People Will Pay For

Constantine's Cultures

"I have management consulting colleagues in Russia who argue that computer programming represents a subculture of such power that it may have greater influence and claims to allegiance than even national culture. Their position is that programmers in Moscow are more like programmers in Minneapolis than either are like their nonprogramming compatriots from the cities in which they live and work. Whatever the causes, this trend toward uniformity may be a real handicap to our profession, especially as we work in teams."

Constantine, Larry L., *The Peopleware Papers: Notes on the Human Side of Software*, Upper Saddle River, New Jersey: The Yourdon Press (0-13-060123-3), 2001, p. 46.

A Socialist's Distress

- British & German Soldiers in the Trenches had more in common with each other than with the capitalists & aristocrats whom, in the Socialist's viewpoint, they fought for.
  - Yet they proudly fought each other
- Does an American programmer have more in common with an Indian programmer than with an American factory worker or trust fund baby?

Yin 陰	**YANG** 陽
Bun: Cultural	*Bu*: Martial
Scholar	Warrior
Mental	Physical
Creative	Logical
Introspection	Teamwork
Contracting	Expanding
Dark	Light
Shaded	Sunny
Cool	Warm
Wet	Dry
Gentle	Strong
Sweet	Sour
Receptive	Active
Moon	Sun
Earth	Heaven
Feminine	Masculine
Process-Oriented	Results-Oriented
Retreating Hand	Punching Hand
Negative Electricity	Positive Electricity
Eastern Philosophy	Western Philosophy

Stakeholder Analysis

Stakeholder Analysis

Copyright © 2001 Patrick McDermott

the University of California

Berkeley Extension

pmcdermott@msn.com

What's a Stakeholder?

- Stakeholder - Anyone who can impact the project or be impacted by it, either now or in the future.
- Yourdon distinguishes certain stakeholders as Shareholders, those who have a vested interest in the outcome

- A.k.a. the Victim

Types of Stakeholders

Sponsor
- Sets future direction of business; sets goals and priorities; evaluates from strategic level. Controls Budget. "Owner"

Power Client
- Determines success criteria, what it has to do to be an improvement; tactics; gives access to resources

User
- Will use the system. "Customer"

Resource
- Controls information or other Resource

Opinion Leader
- Characteristic of an individual, not organizational role. "Champion"

Career Influencers
- Mentor(s), immediate boss, boss's boss

Type Matrix

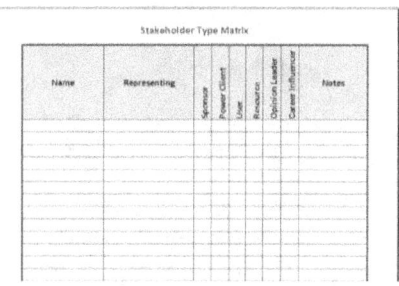

Major User Relations Issues

1. Establishing Credibility
   - Telling the truth
2. Developing a sense of Collaboration
   - Partners in Decision Making
3. Communicating
4. Teaching and Mentoring
   - Being both a teacher and a learner
5. Advising/Providing Feedback
   - Anticipating the Impact

A Partnership

✓ Influence over what happens
✓ Being told about new, significant events
✓ Respect for each other's contributions
✓ Feedback about what has gone well, and not so well
✓ Coming to each other first when there is a problem
✓ Doing your part
✓ Make me look good to my boss

Get the Scoop

✓ Access to people
  ➢ Supervisors, end users and user's users
✓ Freedom of movement in the department and between departments
✓ Access to information
✓ Time taken away from production if necessary

Understanding

✓ Endorsement from management to the user community
✓ Enough time to get the job done
✓ Appreciate my scheduling problems
✓ Tolerance of mistakes; forgiveness
✓ Tell me when you don't understand what I've said
✓ Opportunity to be innovative

Contact

✓ Willingness to renegotiate deliverables
✓ Return phone calls
✓ Knowing what he or she is trying to achieve
✓ Hold off on evaluation
✓ Support

User needs from the Analyst

✓ Basic knowledge about the technology, relatively jargon free
✓ Confidentiality about areas of user deficiency in operational knowledge and areas of operational sloppiness
✓ Understanding, empathy and supportiveness
✓ Challenging status quo in a non-defensive productive way
✓ Being realistic in my promises
✓ Being clear about what I am doing
✓ Communicating frequently, informally and face-to-face

Steps

- Find a Sponsor
  - Higher than all participants
  - Could be a Steering Committee
- Draw a Project Org Chart
- Consider the Stakeholders
  - Favor
  - Discourage
  - Ignore, "Don't Care"
    - Obsolete Browser
    - Email your Résumé

Stakeholder Analysis

- Influence the Project
- Interest in the Outcome
- Impacted by the System
- Intelligence for Analysis

	Influence	Interest	Impacted	Intelligence	Total
Mike	1	2	4	5	12
Mary	3	5	4	5	17
Mel	2	1	2	1	6
Mimi	2	4	3	2	11

Two Rules for Success

 Never Tell them Everything.
   Leave Them Wanting More.

Stakeholder Exercise

- Exercise
- Beyond the Use Case Actors
- Who are the Broad Stakeholders involved in
  - Order taking at amazon.com
  - Registration at UCBx
- Late Project Case Study

Stakeholder Four I's

	Influence	Interest	Impacted	Intelligence	Total
Mike	1	2	4	5	12
Mary	3	5	4	5	17
Mel	2	1	2	1	6
Mimi	2	4	3	2	11

Stakeholder Type Matrix

Name	Representing	Sponsor	Power Client	User	Resource	Opinion Leader	Career Influencer	Notes

Justice, Tom & David W. Jamieson, Ph.D, The Facilitator's Fieldbook, Second Edition, New York: AMACOM American Management Association (0-8144-7314-8 978-0-8144-7314-6), 2006, p. 55.

Stakeholder Case Study

Overview

The company has for the last two years been developing a second upgrade of their inventory, rental agreements and accounting. During this phase the database structure is drastically changing and will require conversion. The methods of billing and tracking accounts receivables are also undergoing considerable modification. New bills will be produced.

Implementation is two months away. The VPs and Sr. VPs will earn their bonuses only if implemented by the scheduled date.

Organization Structure

Operations is headed by Virginia, VP, who reports to Al, Sr. VP, who reports to Mike, Pres. of subsidiary, who reports to Jerry, President of the parent company. James manages and controls inventory. His boss also reports to Mike. Jill manages the billing department and has 30 customer service representatives reporting to her. Jill is a very enthusiastic person with lots of good ideas. She is listened to by MIS. She reports to Virginia. Peter, VP MIS, reports to Lynn, Sr. VP of Finance. The programmers are 90% contractor personnel. Also reporting to Lynn is the Controller, Nancy. The person who manages AP and GL is Sue. She reports to Fred, the Assistant Controller. Lynn reports to Mike with a dotted line reporting to Chuck, CFO of the parent company. Chuck reports to Jerry. Paul, the treasurer, also reports to Lynn.

The project is managed by a steering committee consisting of Lynn, Al and Mike. There is also a user design committee where specifications are developed, test plans are written and executed and problems are discussed. Timelines are managed by a rotating chair of the committee.

Development

Most of the code has been written and unit tested. Some integrated testing has occurred with dozens of errors found. User acceptance testing is scheduled for next week. The conversion program was designed without clear user input or test plan. The conversion program has not been fully tested. The accounting interface specifications still need final approval before coding can begin. Fred is responsible for these interfaces. Fred's assistant, Sue, is responsible for the balancing of the GL and does not want the new system because of the potential problems to the GL. According to operations, the modules do not need to be completed until one month after implementation.

The inventory control training has just begun. The user manuals have been drafted but not completed. Customer support has not yet been trained. The customers have not been alerted.

Because of the radical changes to the database structure, a parallel test will be impossible. Conversion of the database will take three days. So, to stay on-line for the customers, the conversion must occur over the long three-day weekend. The next long weekend is four months away. Operations is happy with the testing. Accounting is not at all happy, since there is no code yet. Inventory control hates the training because they were excluded from the user requirements. Donna, the lead MIS contractor, makes changes to code without informing the user community.

Discussion

Review the case study, and develop a presentation or write-up that provides the following:
- Identify what you think the basic problem is
- Identify the stakeholders
- Categorize each of the stakeholders (sponsor, power client, user, resource, opinion leader, career influencer)
- Consider what each of the stakeholders might need, what information you would want from them, and describe how you would deal with each of them.
- Discuss how you would approach solving the problem.

Note: The technical solution to the problem is not what's important.

Groups
Form, Storm, Norm, Perform

"Once upon a time there was an organization with only three members—Somebody, Everybody and Nobody. Somebody said that an important job needed to be done. Everybody agreed that the job needed doing. Nobody ended up doing it."—Mark Norris, *Survival in the Software Jungle*

FSNP

Copyright © 2004 Patrick McDermott

UC Berkeley
Extension

pmcdermott@msn.com

Collaboration

- Chickens & other Bird Brains
  - Pecking Order
  - Dog Pack "Leader of the Pack"
- Contention of Gilbert & Sullivan: *Topsy Turvy*
- Movie *Casablanca*
  - No one wanted to be there; no script, no plan, etc.
  - But became masterpiece
- Collaborate good/bad
  - How important is collaboration?
  - Would a collaborator have helped Einstein?
    - Assuming his wife wasn't…

Team Life Cycle

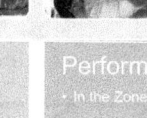

Form	Storm	Norm	Perform
• Excited, but nervous	• Conflict, Turbulence, Bi-polar	• Harmony and Acceptance	• In the Zone

Form

- Ambivalent Feelings
- Excited, but apprehensive
- Need to define tasks
- Need to learn to work together
- Might thrash if objectives are unclear

Jacques-Louis David (1748-1825)
Oath of the Horatii, c. 1784-85

Storm

- Conflict, Turbulence
  - Ambivalent may become Bi-polar
- Some compete for dominance
- Establish a Pecking Order
- Sometimes just "Wrong Foot"
- We accept hierarchy
  - 2nd Lt is youngest, weakest, dumbest
    - But grizzled sergeants obey

Winslow Homer (1836-1910)
The Life Line, c. 1884

Norm

- Team Spirit
- Harmony and Acceptance
- Constructive Disagreements
  - "If everyone agrees, someone is wrong!"
- Can Do the Job

- In a Word: Synergy
  - "The whole is greater then the sum of its parts."

Edward Hicks (1780-1849)
The Peaceable Kingdom, c. 1837

Perform

- In the Zone
- Anticipate each others needs
- Fill in for each when necessary
  - Without management Intervention
- Few teams reach this level
  - Make it your Goal, nonetheless

Edgar Degas (1834-1917)
The Rehearsal on Stage
c. 1874

Morale & Productivity

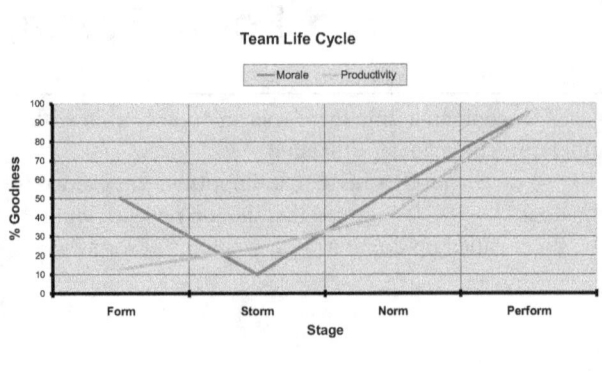

Re-Boot

- Often a new member stirs the mix
  - Existing patterns become open to question
- When a new member joins, Regress
- A New Pecking Order must be Established

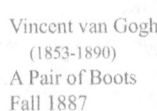

Vincent van Gogh
(1853-1890)
A Pair of Boots
Fall 1887

Team Death Cycle

"You should be glad that bridge fell down—I was going to build twelve more to the same design."—I.K. Brunel

- Adjourn
  - Wrap up & Look back
- Mourn?
  - They're breaking up that old gang of mine
  - It's called a "Post Mortem" for a reason
  - Learn from mistakes
  - Post-parted Depression

Not Always

- Sometimes (~15%) a Lost at Sea participant would have been better alone
- Group dynamix: need right group; if nobody knows nothin': no good.
- Three 100 IQs not smarter than Einstein
- Einstein would not have been better on a committee

Drucker's 3 Team Types

 Baseball
  - Fixed Positions, Set Jobs/Responsibilities
  - Information from the Situation

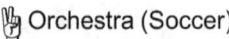 Orchestra (Soccer)
  - Requires a Conductor/Coach
  - Synchronized/Coordinated
  - Information from the Conductor

Tennis Doubles
  - Cover for one another
  - Adapt to partner's Strength & Weaknesses
  - Information from each other

Jacques-Louis David (1748-1825)
Oath of the Horatii
c. 1784-85

Form

Winslow Homer (1836-1910)
The Life Line
c. 1884

Storm

Norm

Edward Hicks (1780-1849)
The Peaceable Kingdom
c. 1837

Edgar Degas (1834-1917)
The Rehearsal on the Stage
c. 1873

Perform

Murderous Meetings

Murderous Meetings

Copyright © 2004 Patrick McDermott

UC Berkeley
Extension

pmcdermott@msn.com

What is a Meeting?

✓ An event where minutes are kept and hours are lost

✓ A gathering where people say nothing and everybody disagrees

✓ Indispensable when you don't want to accomplish anything

✓ Meeting length varies as the square of the number of participants

If you had to identify, in one word, the reason why the human race has not achieved, and never will achieve, its full potential, that word would be "meetings".
—Dave Barry

Groups Gone Bad

- Recognize them, so you can do something
- Fight for Dominance
- Gripe Session
- Group Think
- Superficial Analysis
- No Progress
  - Old Agenda Story
  - We thought it was current

A meeting is an ad hoc team
Formed of individuals
With a cultural background
Teamwork is essential!

Dominating

- Argumentative
  - Wrong
    - But won't admit it
  - Obstinate
- Won't shut up
- Others have no input

Ramblers

- Digresses
- Heckler
- Distracts
- Comedian
- Not Present in Present
  - Side Conversation
  - Problem or Symptom?

Angry

- MOA
  - Mad On Arrival
- With some justification
  - But it wasn't us
- Personality Clash
- Explosion "The Grenade"

No Speak

- Won't Talk
  - Passive
- Not Assertive
- Ignoring Member(s)
  - Chair/Facilitator
  - Individuals
  - Key players

- But later might say "I didn't Agree"!

How to Ruin a Meeting

1. Hogging
2. Bogging
   Getting bogged down
3. Fogging
   Too vague, unfocused
4. Frogging
   Jumping from topic to topic
5. Flogging
   Attacking person, not idea
6. Clogging
   Not completing necessary homework

Bounds & Woods
Supervision

Meeting Health
or
Meeting Hell

Run a Meeting

Running a Meeting takes Mental Energy

You should NOT try to take notes, too

Appoint a Scribe/Notetaker

Team Size

Emanuel Leutze (1816-1868)
Washington Crossing the Delaware
c. 1851

Team Size

The University of California
Berkeley Extension
pmcdermott@msn.com

Copyright © 2008 Patrick McDermott

Scope of Group

Number of Conversations

$$N^2 - N$$

 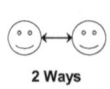

2 Ways

6 Ways

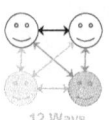

12 Ways

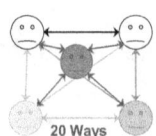

20 Ways

Next number is 2N greater

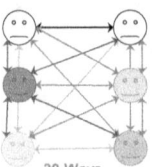

30 Ways

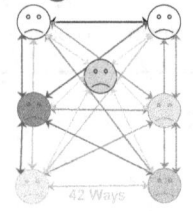

42 Ways

Ramp Up

- Brooks: "You can't get a baby in 1 months by putting 9 women on the job."
- "Adding Staff to a Late Project Will Make it Later"
- 10 minutes in meeting of 12 is 2 Hours!
- The Marginal Utility of Labor
  - The Law of Diminishing Returns
- Boehm sets the compression limit at 75% of Nominal Development Time
  - You can't reduce by > @ ⅓

Team Size vs. Productivity

LOC/Month

Size	Individual Productivity	Total Productivity
1	500	500
2	450	900
3	400	1200
4	350	1400
5	300	1500
5.5	275	1513
6	250	1500
7	200	1400
8	150	1200

 van Vliet, Hans, *Software Engineering, Principles and Practices*, Chichester, England: John Wiley & Sons (0-471-93611-1), 1993, p. 116.

Size	Individual Productivity	Total Productivity
1	500	500
2	550	1100
3	560	1680
4	570	2280
5	525	2625
6	510	3060
7	500	3500
8	500	4000
9	500	4500
10	490	4900
11	450	4950
12	400	4800
13	350	4550

Patrick's Take

Organizational Culture

Artifacts
Values you See In Action

Espoused Values
Values that are Communicated

Underlying Assumptions
(Sometimes Subconscious) Values Driving the Organization

Theory X, Y, Z, & W

Barry Boehm, discussed in "Barry Boehm's "Theory W" Principle of Software Project Management" in Glass, Robert L., *Software Conflict 2.0: The Art and Science of Software Engineering*, Atlanta, Georgia: developer.* Books (0-9772133-0-7), 2006 (*Software Creativity: Essays on the Art and Science of Software Engineering*, 1990), pp. 147-151.

 Theories X, Y, Z [& W]

University of California
Berkeley Extension
pmcdermott@msn.com

Copyright © 2007 Patrick McDermott

Sources

 Theory X (Authoritarian)
Theory Y (Participatory)
 – Douglas McGregor, MIT
 – Scientific vs. Humanistic
Theory Z (Consensus)
Ouchi, William, **Theory Z**: *How American Business can meet the Japanese Challenge*, Reading, Massachusetts: Addison-Wesley (0-201-05524-4), 1981.
 – Japanese Management Theory
 – Consensus
 – Based on Deming
 Boehm Theory W
 – Win Win Management

Theory X

- People inherently dislike work.
- They have to be coerced into working.
- They prefer being told what to do.

"Theory X is based on an assumption that people must be prodded into doing work; this tends to result in an adversarial management-developer relationship, and in fact does not accurately reflect the nature of software people." —Barry Boehm

Theory Y

- People don't inherently dislike work.
- People can exercise self-direction.
- Commitment to objectives depends on resulting rewards.
- People can learn to seek responsibility.
- Work creativity is widely distributed.
- People potential is only partly utilized.

"Theory Y is based on an assumption that people will work well if they are rewarded properly; this tends to result in the creation of a self-oriented work force, and tends to break down when conflict is encountered." —Barry Boehm

Theory Z

- People work best toward goals which they have helped establish.
- Once people have bought into goals, you can trust them to perform.
- If people share a common set of values, they can develop workable project goals.

"Theory Z, the so-called "Japanese-style management," is useful in a single community of workers, but tends to break down when multiple organizations, such as software's managers, customers, developers and maintainers are involved." —Barry Boehm

Theory W

W stands for "Make Everyone a Winner"

1. Establish a set win-win preconditions. Understand what the win conditions for each player really are. Establish objectives which include making those wins possible. Provide a supportive environment in which all participants accept the possibility of a win-win solution.
2. Structure a win-win software process. Establish a realistic process plan, including the flagging of win-lose and lose-lose situations as risks. Provide feedback which keeps involved as negotiation and compromise proceed.
3. Structure a win-win software product. Define a final software product which matches all the win conditions, those of the user and the maintainer.

A Win for Each Player

Management
- Wants the product built with no overruns or surprises.

Customers
- Want the project built as quickly as possible within budget.

Users
- Want lots of functions, a fast and robust product, and user-friendliness.

Developers
- Want an interesting career path, a project built with integrity, and the minimization of documentation writing.

Maintainers
- Want a bug-free product, good documentation, and a product that is easy to change.

Boehm's Steps

1. Separate the people from the Problem.
2. Focus of Interests, not positions.
3. Invent Options for mutual gain.
4. Insist on using objective Criteria to analyze the results.

"Do unto others as you would have them do unto you —if you were like them" —Barry Boehm

Work the Room

Work the Room

College of Alameda
pmcdermott@peralta.edu

Copyright © 2008 Patrick McDermott

The size & arrangement of the room can profoundly affect the success of your presentation

Classroom

- Writing Surface for Notes, References
- Hard to Interact with each other

Theatre

- More People in the Room
- Hard to Interact with each other

U for You

- Group Discussions
- You can see everybody
- They can interact
- Writing Surface for Notes, References

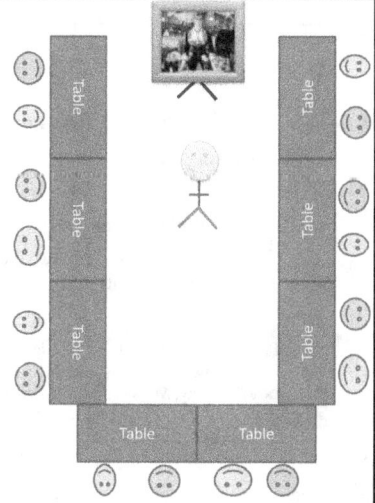

Banquet

- Small Groups
- Hands-On Team exercises

- Eating...

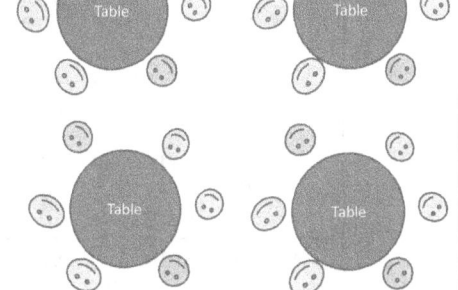

NASA Team-Building
A Team-Building Exercise that's Out of This World

This is about a team-building exercise used at NASA.

<table>
<tr><td>

Technical Team

Mostly Technical people
- The total process was orderly and efficient
- A team member quickly took charge and guided the group
  - Established criteria
  - Evaluated the items
  - Assigned priorities to each
- The group was finished quickly
- Each point was discussed, and unanimously settled

</td><td>

Disorderly Team

The Second Group was chaos:
- Several viewed this class as a way to demonstrate their leadership skills
  - Each tried to take charge
- Degenerated into a series of arguments
- No discernible order or plan
- When the hour was up, still arguing over the final items and had to be called back into the meeting room.

</td></tr>
</table>

"The group was then arbitrarily divided into two ten-person teams, and each went to a separate meeting room for an hour to produce an answer."

The first group was mostly technical people and was orderly and thorough:
"In one case, a team member quickly took charge and guided the group through an orderly process of establishing criteria, evaluating the items, and assigning priorities to each. … This total process was orderly and efficient, each point was discussed and unanimously settled, and the group was finished in only fifteen minutes."

The second group was chaos:
"Several viewed this class as a way to demonstrate their leadership skills, so they each tried to take charge. As a result, the meeting quickly degenerated into a series of arguments with no discernible order or plan. When the hour was up, they were still arguing over the final items and had to be called back into the meeting room."

<table>
<tr><td>

Exercise Results

But the results may surprise you:
- The technical, team members had individually done quite well
  - But their overall team result was little better than their best individual score
- On the disorderly team, none of the individual scores had been very good
  - But the team result was better than their best individual score
- Better than the score of the technical team
  - Even though their individual team members had not done nearly as well

</td><td>

Exercise Conclusion

Arranged agenda and a firm Leader (chair)
- Can be very effective in gathering facts
- BUT can seriously inhibit
  - The generation of new ideas
  - The open communication needed to reach complete agreement

 Humphrey, Watts S., *Managing Technical People: Innovation, Teamwork, and the Software Process*, Reading, Massachusetts: Addison-Wesley, 1997.

</td></tr>
</table>

But the results may surprise you: "When the results were compared, the technical, team members had individually done quite well, but their overall team result was little better than their best individual score. On the disorderly team, none of the individual scores had been very good, but the team result was better than their best individual score. What is more, it was even better than the score of the technical team, even though their individual team members had not done nearly as well."

"When strong leaders take charge, their views tend to dominate the process. While they may request everyone's opinions, their views set the agenda and largely control the final result. An arranged agenda and a firm chairman can be very effective in gathering facts, but they seriously inhibit the generation of new ideas and the open communication needed to reach complete agreement. With an established agenda, members are often reluctant to disrupt the proceedings. Even when they have very good ideas, they will hold back out of shyness or deference to the leader." [*]

Strong Leaders

- When strong leaders take charge, their views tend to dominate the process.
- While they may request everyone's opinions
  - Their views set the agenda
  - They largely control the final result

Buzz Aldrin's boot print
One of the first steps
taken on the moon
Apollo 11, 1969

Rigid Agenda

With an Established Agenda
- Members are often reluctant to disrupt the proceedings
- Even when they have very good ideas, they will hold back
  - Shyness
  - Deference to the Leader
  - Fear of Consequences

Pillars of Creation from Eagle Nebula

"The standoff … highlighted the significance of personal conflicts in technical culture. Conflicts over ideals and style loomed large—they were the lifeblood of innovation. Because code writers relied on logic and mathematics in their designs, they downplayed the role of personality in their technical decisions. But the sense of inevitability, ascribed to all seminal inventions, is an illusion. There are invariably many ways to achieve roughly the same technological ends. Technical choices are often highly personal. While shaped by commercial considerations, technical decisions also reflect human values and psychology.

Facilitation for Innovation

The Eagle Nebula

- Don't!
  - Roll with the flow
- Goal?
  - Innovation
  - Consensus
- Hard to control
  - You probably can't control it
  - You don't want to
- Take turns, equal participation-NO!

Other Observations

- Technicians didn't benefit much from creativity; needed an artistic soul?
- Strong leader can inhibit the creativity of members
- Engineers/Techies solved the problem efficiently, but not necessarily creatively

Andromeda galaxy

"Cutler [the head of the NT development project] saw the benefit of allowing personal differences over technology play themselves out. He rarely stifled conflicts. Usually, he followed the dictum of one of the century's finest research managers, E.R. Piore, the U.S. Navy's most

[*] Humphrey, Watts S., Managing Technical People: Innovation, Teamwork, and the Software Process, Reading, Massachusetts: Addison-Wesley (0201545977), 1997, p 172.

perspicacious chief scientist, who said: "Conflict introduces life in the laboratory. When there's no conflict, a lab is no good." [*]

Nonaka & Takeuchi re Ambiguity

It may sound paradoxical, but:

- The Confusion created by the ambiguity of the mission handed down by Honda's top management provided an extremely clear sense of direction to the team.
- Ambiguity can prove useful at times
  - A source of a new sense of direction
  - A new source of meanings
  - A fresh way of thinking about things
- In this respect, new knowledge is born out of chaos.

"It may sound paradoxical, but the confusion created within the product development team by the ambiguity of the mission handed down by Honda's top management provided an extremely clear sense of direction to the team. Ambiguity can prove useful at times not only as a source of a new sense of direction, but also as a new source of meanings and a fresh way of thinking about things. In this respect, new knowledge is born out of chaos." [†]

---

[*] Zachary, G. Pascal, Showstopper: The Breakneck Race to Create Windows NT and the Next Generation at Microsoft, New York: The Free Press (0-02-935671-7), 1994, p. 224.
[†] Nonaka Ikujiro & Takeuchi Hirotaka, The Knowledge-Creating Company: How Japanese Companies Create the Dynamics of Innovation, New York: Oxford University Press (0-19-509269-4), 1995, p. 14.

Facilitation

Facilitation

acilitation

Copyright © 2006 Patrick McDermott

UC Berkeley

Extension

pmcdermott@msn.com

What's Your Purpose?

Check All That Apply

- ❑ Build a Team
- ❑ Explore Ideas & Possibilities
- ❑ Gain Consensus
- ❑ Solve a Problem
- ❑ Decide an Issue

❑ JAD—Joint Application Design

Assumptions

- Participation is Key
  - All Ideas Considered
  - Commitment Gained
- Teams can out-perform Individuals
  - Many Heads are Better than One
  - Diversity in Opinion, Interest
- Process leads to Outcome
  - Facilitator ➔ Process
  - Leader ➔ Outcome

The Wisdom of Groups

- Coordinate Independent Efforts
- Include Multiple Functions
- Share Information
- Make Decisions
- Solve Problems
- Plan

But Einstein probably wouldn't have done better Relativity on a committee

Facilitator ≠ Leader

- Don't get Involved in Their Decisions
- Stay Neutral
- Probe
- Balance Participation
- You're not a Performer
- Be Interested, not Interesting

- Might not fit your personality

The Facilitator's Job

Coach & Guide

- ✓ Analyze Purpose, Outcome, Context, Members
- ✓ Plan the Structure, Process
- ✓ Monitor and Adapt the Process
- ✓ Control Climate and Mood
- ✓ Manage Group Dynamics
- ✓ Decision Process
- ✓ Follow-up

In The Beginning

- An Organized Group
- The Right Members
- Clear on Purpose
- All Roles Understood
- Logistics Planned

- Agenda

Roles

- Member
- Scribe(s)
- Liaison
- Consultant
- Ad Hoc Member
- Leader
- Sponsor
- Steering Committee

They must be Credible & Empowered!

Goldilocks:
Not too Big, Not too Small

Some Techniques

- Ice Breakers
- Brainstorm
- Parking Lot
- Subgroups
- Snacks
- Collective Memory

Always

- ✓ Listen!
- ✓ Focus on the *Process*
- ✓ Stay Present in the Present
- ✓ Organize, Connect, Summarize
- ✓ Protect the Weak
- ✓ Trust the Group
- ✓ Be Flexible
- ✓ Beware of Groupthink

Handling Conflicts

Options for Handling Conflicts

All Together Now!

Facilitator's Check List

Justice, Tom & David W. Jamieson, Ph.D, *The Facilitator's Fieldbook, Second Edition*, New York: AMACOM American Management Association (0-8144-7314-8 978-0-8144-7314-6), 2006.

Facilitator's Checklist

Copyright © 2007 Patrick McDermott

UC Berkeley

Extension

pmcdermott@msn.com

Justice, Tom & David **Jamieson**, *The Facilitator's Fieldbook*, New York: American Management Association (0-8144-7038-6), 1999.

Simply Put

- Your Responsibility as Facilitator is
 Everything!
- Anything Affects the Meeting's Success
  - Do The Tasks, Or…
  - Convince Yourself they are being Done
- Discuss/Negotiate what You Will Do
- Point Out what is & isn't Done
  - You Have No Authority
  - But You Are Responsible

Core Processes

1. Analyze Information
   - Purpose, Context, Participants
2. Design Meetings
3. Establish Climate
   - Ground Rules, Roles
4. Structure & Processes
   - Help Them Make Decisions Intelligently
5. Managing Group Dynamics
   - Intervene to Enforce & Influence

…

Core Processes, continued

6. Coach Group Leader & Members
7. Evaluate Meeting Effectiveness
   - How We Doin'?
8. Navigate Decision Processes
   - Bag of Tools
9. Ensure Follow-up
   - Record & Results
   - Communication
   - How'd We Do?

Planning: Tasks

- ✓ Goals Agreed Upon
- ✓ Research Context, Goals, Participants
- ✓ Stakeholder Analysis
- ✓ Define Group & Leader
- ✓ Finalize & Publish Agenda
- ✓ Logistics
  - Room
  - Supplies
  - Snacks

Planning: Outcomes

- ☑ Group Organized
- ☑ Membership Decided
- ☑ Purpose Established
- ☑ Roles Assigned
- ☑ Logistics Planned
- ☑ Everyone Understands the Plan
- ☑ Agenda Prepared & Distributed

The Meeting: Tasks

✓ Foundation for Working Together
✓ Manage Data Capture
  • Group Memory
  • Scribe Assigned & Oriented
✓ Facilitate Decision Making
✓ Watch Group Dynamics
✓ Evaluate Process & Progress
✓ To-Dos & Other Promises Tracked
✓ Meeting Close

The Meeting: Outcomes

☑ Goals Achieved
☑ Worked Together
  ☑ A Better Group for the Future
☑ Satisfactory Progress
☑ Design Implemented
☑ Agenda Accomplished
☑ Next Steps Clear
☑ Proper Group Behavior

Follow-Up: Tasks

✓ Prepare the Record/Outputs
✓ Inform & Communicate to Interested Parties
✓ Approvals as Needed
✓ Lessons Learned

✓ **Party**!

Henri de Toulouse-Lautrec (1864–1901)
Ball at the Moulin Rouge, 1889–90

Follow-Up: Outcomes

☑ Record/Outputs Published & Distributed
☑ Results Communicated to Members, Sponsors, Stakeholders
☑ Next Steps Communicated
☑ To-Do's Published
☑ Recommendations for Further Work
☑ Nag, Nag, Nag

A Neutral Process

• What needs to be accomplished?
• Who needs to be involved?
• Design, flow & sequence of tasks
• Communication patterns & completeness
• Levels of participation
• Use of resources
• Group energy & momentum
• The physical environment
• The psychological environment

The Facilitator's Checklist

Planning

- ❑ Group Organized
- ❑ Membership Decided
- ❑ Purpose Established
- ❑ Roles Assigned
- ❑ Logistics Planned
- ❑ Everyone Understands the Plan
- ❑ Agenda Prepared & Distributed

Tasks

- ❑ Goals Agreed Upon
- ❑ Research Context, Goals, Participants
- ❑ Stakeholder Analysis
- ❑ Define Group & Leader
- ❑ Finalize & Publish Agenda
- ❑ Logistics
- ❑ Room
- ❑ Supplies
- ❑ Snacks

The Meeting

- ❑ Goals Achieved
- ❑ Worked Together
- ❑ A Better Group for the Future
- ❑ Satisfactory Progress
- ❑ Design Implemented
- ❑ Agenda Accomplished
- ❑ Next Steps Clear
- ❑ Proper Group Behavior

Tasks

- ❑ Foundation for Working Together
- ❑ Manage Data Capture
- ❑ Group Memory
- ❑ Scribe Assigned & Oriented
- ❑ Facilitate Decision Making
- ❑ Watch Group Dynamics
- ❑ Evaluate Process & Progress
- ❑ To-Dos & Other Promises Tracked
- ❑ Meeting Close

Follow-Up

- ❑ Record/Outputs Published & Distributed
- ❑ Results Communicated to Members, Sponsors, Stakeholders
- ❑ Next Steps Communicated
- ❑ To-Do's Published
- ❑ Recommendations for Further Work
- ❑ Nag, Nag, Nag

Tasks

- ❑ Prepare the Record/Outputs
- ❑ Inform & Communicate to Interested Parties
- ❑ Approvals as Needed
- ❑ Lessons Learned
- ❑ **Party!**

12. Problem Solving
Booleans for Searchers

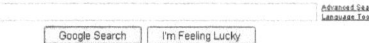

"Have in mind though that even very advanced searchers, such as the members of the search group at Google, use these features less than 5% of the time. Basic simple search is often enough."—Google Advanced Search Help

Booleans for Search

College of Alameda

pmcdermott@peralta.edu

Poor George

- Named After George Boole, 1847
  - "But what Good is it, George??"
- A.K.A. Propositional Calculus, Logical Algebra, Boolean Logic
- Binary: yes/no, on/off, true/false, 0/1
- Two states: `true` and `false`

Choose one from Column A & one from Column B	
Column A	**Column B**
Boolean	Algebra
Logical	Calculus
Propositional	Logic
Symbolic	

George Boole
(1815-1864)

It's Only Words…

The Algorithm
- Inflections: plurals, verb tenses
- Baseball = Earthquake Problem
- Auto vs. Car: Synonyms
- Not about Cannibals
- "Exact Phrase"

"If it was so, it might be; and if it were so, it would be; but as it isn't, it ain't. **That's logic.**"—Tweedledee, in *Through the Looking Glass*

Stop Words

- Words that are too Common
  - On virtually every webpage
- the and a this that, etc.
- Prepositions
- Lists Vary
- Sometimes a common word is important
  - The Algorithm, Of Mice and Men
  - Try "exact quote"

---

1 Rose (Windows), or 16 Roses (Unix)?

1. ROSE   9. rOSE
2. ROSe   10. rOSe
3. ROsE   11. rOsE
4. ROse   12. rOse
5. RoSE   13. roSE
6. RoSe   14. roSe
7. RosE   15. rosE
8. Rose   16. rose

Pierre-Auguste Renoir (1841–1919)
Les Roses dans un Vase, c. 1910–17

For filenames, Windows is Case Insensitive; Unix is Case Sensitive

---

Visualize Truth

3 Little Words
  AND
  OR
  NOT
That's It!

But:

Graduate Seminars
  Don't cover it all!

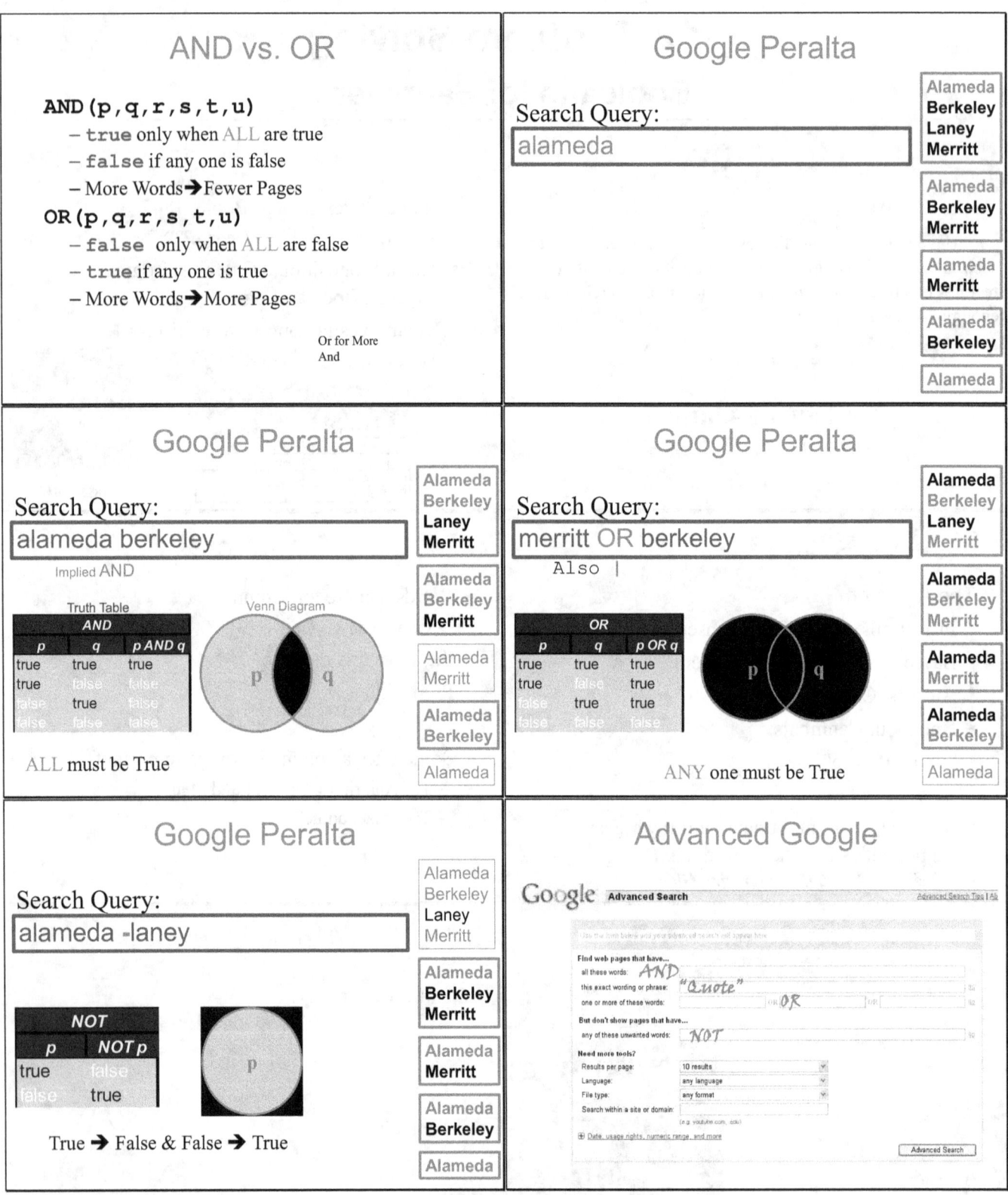

AND vs. OR

AND(p,q,r,s,t,u)
- *true* only when ALL are true
- *false* if any one is false
- More Words➜Fewer Pages

OR(p,q,r,s,t,u)
- *false* only when ALL are false
- *true* if any one is true
- More Words➜More Pages

Or for More
And

Google Peralta

Search Query:

alameda

Alameda **Berkeley Laney Merritt**	
Alameda **Berkeley Merritt**	
Alameda **Merritt**	
Alameda **Berkeley**	
Alameda	

Google Peralta

Search Query:

alameda berkeley

Implied AND

Truth Table
AND

p	q	p AND q
true	true	true
true	false	false
false	true	false
false	false	false

Venn Diagram

ALL must be True

| Alameda Berkeley **Laney Merritt** |
| Alameda Berkeley **Merritt** |
| Alameda Merritt |
| Alameda Berkeley |
| Alameda |

Google Peralta

Search Query:

merritt OR berkeley

Also |

OR

p	q	p OR q
true	true	true
true	false	true
false	true	true
false	false	false

ANY one must be True

| **Alameda** Berkeley **Laney** Merritt |
| **Alameda** Berkeley Merritt |
| **Alameda** Merritt |
| **Alameda** Berkeley |
| Alameda |

Google Peralta

Search Query:

alameda -laney

NOT

p	NOT p
true	false
false	true

True ➜ False & False ➜ True

| Alameda Berkeley Laney Merritt |
| Alameda **Berkeley Merritt** |
| Alameda **Merritt** |
| Alameda **Berkeley** |
| Alameda |

Advanced Google

Google Advanced Search

Advanced Search Tips | All

Find web pages that have...
all these words: *AND*
this exact wording or phrase: *"Quote"*
one or more of these words: *OR*

But don't show pages that have...
any of these unwanted words: *NOT*

Need more tools?
Results per page: 10 results
Language: any language
File type: any format
Search within a site or domain:
(e.g. youtube.com, .edu)

⊕ Date, usage rights, numeric range, and more

Advanced Search

Booleans for Programmers

"If it was so, it might be; and if it were so, it would be; but as it isn't, it ain't. **That's logic.**"—
Tweedledee, in *Through the Looking Glass*

Booleans

George Boole
(1815-1864)

Copyright © 1999 Patrick McDermott

College of Alameda

pmcdermott@peralta.edu

Perfect Logic:
I am a nobody.
Nobody is perfect.
∴ I am perfect.

Poor George

- Named After George Boole, 1847
  – "But what Good is it, George??"
- A.K.A. Propositional Calculus, Logical Algebra, Boolean Logic
- Binary: yes/no, on/off, true/false, 0/1
- Two states: `true` and `false`

Choose one from Column A & one from Column B	
Column A	**Column B**
Boolean	Algebra
Logical	Calculus
Propositional	Logic
Symbolic	

A Good Conductor

A Conductor	
Amps In	**Amps Out**
1	1
2	2
3	3
4	4
5	5
6	6

A Nonconductor	
Amps In	**Amps Out**
1	0
2	0
3	0
4	0
5	0
6	0

Insulator

A Conducting Nonconductor?

What to Call it???

A ☐ Conductor	
Amps In	**Amps Out**
1	0
2	0
3	0
4	4
5	5
6	6

Conditionals

- The criteria for execution
- A `bool`

! Yes or No: No **Maybe**s
  – Law of the excluded middle
  – No **Fuzzy Logic**

Ps and Qs, not x's and y's
"Mind your Ps and Qs"

Comparison Operators

- Comparisons:
  `<` **Less than**
  `>` **Greater than**
  `<=` **Less than or Equal** ≤ [Same as ! >]
  `>=` **Greater than or Equal** ≥ [Same as ! <]
  `==` **Equal** [Note: 2 = signs]
  "Double equal", "Logical Equal", "Equal Equal"
  `!=` **Not Equal** ≠

  Equalities and Inequalities

Visualize Truth

3 Little Words
And
Or
Not
- That's It!

But Graduate Seminars
Don't cover it all!

Spoken English
– Can be Ambiguous

Choose a tool to
understand:
- Truth Tables
- Venn Diagrams
  – John Venn
- Symbolic Logic
  – George Boole

Boolean Operators

&& "and"
All are TRUE
More Conditions → Fewer Iterations

|| "or" ¦¦ ‖
At Least One is TRUE
More Conditions → More Iterations

! "not" ¬
"Exclamation", "Bang"
Reverse the Verdict

AND &&

Both

AND		
p	q	p && q
true	true	true
true	false	false
false	true	false
false	false	false

$A \cap B$

$a \wedge b$

*BOTH,
or ALL*

Intersection

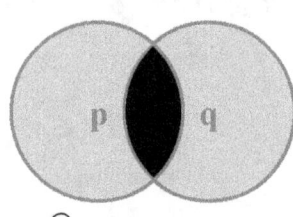

⊗ **Boolean Product x**

OR ‖

**Either or Both
any or all**

OR		
p	q	p ‖ q
true	true	true
true	false	true
false	true	true
false	false	false

$A \cup B$

$a \vee b$

Latin *vel*
*One or the Other,
or BOTH*

"Logical Or"

Union

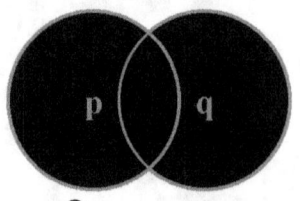

⊕ **Boolean Sum +**

XOR ^

One or the Other

Exclusive OR		
p	q	p ^ q
true	true	false
true	false	true
false	true	true
false	false	false

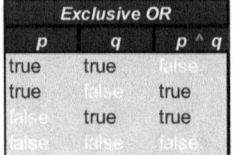

There is no C++ ^^ operator
Simulate using
(p||q) && !(p&&q)
C# has ^ but no ^^
(can't short circuit)

Latin *aut*
*Either
One or the other,
But not BOTH*

Disjunctive

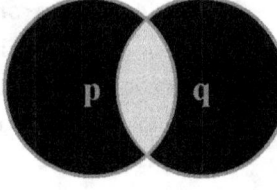

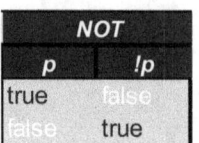

NOT !

Reverse

NOT	
p	!p
true	false
false	true

In XL & Access,
<> Means "not equal"

¬ A

[a]

~ a

*What is true becomes false
What is false becomes true*

"The current king of France is bald."

Negation

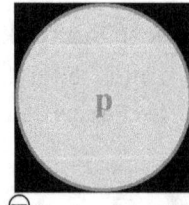

⊖ **Boolean Negation -**

Creativity

reativity

UC Berkeley
Extension
pmcdermott@msn.com

Creative Innovations

- Work of Art
- Writing a Book
- A New Marketing Ad Campaign
- Discovery of DNA Double Helix
- Cancer Cure
- Inventing Light Bulb
- A New Hat
- Developing a Computer System

Greatest Innovation?

- What is the Greatest Innovation of all Time?

- What is the most Important Breakthrough enabling the Information Age?

Contrarian

- **Genius is the ability to believe two completely contradictory ideas at the same time.**
- The Opposite of a Profound Truth is another Profound Truth
- Creative Destruction (Joseph Schumpeter)
- Middle Way
  - Goldilocks' stress: too little as bad as too much—unless there's an inner drive.

Human Salvation lies in the hands of the Creatively Maladjusted.

Martin Luther King, Jr.

Don't Stifle Creativity

✓ Encourage Employees to take more risks
✓ Use creative problem-solving techniques, which can help groups and individuals view any situation from a different perspective
✓ Encourage employees to challenge their own perceptions of products and processes
✓ Encourage "visioning"
✓ Employ rebels
✓ Allow time for pet projects
✓ Ensure senior manager's support

- Wetlaufer, Suzy, "What's Stifling the Creativity at Coolburst?" in Harvard Business Review, *On Breakthrough Thinking*, Boston: Harvard Business School Press (1-57851-181-X), 1999, p. 139-142.

All that is Human must Retrograde if it does not Advance.

Edward Gibbon, *The Decline and Fall of the Roman Empire*

The Bicycle Theory

The Role of Innovation
Change or Die

- Increase institutional intelligence, or corporate IQ.
- Need a high corporate IQ to succeed.
  - Not simply having a lot of smart people
    - although it helps to start with smart people
- A measure of
  - How easily you share information broadly
  - How well people can build on each other's ideas
- Sharing both history and current knowledge.
- Contributions come from
  - Individual learning
  - Cross-pollination of different people's ideas

Innovations Need Innovators

- Miracle occurs during break
- Are inventors made or born?
- Is Xerox PARC's arrangement what worked, or what people thought would work?
- If you take dodos and put them at PARC, you'd get dodo ideas; and some folks would be creative no matter what.
- BUT, you can kill creativity.

Don't Kill Creativity

- Challenge
- Freedom
- Resources
- Work-group features (diversity, excitement, respect for one another)
- Supervisory encouragement
- Organizational support

Amabile, Teresa "How to Kill Creativity" in Harvard Business Review, *On Breakthrough Thinking*, Boston: Harvard Business School Press (1-57851-181-X), 1999, pp. 7-18.

Management

- Flatter, less bureaucratic
- Should genius waste time on managing, even themselves?
- Many don't want to manage
  - Especially without the pay
- "But extending greater freedom and scope to the employee might bring added dividends of innovation and creativity."
  - Donkin, Richard, *Blood Sweat & Tears: The Evolution of Work*, New York: Texere (1-58799-076-8), 2001, p. 275.

Drucker's Internal Sources

- Unexpected occurrences
  - IBM and Libraries, not businesses
  - HP & Disney
- Incongruities
  - It's the time in port, stupid
- Process needs
  - Pulitzer & Advertising (World Series)
- Industry and market changes
  - McD's & Starbucks

Drucker's External Sources

- Demographic changes
  - Dent's boom ahead
- Changes in perception
  - Itch becomes allergy
- New knowledge
  - Computer, moon shot
  - If we go to moon again, just as hard

  - Drucker, Peter "The Discipline of Innovation" in Harvard Business Review, *On Breakthrough Thinking*, Boston: Harvard Business School Press (1-57851-181-X), 1999, pp. 145-156.

Real Artists Ship

  - Steve Jobs, *Insanely Great*
- Champignon and hieroglyphics
- "Someone else will develop it".
- Like business plan—needs to be implementable and implemented.
- Some new patents violate this principle.

Personal Approaches

- Can use Icebreaker
- Creative people usually keep on rolling with the flow, says a certain Rolling Stone.
  - Don't try to write grammatical sentences with cuhrectly spellt wurds.
- Stephen J. Gould's Outline
- And don't forget: if you take one person's idea, it's plagiarism, and despicable. But 2's Research!
- Unpleasant and Difficult
  - Gestation; subconscious; Only learn what you almost knew
- Babe Ruth Dual King

Political Economy

- Undirected
  - Internet
  - Open sores, I mean source (Saint iGNUtius)
- Managing Einsteins
  - But remember: Nobody actually did manage Einstein
  - Like herding cats
  - "Don't hire her, she'll be hard to manage"

The Invisible Hand

As Adam Smith told us, an individual generally "neither intends to promote the public interest, nor knows how much he is promoting it … by directing [his] industry in such manner as his produce may be of greatest value, he intends only his own gain, and he is in this, as in many other cases, led by an invisible hand to promote an end which was no part of his intention. … By pursuing his own interest he frequently promotes that of the society more effectually than when he really intends to promote it."

Smith, Adam, *An Inquiry into the Nature and Causes of The Wealth of Nations*, London: W. Strahan & T. Cadell in the Strand, 1776, Book IV, Chapter 11.

Dear Future CIO:

You probably can't cause creativity, but you can certainly kill it.

Sometimes you need to point the way, then get out of the way.

The Deming Way for Systems

Deming, W. Edwards, *Out of the Crisis*, Cambridge, Massachusetts: The MIT Press (0-262-54115-7), 2000 (1982).

W. Edwards Deming
1900-1993

The University of California
Berkeley Extension
Copyright © 2007 Patrick McDermott
pmcdermott@msn.com

Japan's Guru

- Japan's greatest Business Guru
  - Not some aesthete who lived in the mountains pondering his navel
- Surprise: He's not even Japanese, but American!
- Major use of Σtatistics!
- Taught the Japanese about Quality
  - "Made in Japan" meant "cheap and flimsy"
- Deming is famous for his Fourteen Points

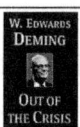

Instant Pudding

- Hope for Instant Pudding
- NSB: "No silver bullet"
  - ACM article by Frederick Brooks, Reprinted in Brooks, Frederick P., Jr., *The Mythical Man-Month: Essays on Software Engineering, 20th Anniversary Edition*, Reading, Massachusetts: Addison-Wesley (0-201-83595-9), 1995 (1975).
- You don't just "Adopt Quality", "Get CASE tools", "Become Object Oriented", or "Install CRM" and magically solve all problems and fix everything.

Fads constantly offer various purported silver bullets, most of which weren't even lead bullets, but paper bullets.

False Starts

- Fads
- Don't join the Methodology of the Month Club
  - Stay with a new methodology long enough to realize some benefit

Some companies happily embrace the fad of the moment, and never actually recover the innovation costs of one methodology, tool or package before going on to the next.

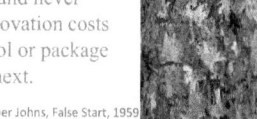

Jasper Johns, False Start, 1959

Automation as Transformation

- The supposition that solving problems, automation, gadgets and new machinery will transform industry
- Don't adopt technology for technology's sake
- If IT Doesn't Change Your Way Of Doing Business, Don't Bother

"Computation of savings from use of a gadget (automation or robotic machinery) ought to take account of total cost, as an economist would define it. In my experience, people are seldom able to come through with figures on total cost."

Search for Examples

- Cookbook methodologies and benchmarking are examples
- If it worked at XYZ company it will work here
  - Assuming it actually Did

"Oh good, we have a methodology, we can all turn our brains off and stop thinking!"

Obsolescence in Schools

Not here, of Course
- Lifelong learning is the name of the game in systems development
- It's hard for the schools to keep up
- Most university academic courses are, well, academic, & often behind the times

The Unmanned Computer

- Autopilot
- The computer can be a curse or blessing
  - But you must still use your brain
- Users too often accept the word of the computer as unquestionable truth
- Programmers, who of all people should know better, sometimes do it, too
- Example: CASE tools and code generators

Just Meet Specifications

- The supposition that it is only necessary to meet specifications
- Deming cites an example of a programmer:
  - "She learns, after she finishes the job, that she programmed very well the specifications as delivered to her, but that they were deficient. If she had only known the purpose of the program, she could have done it right for the purpose, even though the specifications were deficient."

You should be able to explain why any feature makes sense from a business perspective before putting it into a system.

Inadequate Testing

- Inadequate testing of prototypes

- 'Nuff said!

Bruce McCandless II
tests a Mobile Foot Restraint
Space Shuttle Challenger, 1984

The 14 Points (1-7)

1. Create constancy of purpose toward improvement of product and service, with the aim to become competitive and to stay in business, and to provide jobs.
2. Adopt the new philosophy. We are in a new economic age. Western management must awaken to the challenge, must learn their responsibilities, and take on leadership for change.
3. Cease dependence on inspection to achieve quality. Eliminate the need for inspection on a mass basis by building quality into the product in the first place.
4. End the practice of awarding business on the basis of price tag. Instead, minimize total cost.
5. Improve constantly and forever the system of production and service, to improve quality and productivity, and thus constantly decrease costs.
6. Institute training on the job.
7. Institute leadership.   ...

The 14 Points, Continued

8. Drive out fear, so that everyone may work effectively for the company.
9. Break down barriers between departments.
10. Eliminate slogans, exhortations, and targets for the work force asking for zero defects and new levels of productivity.
11a. Eliminate work standards (quotas) on the factory floor. Substitute leadership. b. Eliminate management by objective. Eliminate management by numbers, numerical goals. Substitute leadership.
12a. Remove barriers that rob the hourly worker of his right to pride of workmanship. b. Remove barriers that rob people in management and in engineering of their right to pride of workmanship.
13. Institute a vigorous program of education and self-improvement.
14. Put everybody in the company to work to accomplish the transformation.

Deming's 14 Points for Management

From W. Edwards Deming, *Out of the Crisis*. [10]

      1. Create constancy of purpose toward improvement of product and service, with the aim to become competitive and to stay in business, and to provide jobs.

      2. Adopt the new philosophy. We are in a new economic age. Western management must awaken to the challenge, must learn their responsibilities, and take on leadership for change.

      3. Cease dependence on inspection to achieve quality. Eliminate the need for inspection on a mass basis by building quality into the product in the first place.

      4. End the practice of awarding business on the basis of price tag. Instead, minimize total cost.

      5. Improve constantly and forever the system of production and service, to improve quality and productivity, and thus constantly decrease costs.

      6. Institute training on the job.

      7. Institute leadership.

      8. Drive out fear, so that everyone may work effectively for the company.

      9. Break down barriers between departments.

      10. Eliminate slogans, exhortations, and targets for the work force asking for zero defects and new levels of productivity.

      11 a. Eliminate work standards (quotas) on the factory floor. Substitute leadership. b. Eliminate management by objective. Eliminate management by numbers, numerical goals. Substitute leadership.

      12 a. Remove barriers that rob the hourly worker of his right to pride of workmanship. b. Remove barriers that rob people in management and in engineering of their right to pride of workmanship.

      13. Institute a vigorous program of education and self-improvement.

      14. Put everybody in the company to work to accomplish the transformation.

Tech Enablers

Technology Enablers

Copyright © 2003 Patrick McDermott

UC Berkeley

Extension

pmcdermott@msn.com

Sharp, Alec & Patrick McDermott, *Workflow Modeling: Tools for Process Improvement and Application Development*, Boston: Artech House (1-58053-021-4), 2001.

Political Economy

David Ricardo, *Principles of Political Economy and Taxation*, 1817

Politics = Poly (γρεεκ Many) + Ticks?

a : the art or science of government
b : the art or science concerned with guiding or influencing governmental policy (Merriam-Webster)

Related Word: Policy
1: prudence or wisdom in the management of affairs
2: a definite course or method of action selected from among alternatives and in light of given conditions to guide and determine present and future decisions (Merriam-Webster)

Economics: TNSTAAFL—No Free Lunch

The Science of balancing unlimited human wants with limited resources; The Art of allocating scarce resources to fulfilling human wants and needs.

Ill-Fitting Solutions

- Two Cultures—Bridge the Gap
  - Technology
  - Business

- Solution in Search of a Problem
- Résumé Technology
- Three Solutions:
  - ✓ Communicate
  - ✓ Communicate
  - ✓ Communicate

Unintended Consequences

- Emergence's Evil Twin

Johnson, Steven, *Emergence: The Connected Lives of Ants, Brains, Cities and Software*, New York: Scribner, 2001.
Michael Crichton, *Prey*, New York: HarperCollins, 2002.

  - Freeway Fliers & Contract Programmers
  - Email & Spam: Productivity Paradox
  - Labor Saving Devices and Long Hours
  - Environmental Damages

Edward Tenner, **Why Things Bite Back**: Technology and the Revenge of Unintended Consequences, New York: Vintage Books, 1996.

- The Only Defense: Expect the Unexpected

As Consultants are Wont to Say

- We can do it **Faster**…
- We can do it **Cheaper**…
- We can do it **Better**…
  - —choose no more than *two* of the above.

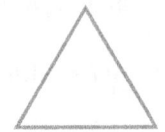

The Enablers

Being Right is only half the Battle!

Your solution can be technologically perfect, but fail!

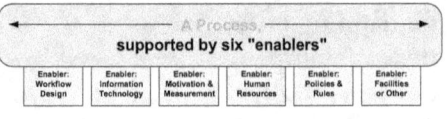

A Process,
supported by six "enablers"

| Enabler: Workflow Design | Enabler: Information Technology | Enabler: Motivation & Measurement | Enabler: Human Resources | Enabler: Policies & Rules | Enabler: Facilities or Other |

The *Enablers* are what enable your solution to succeed.

1. Workflow Design

- Bottlenecks
- A Coordinator or Expeditor Role implies complexity or problems
  - Handoffs
  - Exceptions—Pareto Principle: 80/20
- Would a Customer willingly Pay for it?

- I could write a book

2. I.T.

- Information & Technology
- Larry, The Unknown Tech Worker
- The Future is Ahead of Us
  - Never be First—or Last
- "Machines should work. People should think."
  - Thomas J. Watson, Chairman of IBM
- Problems
  - Missing Information
  - Duplicate Entry
  - Irreconcilable Sources

3. Motivation & Measurement

- Time on Phone
- Auditors & Copy Editors
- Carl's On-Time Performance
- Don't Evaluate with an Indicator

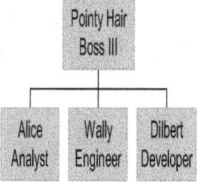

W. Edwards Deming, *Out of the Crisis*, Cambridge, Massachusetts: The MIT Press, 2000 (1982).

- Process Improvement or Decision Support
  - Are Managers promoted for Improvement, or Building an Empire?
  - Kaizen (改善) not Breakthrough

4. Human Resources

- Training
- Job Descriptions
- Org Chart

- Right People
- Right Jobs
- Right Skills

Pointy Hair Boss III

Alice Analyst | Wally Engineer | Dilbert Developer

5. Policies & Rules

- See The Great Business Guru, Scott Adams

- Recursive Feasibility Study
- Approvals & Inflation

- Reward Inertia
  - Punish Innovation?

6. Facilities

- Transport or Communications Delays
- Collaboration versus Quiet
- Copier/Fax, Supplies
- Clerical Support

- … or Other
- e.g. Research Opportunities

Kaizen

Kaizen

改善

The University of California
Berkeley Extension
pmcdermott@msn.com

Masaaki Imai

- *Kaizen*
- *Gemba Kaizen*

KAIZEN

(Ky ' zen) The Key to Japan's Competitive Success

MASAAKI IMAI

Continuous Improvement

- You must continuously improve your processes to keep a quality product in production.

"Better" is a Moving Target

- What's Better?
- McDonalds is Quality to a kid
  - Chez Panisse unbearable.
- Quality is what the customer wants.

Which is Faster?

- A jaguar, an antelope or a human?
- It depends on the distance.
- Jaguar is faster than an antelope for about five seconds. The cat will go hungry if it's not able to catch the antelope in a short burst of a few seconds.
- Over a day a human is faster; that's why humans can hunt antelope and jaguar: the animals can run faster, but can't walk farther, than humans.

Consumer Price Index

- Attempts to measure changes in <u>price</u>, not <u>quality</u>.
- Bigger is better
- Small is beautiful

Keep It Up

- Continuous improvement is necessary just to stay in the same place.
- Even our management and technical techniques need *kaizen* applied to them. We must continue to strive for better ways to manage our processes or quality will deteriorate.

Requirements Kaizen

Sometimes a change in Requirements reveals problems with your system that you didn't even know were there.

"Change is constant, and your system should always improve every time you work on it."—H1OOAD, p. 141

Knowledge Management

Knowledge Management

Patrick McDermott
The University of San Francisco

pmcdermott@peralta.edu
Copyright © 2003 Patrick McDermott

Knowledge Management

- Buried in jargon
- Perpetually in search of itself
- A consultant's dream
  - Promises without end
  - Certainties that are impregnable
  - Definition that is impossible

Learning Organization

- Perfect for gurudom
  - Murky, confusing and filled with abstruse jargon
  - If-I-can't-understand-it-then-it-must-be-good
- A magical and reverential search
- A "big conceptual catchall"

- Readers came away saying, "But what do we do Monday morning to put these ideas into practice?"

KM Issues

✓ The difference between data, information and knowledge
✓ The difficulties organizations have in measuring their intellectual capital
✓ The process of knowledge creation
✓ The concept of knowledge markets
✓ Strategies for implementing knowledge management
✓ The human aspects of knowledge creation and transfer

The New Meaning of Knowledge

[Peter] Drucker reminds us that knowledge has meant different things throughout history. For hundreds of years, knowledge was applied to a person's "being," and two theories dominated in both the West and East. One theory, associated with Plato and Socrates in the West and the Taoist and monks in the East, held that the purpose and function of knowledge was to enable self-knowledge through intellectual, moral, and spiritual growth. A competing theory, associated with Protagoras in the West and Confucius in the East, held that the purpose and function of knowledge was the acquisition of logic, grammar, and rhetoric to enable the holder of know what to say and how to say it.

Somewhere around 1700, the meaning of knowledge changed radically. Knowledge began to be applied to "doing," not just to "being." That change in the meaning and purpose of knowledge, writes Drucker, initiated one of three revolutions in the application of knowledge that created and then destroyed both communism and capitalism and ultimately led to the creation of a postcapitalist knowledge society.

3 Revolutions

The Age of the Artisan

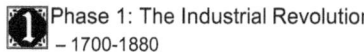 Phase 1: The Industrial Revolution
 – 1700-1880
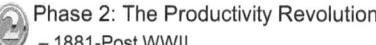 Phase 2: The Productivity Revolution
 – 1881-Post WWII
Phase 3: The Management Revolution
 – Post WWII-2020

Drucker's Post Capitalist Era

Age of the Craftsworker

- Stand at one spot and observe the construction of the product in its entirety
- One person often accomplished the entire process, not just the manufacturing, but even marketing, sales, design, and service.

- Today:
- You would have to visit several *continents* to view the entire process

The Industrial Revolution

- The Age of the Factory
- Adam Smith, *The Wealth of Nations*, 1776
- Watt's Steam Engine

Gare St.-Lazare, Paris
Claude Monet
c. 1877

Smith, Adam
An Inquiry into the Nature and Causes of The Wealth of Nations
London: W. Strahan & T. Cadell in the Strand, 1776

The Productivity Revolution

- The Age of the Specialist
- Drucker Dates it from 1881
  - Frederic Winslow Taylor

J. Howard Miller
1942

The Management Revolution

- Age of the Professional
- GI Bill
- Of Divisions & Modern Major Generals

When I can tell at sight a Mauser rifle from a javelin,
When such affairs as sorties and surprises I'm more wary at,
And when I know precisely what is meant by "commissariat",
When I have learnt what progress has been made in modern gunnery,
When I know more of tactics than a novice in a nunnery –
In short, when I've a smattering of elemental strategy …

Gilbert & Sullivan
The Pirates of Penzance
Opened April 3, 1880

Factors of Production

- Land
  - Agriculture & Natural Resources
- Labor
- Capital
  - "The Means of Production/Tools"

- Entrepreneurial Ability
  - Now Hired Managers

- Technology?
  - Knowledge?

The Post Capitalist Era

"The organization's function is to put knowledge to work."

- Focus on What you do well
  - Outsource the rest
- An Organization of Equals
- Constant Change
- Decentralized
- A Mobile Society
- A Competitive Society

226

Maeda on Simplicity

John Maeda of the MIT Media Lab has proposed The Laws of Simplicity [11]

1 REDUCE - The simplest way to achieve simplicity is through thoughtful reduction.
2 ORGANIZE - Organization makes a system of many appear fewer.
3 TIME - Savings in time feel like simplicity.
4 LEARN - Knowledge makes everything simpler.
5 DIFFERENCES - Simplicity and complexity need each other.
6 CONTEXT - What lies in the periphery of simplicity is definitely not peripheral.
7 EMOTION - More emotions are better than less.
8 TRUST - In simplicity we trust.
9 FAILURE - Some things can never be made simple.
10 THE ONE - Simplicity is about subtracting the obvious, and adding the meaningful.

THREE KEYS

1 AWAY - More appears like less by simply moving it far, far away.
2 OPEN - Openness simplifies complexity.
3 POWER - Use less, gain more.

SHE: Shrink, Hide, Embody
SLIP: Sort, Label, Integrate, Prioritize

Basics are the Beginning.

Repeat yourself Often.

Avoid creating Desperation.

Inspire with Examples.

Never forget to Repeat yourself.

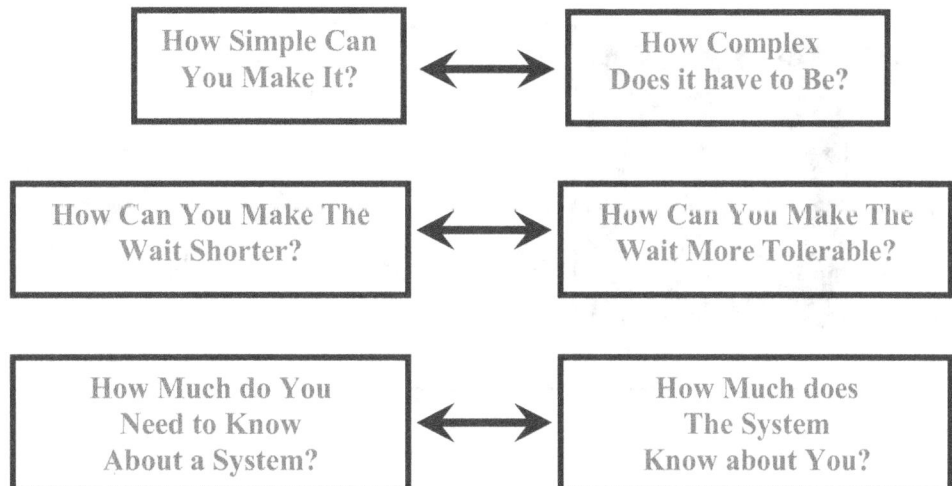

Back of the Napkin Thinking

Roam, Dan, *The Back of the Napkin: Solving Problems and Selling Ideas with Pictures*, New York: Portfolio / Penguin Group (978-1-59184-199-9), 2008.

I keep six honest serving-men
  (They taught me all I knew);
Their names are What and Why and When
And How and Where and Who.
—Rudyard Kipling

Backs of
Napkins

University of California
Berkeley Extension

pmcdermott@msn.com

Copyright © 2008 Patrick McDermott

The 6 Types of Problems

1. Who and What problems. Challenges that relate to things, people, and roles. ✝ What is going on around me, and where do I fit in? Who is in charge and who else is involved? Where does responsibility lie?
2. How much problems. Challenges that involve measuring and counting. ♨ Do we have enough of X to last as long as we need? How much of X do we need to keep going? If we increase this over here, can we decrease that over there?
3. When problems. Challenges that relate to scheduling and timing. ⊕ What comes first, and what comes next? We've got a lot of things to do: When are we going to do them all?
4. Where problems. Challenges that relate to direction and how things fit together. 🜨 Where are we going now? Are we headed in the right direction, or should we be moving elsewhere? How do all these pieces fit together? What's most important and what matters less?
5. How problems. Challenges that relate to how things influence one another. ⚒ What will happen if we do this? What about that? Can we alter the outcomes of a situation by altering our actions?
6. Why problems. Challenges that relate to seeing the big picture. ❓ What are we really doing, and why? Is it the right thing, or should we be doing something different? If we need to change, what are our options? How can we decide which of those options are best?

1A. Who: Portrait

Edward Hopper (1882-1967)
Self-Portrait, 1925–30

Élisabeth Vigée-Lebrun (1755-1842)
Self-Portrait, 1782

1B. What: Picture

2. How Much: Chart

The Law of Gravity

Pie in the Sky

3. When: Timeline

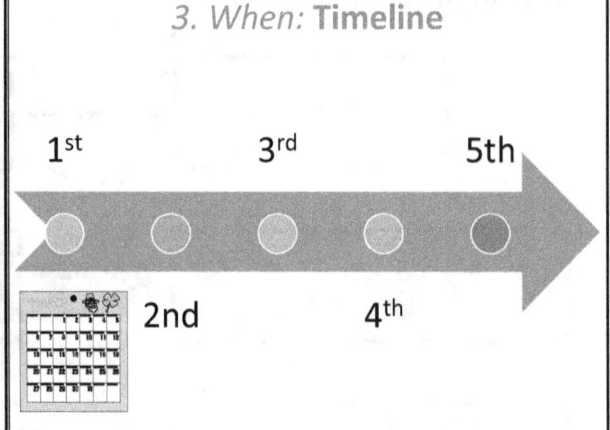
1st   3rd   5th
2nd   4th

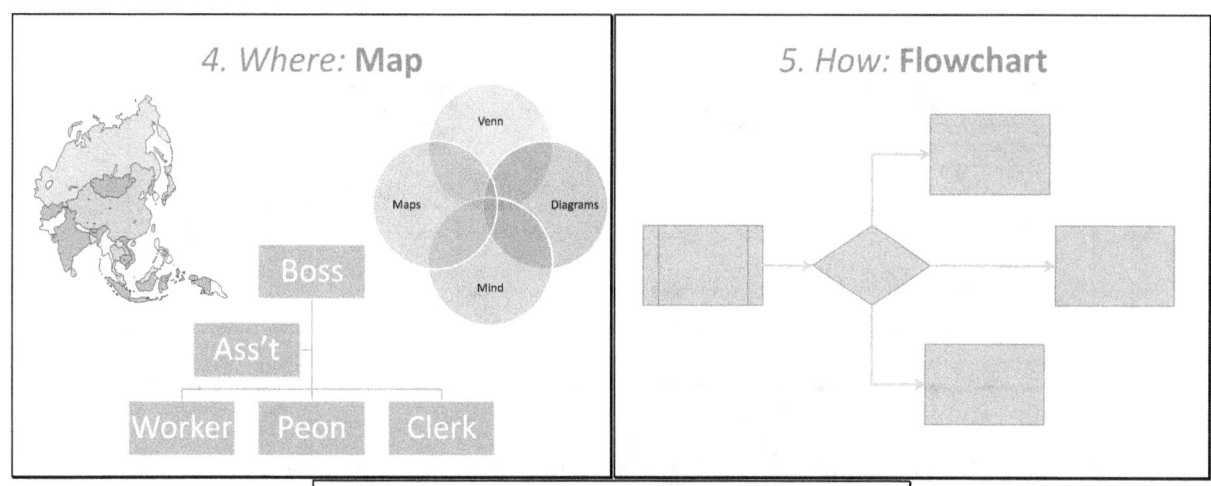

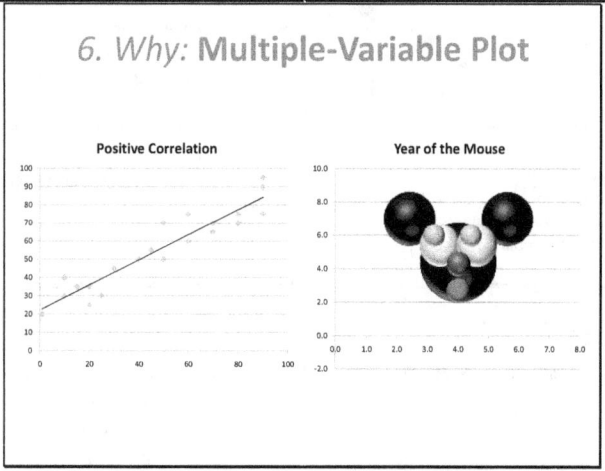

Paradox in Projects

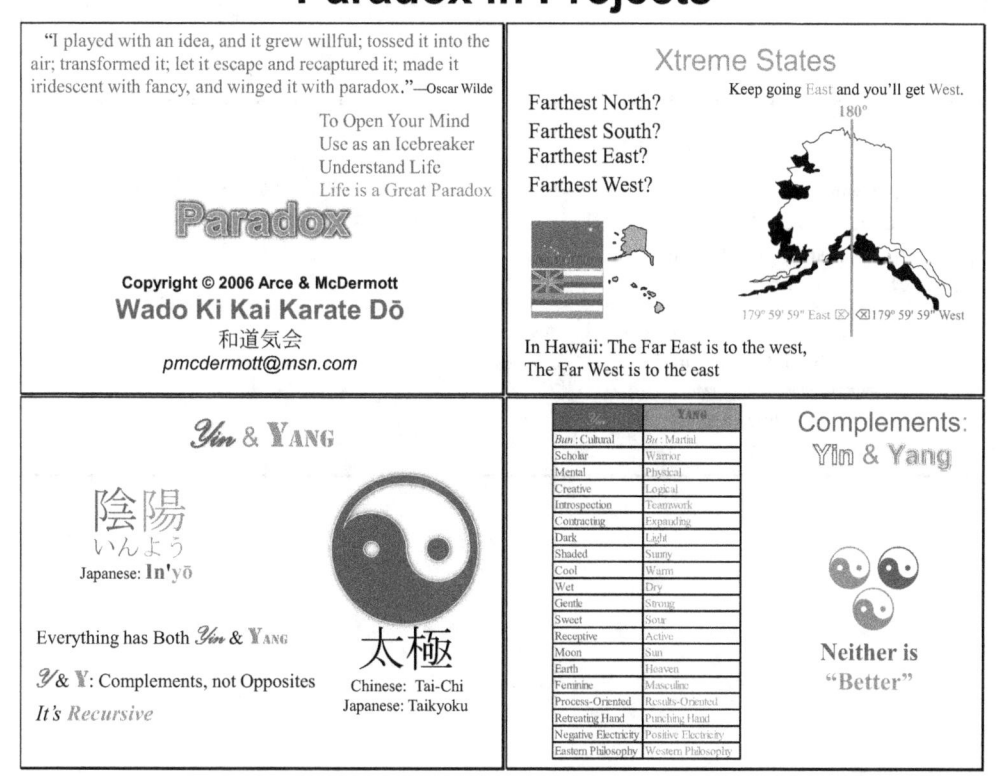

Truth in Paradox

To know what's really good, you have to know what's bad.
Both extremes, communism and Nazism, were totalitarian.
Laughing and crying look the same in photographs.
Love & Hate can easily Reverse.
A vibrant economy requires Creative Destruction.

Genius is the ability to believe two completely contradictory things simultaneously.—Albert Einstein

There is Strength in Weakness:
If I owe you $50 thousand, and can't pay, I have a Problem.

If I owe you $50 million, and can't pay, YOU have a Problem.

All generalizations are false—Including this one.

29th Infantry Division

Blue & Gray
WW I: Belleau Woods
WW II: Omaha Beach

A Samurai was expected to understand both cultural (bun) and military (bu) subjects. They were warrior bureaucrats!

文武
Cultural & Military
The Pen and The Sword

"Literary and martial skills are like the two wheels of a cart, the two wings of a bird."

There are but two powers in the world, the sword and the mind. In the long run the sword is always beaten by the mind.—Napoleon

The First Law of Logic
for Analysts

- Logic doesn't always Work!
- Less is More.
- Go Slow to go Fast.
- Never say "Never".
- Expect the Unexpected.
- For spellcheck, a small dictionary
- In AI, the hardest problems are the easiest; the easiest are the hardest–Hans Moravec
- Japanese and American management is 95 percent the same and differs in all important respects.
- If Everybody agrees, Somebody is Wrong!

Relativity
July 1953
M.C. Escher
(1898-1972)

Embrace Contradiction

- Real knowledge is knowing how ignorant you are.–Confucius
- You can kill with kindness.
- Are your feet cold? Put on a hat.
- There is no such thing as Nothing.
- The greatest Truths are told in fiction.
- The most valuable container should have no lock.
- To remember something, stop trying to remember it.
- If you want something done, assign it to someone who is busy.
- Dickens was right: This *is* the best of times, and the worst of times.

Luttwak's Strategic Paradox

- The best defense is a good offense.
- A fighter plane needs great speed so it can get behind the enemy plane.
- A bad road can be good *precisely because it is bad.*
- *Si vis pacem, para bellum*
  - If you want peace, prepare for war

Get the Other Viewpoint

Luttwak concludes that "when scarce development resources must be allocated between competing scientific concepts and engineering configurations, it is unwise to rely on scientific and engineering judgment alone."

⊞ Nothing Fails like Success

Luttwak, Edward N., *Strategy: The Logic of War and Peace*, Cambridge, Massachusetts: Belknap Press / Harvard University Press (0-674-83995-1), 1987, p. 29.

Beware of "Victory Disease"

Opposite Approaches

- The Hawthorne Effect
- Lt. Columbo (Peter Falk)
- Opposites can be Equally Effective
  - Disciplinarian versus GI General
    - Patton vs. Bradley
  - Boston Latin and Science Academy
  - Co-ed versus All-Boy, All-Girl
  - Decentralized vs. Centralized
- Jackie Chan vs. Bruce Lee
  - Not afraid to be a Coward

Remember

Opposite Approaches can Both work well

Choose The Middle Way

Expect Unintended Consequences

Oxymorons

An oxymoron is a (seemingly) self-contradictory phrase.

Acute dullness
Al most perfect
Bad health
Bittersweet
Blameless culprit
Cardinal sin
Clearly confused
Conservative liberal
Constant variable
Deafening silence
Definite maybe
Deliberately thoughtless
Even odds
Exact estimate
Express mail
Extensive briefing
Freezer burn
Friendly takeover
Friendly fire
Genuine imitation
Good grief!
Government efficiency
Holy war
Home office
Idiot savant
Instant classic
Intense apathy
Jumbo shrimp
Justifiably paranoid
Larger half
Least favorite
Linear curve
Liquid gas

Mild interest
Military intelligence
Minor miracle
Modern history
Nonalcoholic beer
Nondairy creamer
Normal deviation
Old news
Only choice
Open secret
Original copies
Passively aggressive
Player coach
Pretty ugly
Qualified success
Randomly organized
Real potential
Rock opera
Rolling stop
Same difference
Silent scream
Simply superb
Sweet sorrow
Taped live
Terribly enjoyable
Tragic comedy
Unbiased opinion
Uncrowned king
Unsung hero
Vaguely aware
Wall Street ethics
War games
Working vacation

Pareto Charts

SEE also Koch, Richard, *The 80/20 Principle: The Secret to Success by Achieving More with Less*, New York: Currency / Doubleday (0-385-49174-3), 1999 (1998), pp. 142ff. Especially 144.

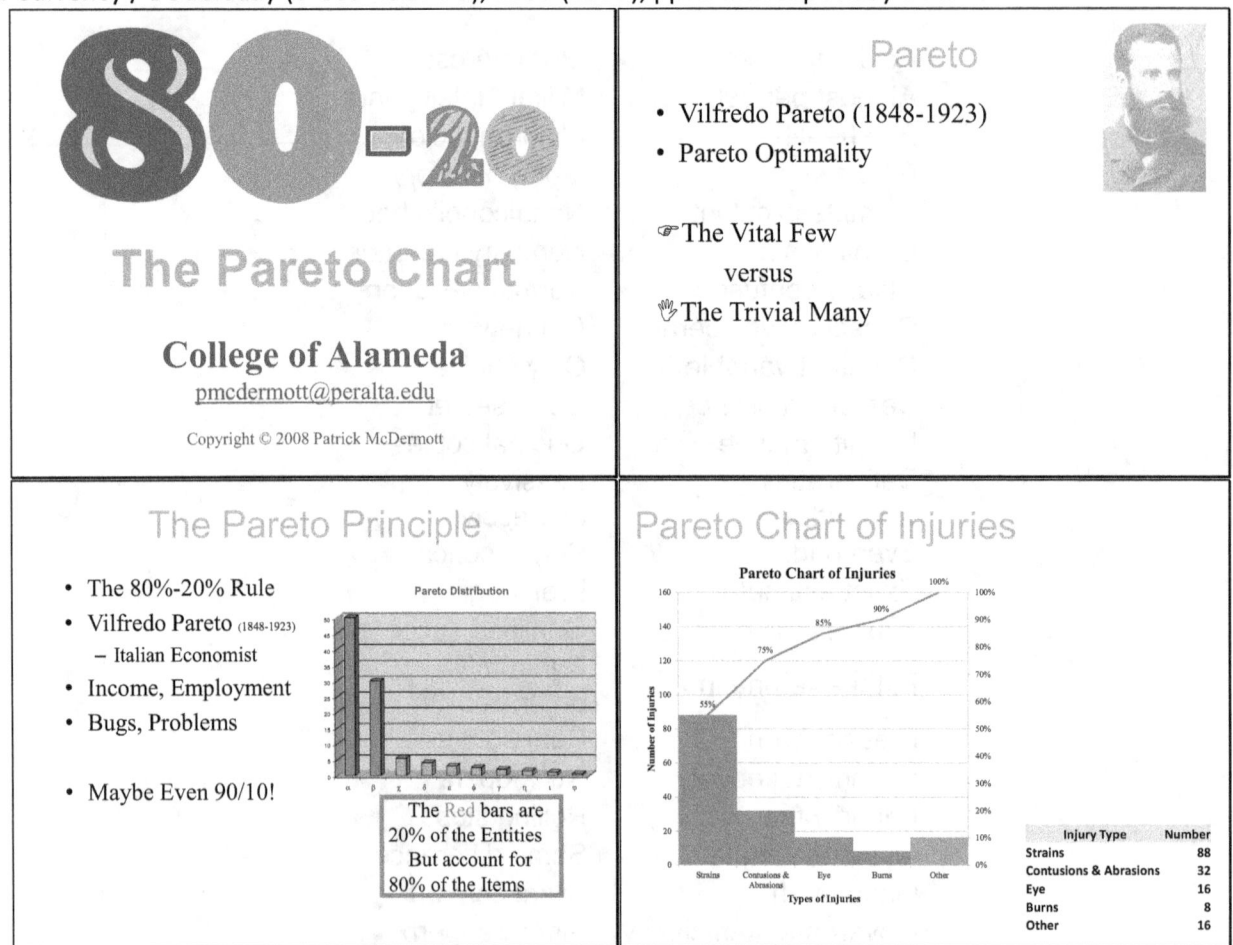

How to Make a Pareto Chart

1. Get the data; sort it by frequency, highest first, except "Other" is always last. Enter them on your spreadsheet.
2. Sum the numbers
3. Compute the Running Totals
4. Compute the cumulative percents
5. Add a Clustered Column chart
6. Select Percentage, Format Secondary Axis
7. Change Chart Types of the Percentage Group to Line
8. Select Count, set Primary Axis to max Total; Secondary Axis max 100
9. Add Data labels on %
10A. Cleanup: Delete the Legend
10B. Cleanup: Add Title
10C. Re-Color "Other"
10D. Add Labels
10E. Re-Size Aesthetically

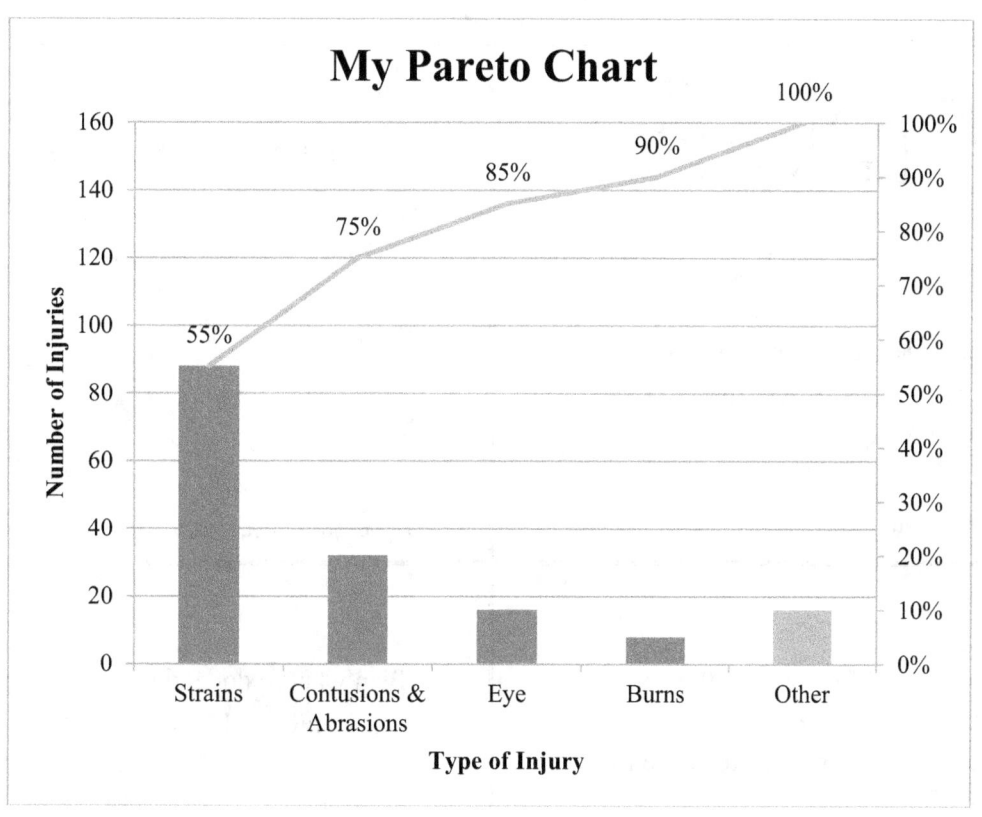

PDCA

Plan-Do-Check-Adjust

Copyright © 2003 McDermott & Arce
Wado Ki Kai Karate Dō
和道気会
pmcdermott@msn.com

"Shewhart" or "Deming" Cycle

P.D.C.A.

The Learning Cycle—This Works!

1. **Plan**
2. **Do**
3. **Check**
4. **Adjust**

↻Repeat
∞Forever

Decide, Do, Reflect, Connect

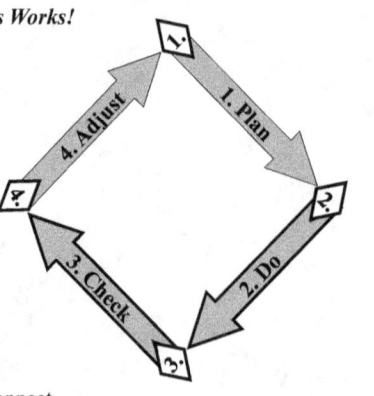

Plan

- The 6 P's: Proper Preparation Prevents Particularly Poor Performance
- "I'm in too much of a hurry to waste time on a plan"
  - Woodcutter too busy to sharpen the axe
- Go Slow to go Fast
- If you fail to plan, you plan to fail

Do

- Plan what to do, and then do the plan
- Companies and Plans
  - Companies that Plan do Better
  - Companies that Follow the Plan do Worse
- Take Heart
  - Atavism and language acquisition
- If Not Sure, Back Up first
  - An Exit Strategy

Check

- There are bugs in every system
- Make it prove it's right
- If you see something wrong, fix it
- It's a Moving Target
  - Car Improvement & CPI

Adjust

- Adjusted Aiming Point
- "I'm not very good as a writer, but I'm a great re-writer"
  - Many writers: Michener, London, etc.
  - Guy Kawasaki: churn
  - Reagan's 10-year speech, Gore's 30-year talk

改善
Kaizen
"Continuous Improvement"

Unpleasant & Difficult

Tasks that are hard to accomplish can be grouped into two categories: unpleasant work, and difficult work. Embrace contradiction: Opposite approaches are needed for these two categories. For the unpleasant, the Nike motto is best: "Just do it". It's not going to get any better, so get it over with; the time you'll spend dreading it will increase the total unpleasantness, so unless you can avoid it permanently (probably the best approach of all), get it over with.

For the difficult, the approach is reversed. Use the Power of Positive Procrastination. Sleep on it. Let it sit in your subconscious for a while. Do some thinking about it from time to time, but delay the decision as long as possible. If no answer is required for several weeks, start a folder on the problem, then put it aside. Pick up the folder every few days and think about it a little, but don't force it. A certain Zen acolyte was given an especially tricky *koan*, a difficult riddle as an exercise to help him gain understanding. When he asked how long it would take to master the koan, he was told, "About two years". "But what if I study really, really hard?" "Then it will take you about twenty years!" was the reply.

> Over time,
>
> Unpleasant tasks become *more* Unpleasant, but
>
> Difficult tasks become *less* Difficult.

One technique for managing difficult questions in meetings and facilitated sessions is the parking lot. It allows you to defer difficult questions in the hope they will resolve themselves. In this technique, you take a sheet of paper or board and label it "Parking Lot". When something comes up you can't resolve, simply note it on a Post-It note and place it on the parking lot. Since it's visible, and will be taken care of, you can safely ignore it for the time being. At the end of the meeting, or each day for a multi-day meeting, review the parking lot. You'll be surprised how many of the items will take care of themselves. Those that haven't by the end of the session are assigned to someone, and recorded on a task list for follow-up. The parking lot can also park unnecessary detail. In a CRC Card Session, I use the back of the card for a similar purpose. Someone will have been sent to the session with strict instructions: "Make sure you tell them about the new manufacturing classification we need." So at every turn, this poor guy tries to bring up this low-level detail. No problem, just write it on the back of the CRC card. He now sees it's been recorded and will shut up about it, and you *have* recorded it so won't forget it.

Now the tough part. What if a problem is both unpleasant *and* difficult? I'll leave that as a koan for the reader.

Why Write a `Function()`?

Adapted from McConnell, Steve, *Code Complete: A Practical Handbook of Software Construction*, Redmond, Washington: Microsoft Press (1-55615-484-4), 1993, pp. 74-79.

1. Reduce complexity
2. Avoid duplicate code
3. Limit effects of changes
4. Hide sequences
5. Improve performance [*]
6. Make central points of control
7. Hide data structures
8. Hide global data
9. Hide pointer operations
10. Promote code reuse
11. Plan for a family of programs
12. Make a section of code readable
13. Improve portability
14. Isolate complex operations
15. Isolate nonstandard language features
16. Simplify complicated Boolean tests
17. Get more points on school project

---

[10] Deming, W. Edwards, *Out of the Crisis*, Cambridge, Massachusetts: The MIT Press (0-262-54115-7), 2000 (1982), pp. 23-24.

[11] Maeda, John, *The Laws of Simplicity: Design, Technology, Business, Life*, Cambridge, Massachusetts: The MIT Press (0-262-13472-1 978-0-262-13472-9), 2006, summary on p. ix.

---

[*] Maybe.

13. Design

Artificial Intelligence

AI
Artificial Intelligence

Copyright © 2006 Patrick McDermott

UC Berkeley
Extension
pmcdermott@msn.com

Long Before Machines are Intelligent, They Will Demand Human Rights

Human Smartest?

"Before [the 21st] century is over "human beings will no longer be the most intelligent or capable type of entity on the planet.".

"Once a computer achieves a human level of intelligence, it will necessarily soar past it."

"There are more than enough new computing technologies now being researched, including three-dimensional chips, optical computing, crystalline computing, DNA computing, and quantum computing, to keep the law of accelerating returns [Moore's Law] going for a long time."

Kurzweil, Ray, *The Age of Spiritual Machines: When Computers Exceed Human Intelligence*, New York: Viking (0-670-88217-8), 1999.

Double E

- Emergence & Evolution
- The Emergence Paradox
  - Lots of Dumb → Smart
- Swarm Intelligence
- Nanotechnology
- Evolutionary Programming
- Data Mining

Berry, Michael J.A. & Gordon Linoff,
Data Mining Techniques: For Marketing, Sales, and Customer Support,
New York: Wiley Computer Publishing (0-471-17980-9), 1997.

Intelligent?

- Strange to say, the Deep Blue team, AI's reigning heroes, is not impressed with AI: "Several members of the team would probably consider it an insult to call Deep Thought an Expert System. In fact, at least two members of the team had used the word "bull****" to describe "expert systems", or for that matter Artificial Intelligence."
- At CMU, Hsu had to take remedial for AI.
- "But Deep Blue is not intelligent. It is only a finely crafted tool that exhibits intelligent behavior in a limited domain." Unlike Garry Kasparov, it can't come up with accusations of cheating against its opponent.

GIGO

- Garbage In, Garbage Out
- Can't Vacuum
  - Can't make full size robot, why nano?
- Not the Same
  - Galapagos Lizard
  - Laser, not eyes
  - Compare letters
  - Names
  - Only Keep what there is a Place for

Asimov's Laws Assume They Understand

1. A robot may not injure a human being, or, through inaction, allow a human being to come to harm.
2. A robot must obey the orders given it by human beings except where such orders would conflict with the First Law.
3. A robot must protect its own existence as long as such protection does not conflict with the First or Second Law.

From Handbook of Robotics, 56th Edition, 2058 A.D., as quoted in *I, Robot*.

➢ Hope They Like Pets

Moravec's Paradox

- What is easiest for people is hardest for machines, and what is hardest for people may be easy for machines
- "It is comparatively easy to make computers exhibit adult level performance on intelligence tests or playing checkers, and difficult or impossible to give them the skills of a one-year-old when it comes to perception and mobility."
  – Hans Moravec, 1988

Moravec Explains

- We should expect the difficulty of reverse engineering any human skill to be roughly proportional to the amount of time that skill has been evolving in animals.
- The oldest human skills are largely unconscious and so appear to us to be effortless.
- Therefore, we should expect skills that appear effortless to be difficult to reverse engineer, but skills that require effort may not necessarily be difficult to engineer at all.

What's Easy

Skills that have been evolving for millions of years: recognizing a face, moving around in space, judging people's motivations, catching a ball, recognizing a voice, setting appropriate goals, paying attention to things that are interesting; anything to do with perception, attention, visualization, motor skills, social skills and so on.

What's Hard

Skills that have appeared more recently: mathematics, engineering, human games, logic and much of what we call science. These are hard for us because they are not what our bodies and brains were primarily designed to do. These are skills and techniques that were designed recently, in historical time, and have had at most a few thousand years to be refined, mostly by cultural evolution.

Efficiency

Efficiency

College of Alameda

pmcdermott@peralta.edu

Copyright © 2010 Patrick McDermott

Hello!

- The Greatest Sins in Programming have been done in the Name of Efficiency

- Next Release catches up anyway
- Flying Fish

Terabytes

- TB < $100.00
- Prog $100/hr.

1,000,000,000,000

---

5 Types

Trade Off
1. Main Memory/Semi-Conductor/RAM
2. Storage/Hard Drive/Offline
3. Processing Time/Cycles
4. Programmer Time
5. User time

Often Wrong

- Guess Wrong
- It Changes
- Interfere with Optimizer

Page Swapping

- MRU Algorithm (KISS)

Stack versus Heap

- Stack
  - Small
  - Short-term
- Heap
  - Big
  - Long-term
- Definition of Large changes
- Ratios: Size vs. Duration changes

Copy

$$Time = K + F*FileCount + B*Megs$$

Futurism

Futurism

***The* University of California**

Berkeley Extension

pmcdermott@msn.com

Copyright © 2008 Patrick McDermott

The Future is Ahead of Us

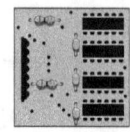

DNA's 3

1. Anything that is in the world when you're born is normal and ordinary and is just a natural part of the way the world works.

2. Anything that's invented between when you're fifteen and thirty-five is new and exciting and revolutionary and you can probably get a career in it.

3. Anything invented after you're thirty-five is against the natural order of things.

From *The Salmon of Doubt* by Douglas N. Adams, 2002

If No Automobiles...

- You'd think I was crazy to suggest it
- Must run a ribbon of concrete from *every* building to *every* other building!
- Fuel is a *mile underground* on the *opposite side of the planet*!
- 40,000 people a year would *die* in accidents!

Three Laws of Arthur C. Clarke

Law 1. When a distinguished but elderly scientist says something is possible, he is almost certainly right. When he says it is impossible, he is very probably wrong.

Law 2. But the only way of discovering the limits of the possible is to venture a little way past them into the impossible.

Law 3. Any sufficiently advanced technology is indistinguishable from magic.

If No TV...

- We'll jiggle electrons
  - So small no one has ever seen one
- Miles away, a little box will sympathetically jiggle its electrons, and reproduce the picture and sound!

- I see Dead People!!!

Glass & Constantine on Software Quality

Software Quality

College of Alameda
pmcdermott@peralta.edu

Copyright © 2007 Patrick McDermott

Glass's Quality 7

1. Reliability
2. Usability (Human engineering)
3. Understandability
4. Modifiability
5. Efficiency
6. Testability
7. Portability

Glass, Robert L., *Facts and Fallacies of Software Engineering*, Boston: Addison-Wesley (0-321-11742-5), 2003, pp. 129-131.

➢ Order: "If any two software people agree, they probably constitute a majority."

Glass: Quality !=

- Quality is *not*:

  ✓ User Satisfaction
  ✓ Meeting Requirements
  ✓ Meeting Cost & Schedule Targets
  ✓ Reliability

- It goes beyond those

The Great Law of Usability

- Goal: Reduce the Human Memory Load
- A System should be usable
  Without training, assistance or manuals
  By someone who knows the application
  but not the software

- Actually, an Ideal Goal ☺

Constantine, Larry L.
The Peopleware Papers: Notes on the Human Side of Software
Upper Saddle River, New Jersey: The Yourdon Press (0-13-060123-3), 2001.

Problem Solving

- Orderly Progression
  – Step By Step
- Solution by subdivision
  – Divide & Conquer
- Component independence

- Component integrity

- Structural fit
  – Model the World

Model The World

- Reflecting the "natural" structure of the problem domain in software saves us from solving problems that don't need solving.
- Instead of inventing whole new architectures, use the serviceable ones that already exist "out there".
- Software is simply structured the way people already think about the problem
  – Maintenance, expansion, reuse easier

Software's Slow Advance

Computing's advances have come from

Hardware, Not Software

College of Alameda
Copyright © 2006 Patrick McDermott
pmcdermott@peralta.edu

Anders Hejlsberg: ["Father" of C#]: I guess I'm becoming less and less of a believer in revolutionary approaches to language design. It really is amazing how much the capabilities of computing have evolved, yet we're basically still using the same kinds of programming languages. It gives me hope that we can go even further with an evolutionary approach where we don't just invalidate all the work that went before.

Robert Glass: *Hype,* and the notion of *one-size-fits-all* undermine out ability to put together project-focused, strong, sensible solutions. We continue to seek the Holy Grail while knowledgeable people tell us over and over again that we are not going to find it.

More Moore?

- Array of 100 items versus 100,000,000
  - No person on earth owned such a computer
  - Both arrays took me about as long to program
- If Moore's Law is correct
  - 2011 is 47,453,133 times 1960 (Cobol released)
  - Autos don't get 1,000,000,000,000,000 mpg
  - But if there was a Microsoft ® Auto
    - Freeze every 1,000 miles or so, needs to be restarted
    - Every 10,000 miles or so, blows up killing all aboard

If builders built buildings the way programmers write programs, then the first woodpecker that came along would destroy civilization.

Software

- If Software was like Hardware
  - No one would need to be "a programmer"
    - "The (part-time) programmer for the world"
  - New programmer == 1 billion old programmers!
- We can do things we couldn't
  - But not 50 billion times as good
  - All advances essentially due to Hardware
- Linux is More of the Same

Essence & Accident

- Fred Brooks' "No Silver Bullet" is still true
- Programming is less than half the problem
- Eliminate Programming Phase entirely
  - You wouldn't even double productivity
    - not to mention an order-of-magnitude improvement

"Not only are there no silver bullets in view, the very nature of software makes it unlikely there will be any—no inventions that will do for software productivity, reliability, and simplicity what electronics, transistors, and large-scale integration did for computer hardware."

Humans

- After 100,000 years
  - Need same Nutrients
  - Need same Rest
  - Have same Emotions
- Progress?
  - War
  - Crime
  - Prejudice
  - Stupidity
  - Cruelty

- BUT Optimism
- More Secure
- More Interesting
- Longer Lives
- We Might be the last generation that thinks 100 is Old.

Heinrich Hoerle
Men-Machines
1930

8. Software Economics

Digital Harmony

Quantity Era	Quality Era	Harmony Era
Mechanical technology	Programmable control	Direct information access
Economies of scale	Economies of speed	Economies of convenience
Advance-planning emphasis	Customer feedback emphasis	Personalized emphasis
Hierarchical organizations	Team-based organizations	Architectural organizations
Value from volume	Value from performance	Value from coherence
Technology islands	Technology overlap	Technology merger
Environmental exploitation	Environmental concern	Environmental renewal

Penzias, Arno, *Digital Harmony: Business, Technology & Life After Paperwork*, New York: HarperBusiness (0-88730-785-X), 1996 (1995).

MACHINES of *Loving Grace*

```
I like to think (and
the sooner the better!)
of a cybernetic meadow
where mammals and computers
live together in mutually
programming harmony
like pure water
touching clear sky

              I like to think
            (right now, please!)
          of a cybernetic forest
       filled with pines and electronics
        where deer stroll peacefully
                past computers
             as if they were flowers
            with spinning blossoms
```

MACHINES of *Loving Grace*

```
        I like to think
         (it has to be!)
      of a cybernetic ecology
   where we are free of our labors
     and joined back to nature,
        returned to our mammal
         brothers and sisters
        and all watched over
   by machines of loving grace
```

Richard Brautigan, 1967

The Strategy of Musashi

Miyamoto Musashi (宮本武蔵 1584-1645) was one of Japan's greatest strategists. Although he was actually a master of Kendō, the Way of the Sword, *Time* Magazine called him "Japan's answer to the Harvard MBA!" *Time* went on to say: "On Wall Street, when Musashi talks, people listen." In *Go Rin no Sho* (五輪の書), *The Book of Five Rings*—actually a letter to his sword fighting students written shortly before his death—the "Sword Saint" enumerates nine principles of strategy. These precepts have surprisingly broad application to systems analysis.

1. **Do not think dishonestly**. Notice it says do not *think* dishonestly. In Systems Analysis, it is bad policy to fool others, but it's even more foolish to fool yourself. In *Rapid Development*, Steve McConnell elaborates 36 classic mistakes in software development, lucky 13

being "Wishful Thinking", as in "The schedule is impossible but if we work hard we can make it"; or "We haven't coordinated the interfaces but we are good communicators so it will be easy"; or "No need to ask the users because we know what they want". Overly optimistic schedules are a way of life in systems (McConnell's classic mistake number 14), as is the persistent belief, despite all evidence to the contrary, that you'll make up your schedule slippage in the next phase (number 26), or that your new tool or method will save plenty of time (number 34).

2. **The Way is in training**. Being a systems analyst requires lifelong learning. Technology is changing at an ever more rapid pace; if you don't believe me, just go into a bookstore in late spring or early summer and see how many computer books already claim copyrights for the coming year! Read a book, or better, take a course from me.

3. **Become acquainted with every art**. You have to understand the world to understand any system. If you are naturally interested in a variety of arts, you'll enjoy the work of a systems analysis, since broad curiosity is almost essential to succeed. To help the accounting department, for example, you'll need to understand the art of accounting. Curiosity killed the cat but is good for the systems analyst. Always strive to be eclectic, picking the best from any art. You'll notice in this book I've been eclectic. Okay, okay, so maybe "random" is a better word for me, but you get the idea: you should open your mind, and bring ideas and analogies from other disciplines.

4. **Know the Ways of all professions**. To help your users, you need to understand something about what they do. Computers now touch on every field, but as I keep telling you, you need to understand both business and technology to be a Systems Analyst.

5. **Understand profit and loss**. Understand Economics. (My observation has been that, as a group, Economics majors make the best systems analysts, but since I am part of that august group, I would understand if you discounted that observation.) Money makes the World go around, and also systems. Most computer systems are *business* systems, and so must cover their costs and have a favorable ROI (Return on Investment).

6. **Develop and trust your intuition**. Go with the flow, your gut intuition, or *hara* (腹). About the only way to achieve this is through experience: Good judgment comes from experience. Unfortunately, experience comes from bad judgment.

7. **Perceive what cannot be seen with the eye**. At one level, that's all we do: we certainly cannot see any of the computer's electron-level activities. But as analysts, we can use models and other tools to see the unseen. See Chapter 8 for more on this topic.

8. Software Economics

8. **Pay attention even to trifles**. The devil is in the details. All analysts know how a trivial piece of information can change everything. The trick, of course, is knowing which trifles will become important later. I've also seen this principle punctuated: "Pay attention! Even to trifles", for those of you who don't pay attention.

9. **Do not do anything useless**. Efficiency, economy and no redundancy. Constantly reflecting on your own techniques and improving them (改善 kaizen) will help you follow this dictum. But also be sure the system itself, not just your development methods used to create it, follows this rule. Featuritis, where we add features for no conceivable end except the feature itself is an example of a failure to observe this principle.

Reasons for Death March Projects

Ed Yourdon lists common reasons for Death March Projects. [1]

1. Politics, politics, politics
2. Naive and/or devious promises made by marketing, senior executive, inexperienced project managers, etc.
3. Naive optimism of youth: "We can do it over the weekend"
4. The "startup" mentality of fledgling entrepreneurial companies
5. The "Marine Corps" mentality: Real programmers don't need sleep
6. Intense competition caused by globalization of markets
7. Intense competition caused by the appearance of new technologies
8. Intense pressure caused by unexpected government regulations
9. Unexpected and/or unplanned crises—e.g., your hardware/software vendor just went bankrupt, or your three best programmers just died of bubonic plague

Reasons for Participating in Death March Projects

Yourdon details 36 reasons why people participate, and discusses 9 in depth. He also discusses the possibility the participant didn't know the project was a Death March.

1. The risks are high, but so are the rewards
2. The "Mt. Everest" syndrome
3. The "buzz" of working intensely with other committed people
4. The naiveté and optimism of youth
5. The alternative is unemployment
6. It's required in order to be considered for future advancement
7. The alternative is bankruptcy or some other calamity
8. It's an opportunity to escape the "normal" bureaucracy
9. Revenge [As in "I'll show 'em!"]

Here is the extended list, attributed to a Brainstorming session by Kevin Huigens.

Everybody wants to feel wanted	Perceived opportunity
Perceived money gain	Can't afford to lose job
Brought in from the outside to lead the project	Don't care whether project fails, get to work with cool technology
Willing suspension of disbelief	On-the-job-training on new technology
Eternal optimism	Challenge
Plain stupidity	Chance to prove yourself
To get the job done	It's the only project
Your friend is running the project	Your brother is running the project (It'd take more than friendship)
Your boss said so	You have no other life
Nothing better to do	Stock options
Existing pay vs. expectation of raise	Love is blind
Résumé building	Ignorance
Camaraderie	Expectations for how long it will take are too low

---

[1] Yourdon, Edward, *Death March, Second Edition*, Upper Saddle River, New Jersey: Prentice-Hall (978-0-13-143635-0 0-13-143635-X), 2007 (2004), Table 1.1, p. 6; Table 1.2, p. 16; p. 17.

Zen & the Art of Software Economics

McDermott, Patrick,
Zen and the Art of Systems Analysis:
Meditations on Computer Systems Development,
New York: iUniverse (0-595-25679-1), 2003 (2002).

Zen & the Art of Economic$
Economic Analysis & Systems Analysis

The University of California
Berkeley Extension
pmcdermott@msn.com

Copyright © 2007 Patrick McDermott

What's I.S. Goal?

✓ Efficiency
– Faster, Cheaper
– Save Time
– Doing things Right

✓ Effectiveness
– Better, Smarter
– Information as an Asset
– Doing the Right Thing
– "It's no use running faster if you're on the wrong track."

✓ Innovation
– New Area
– Something You Didn't do Before
– Doing New Things

Optimist: The Glass is half Full
Pessimist: The Glass is half Empty
Economist: The glass is 50% efficient

Internet Categories

➤ Content
– Entertain or Inform: **Eyeballs**
➤ Community
– Social
• YouTube, Amazon reviews
➤ Commerce
– Sell, Sell, Sell
• Meta Categories
– ISPs
– Portals
– Web Services

"Both Magritte and Escher use realism in exploring the worlds of paradox and illusion; both have a sure sense for the evocative power of certain visual symbols, and—something which even their admirers often fail to point out—both of them have a sure sense of the graceful line."—Crab (Douglas Hofstadter, *GEB*)

Planning Paradox

◎ Companies that plan are more successful than those that don't. But companies that actually *follow* their plans are <u>less</u> successful than those that do not follow their plan.

◎ Target Seeking Arrows

◎ The Most Common Plan:
🎯 A Budget

Target with Four Faces
Jasper Johns, c. 1955

Quality Control

The original meaning of QC:
"As good as it needs to be, and NO BETTER."

• What's a few Bugs between friends?
• Steve Ballmer's $2 million bug cleanup
• Yourdon's "Good Enough" Software
– ⊘ Zero Defects, ⊘ 6 σ

Yourdon, Edward, *Rise & Resurrection of the American Programmer*, Upper Saddle River, New Jersey: Yourdon Press (0-13-121831-X), 1996.

The Terrible Twins

➤ Analysis Paralysis
– The Winchester Mystery Model
– Its own (first class) airplane seat

➤ Scope Creep
– "The main thing is to keep the main thing the main thing."—James Thurber
– Just say "No"
– Allow 10%
– Re-negotiate

Self-Fulfilling Prophecies

When people believe something is going to happen, because of their belief, they can unintentionally cause the event to actually happen

✓ Run on a Bank
✓ Stock Market goes Up or Down
✓ Project Succeeds or Fails

Measuring Distorts

Never use an Indicator as an Evaluator
– Army Spit Shine
– Phone Calls (Mis-)Handled
– Lines of Code
– More Time Testing
– Teach to the Test
– Heisenberg Uncertainty Principle
• "Observing changes the Observed"

"Not everything that can be counted counts, and not everything that counts can be counted."—Albert Einstein

Mallory vs. Hillary

- Who was first to climb Mount Everest?
- George Mallory (1886-June 8,1924)
  - "Because it is There!"
  - And he's still There
- Edmund Hillary & Sherpa Tenzing Norgay
  - May 29, 1953
  - No doubt: The 1st <u>Successful</u> Climb

- Always consider the Costs

Economic Costs

- Fixed Cost versus Variable Cost $
  - Periodic vs. Per Unit
  - Systems are usually fixed cost   ¥
    - Even if broken!

- Sunk Costs are Junk Costs
  - Don't Throw Good Money after Bad   €

- Opportunity Cost   ¢
  - What Might Have Been   ₩

Learning Curve

- Like *The Ugly American*, who was not Ugly inside
- "Steep learning curve" means it's *easy* to learn

A "Learning Curve"

Unit Cost ($ per unit) vs Total Production (millions of units)

Mix Apples & Oranges

Apples and Oranges *are* Comparable
  - A Small, inexpensive fruit
  - Good School Lunch Choice
  - Make Delicious Fruit Salad

Paul Cézanne (1839-1906)
Apples & Oranges, 1895

René Magritte (1898-1967)
Ceci n'Est Pas une Pomme
"This is not an Apple", 1964

René Magritte (1898-1967)
La Chambre d'écoute
"The Listening Room", 1952

This is not a PC:

Specs

Algorithms

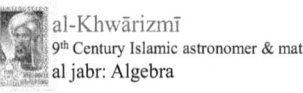 al-Khwārizmī
9th Century Islamic astronomer & mathematician
al jabr: Algebra

The Algorithm

College of Alameda

Copyright © 2006 Patrick McDermott

pmcdermott@peralta.edu

The King of Hearts

"Begin at the beginning, and go on till you come to the end: then stop."

—K♥ The King of Hearts

in Lewis Carroll,
Alice's Adventures in Wonderland

• Don't forget to STOP!

An Algorithm is

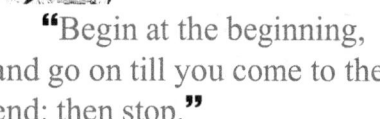

Artist Drawing a Lute
with the Help of a Mechanical Device
Albrecht Dürer, c. 1525

A finite procedure,
written (or could be) in a fixed symbolic vocabulary,
governed by precise instructions,
moving in discrete steps, 1, 2, 3…,
whose execution requires no
   insight, cleverness, intuition, intelligence, or perspicuity,
and that sooner or later comes to an end.

Berlinski, David, *The Advent of the Algorithm: The Idea that Rules the World*, New York: Harcourt (0-15-100338-6), 2000, p. xviv.

The *Entscheidungsproblem*
   Given a description of a program and a finite input, decide whether the program finishes running or will run forever, given that input.

How to Get Rich

J. Paul Getty's secret:
The Sure-fire way to get *Rich*!

Rise Early → Work Hard →

Some Algorithms

- The Great Google {Secret} Search Algorithm
- Long Division
- Linear Programming
- Sorting
- McDonald's Recipe
  - But not Julia Childs'
- Bake a Cake
  - From a Package
  - But NOT "from scratch"
  - Cake can lead to a Long Life!

How To Live a Long Life!

Eat Chocolate Cake

Every Day

Bubble Sort

- Look at each item in turn
- If the next item is less, swap them
- Keep doing it until they are in order

T
L
A

	0	1	2
	T	L	A
	L	A	L
	A	T	T

What's Goodness?

- Donald Knuth
- *The Art of Computer Programming*
  - Not *Science*
1. Finite
2. Definite
3. Input
4. Output
5. Effective

- Efficient
  - ✓ Processing
  - ✓ Memory
  - ✓ Storage
- Easy to Code
- Easy to Maintain
  - ✓ Robust
  - ✓ Understandable

MACHINE

HUMAN

amazon.com

- Bestsellers
- Every Hour
- Not Total
- Current Hot Titles
  - Wild fluctuations cool!
- Steady sellers
  - Wild fluctuations bad!
  - Few or rare sales
- Stock versus Flow
  Author: Most recent or best seller?

- Best Reviewers
- Sheer Numbers
- Positive Votes
- Negative Votes
  - Academia Bad = Good
- Gaming the System
  - Campaigns
  - Vote For Myself

14. Estimating

The **Black** Art: Estimating

McConnell, Steve, *Software Estimation: Demystifying the Black Art*, Redmond, Washington: Microsoft Press (978-0-7356-0535-0 0-7356-0535-1), 2006.

Estimating

Copyright © 2006 Patrick McDermott

UC Berkeley

Extension

pmcdermott@msn.com

Resources

- CoCoMo
- Function Points
- CPM Critical Path
- Various Estimating Tools
- Microsoft ® Project

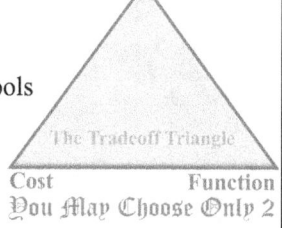

Time

The Tradeoff Triangle

Cost   Function

You May Choose Only 2

- I recommend: Voodoo, or Zen!

Emergence in Estimation

- My Economic Crystal Ball
  - Knowing a Lot Can Help
- Rules of Thumb aren't all that Dumb
- Law of Large Numbers
  - A lot of inaccurate guesses can add up to a very accurate estimate
- The Proof: Las Vegas
  - They don't know who will win
  - But they know how many will win

Techniques

- Count, Compute, Judge
- Decomposition & Recomposition
- Calibration & Historic Data
  - Industry Average
  - Organizational Data
  - Project Specific Data
- Expert Judgment
  - Individual
  - Delphi Technique
- Estimation by Analogy

Politix

- What Gets Done
- The Incredible Shrinking Estimate
- Is it a Lie if Nobody Believes it?
- Low Ball It
  - Government Contracts
  - Auto Industry
- The Estimate is inversely proportional to the estimator's desire to do the project

Strange Attractors

- The Earth is 4,600,000,006 Years Old
- T-Shirt Size
  - S M L XL
- The Cone of Uncertainty
- It's not the average, it's the variance from expectation, that causes disappointment
- The calendar can affect acceptability
  - January 10 can be a harder sell than June 30!
  - Bonus!

Critical Path

```
                        3.0
                   ┌──────────────┐
                   │Paint Interior│
                   └──────────────┘
  2.0         3.5                      1.0
┌──────────┐ ┌──────────┐           ┌─────────┐
│   Lay    │→│  Put Up  │           │Inspector│
│Foundation│ │  Walls   │           └─────────┘
└──────────┘ └──────────┘
                    5.5
                   ┌──────────────┐
                   │Paint Exterior│
                   └──────────────┘
```

On the Critical Path

Function Points

$$4 \times \mathbf{I} + 5 \times \mathbf{O} + 4 \times \mathbf{E} + 10 \times \mathbf{L} + 7 \times \mathbf{F}$$

Type	Complexity Level		
	Simple	Average	Complex
Input ($\mathbf{I}$)	3	4	6
Output ($\mathbf{O}$)	4	5	7
Inquiry Types ($\mathbf{E}$)	3	4	6
Logical Internal ($\mathbf{L}$)	7	10	15
Interfaces ($\mathbf{F}$)	5	7	10

van Vliet, Hans, *Software Engineering, Principles and Practices*, Chichester, England: John Wiley & Sons (0-471-93611-1), 1993 , p. 111.

McConnell's Sanity Check

1. Was a standardized procedure used to create the estimate?
2. Was the estimation process free from pressure that would bias the results?
3. If the estimate was negotiated, were only the inputs to the estimate negotiated, not the outputs or the estimation process itself?
4. Is the estimate expressed with precision that matches its accuracy? (For example, is the estimate expressed as a range or coarse number if it's early in the project?) ...

McConnell's Sanity Check II

5. Was the estimate created using multiple techniques that converged to similar results?
6. Is the productivity assumption underlying the estimate comparable to productivity actually experienced on past projects of similar sizes?
7. Is the estimated schedule at least 2.0 x StaffMonths⅓? (That is, is the estimate outside of the Impossible Zone?)
8. Were the people who are going to do the work involved in creating the estimate? ...

McConnell's Sanity Check III

9. Has the estimate been reviewed by an expert estimator?
10. Does the estimate include a nonzero allowance for the impact that project risks will have on effort and schedule?
11. Is the estimate part of a series of estimates that will become more accurate as the project moves into the narrow part of the cone of uncertainty?
12. Are all elements of the project included in the estimate, including creation of setup program, creation of data conversion utilities, cutover from old system to new system, etc.?

Remember

✓ Don't Confuse an Estimate with a Target
✓ Don't let *them* confuse a Target with a Commitment

• Executives are trained negotiators, Engineers are not

• Just Say "No" to Bill Gates

Estimate Sanity Check

The following sanity check indicates how useful your current project estimate is likely to be in managing your project. For each Yes answer, give the estimate one point.

Yes

____ 1. Was a standardized procedure used to create the estimate?

____ 2. Was the estimation process free from pressure that would bias the results?

____ 3. If the estimate was negotiated, were only the inputs to the estimate negotiated, not the outputs or the estimation process itself?

____ 4. Is the estimate expressed with precision that matches its accuracy? (For example, is the estimate expressed as a range or coarse number if it's early in the project?)

____ 5. Was the estimate created using multiple techniques that converged to similar results?

____ 6. Is the productivity assumption underlying the estimate comparable to productivity actually experienced on past projects of similar sizes?

____ 7. Is the estimated schedule at least $2.0 \times \text{StaffMonths}^{1/3}$? (That is, is the estimate outside of the Impossible Zone?)

____ 8. Were the people who are going to do the work involved in creating the estimate?

____ 9. Has the estimate been reviewed by an expert estimator?

____ 10. Does the estimate include a nonzero allowance for the impact that project risks will have on effort and schedule?

____ 11. Is the estimate part of a series of estimates that will become more accurate as the project moves into the narrow part of the cone of uncertainty?

____ 12. Are all elements of the project included in the estimate, including creation of setup program, creation of data conversion utilities, cutover from old system to new system, etc.?

____ TOTAL

Gilb's 10 Principles of Estimation

Tom Gilb asks whether you really do want to predict software project costs, or if you actually want to *control* them. He offers these ten principles: [12]

1. The Dependency Principle

All system attributes are affected by all others.

2. The Sensitivity Principle

Even the slightest change in one attribute can cause uncertainly large changes in any other attribute.

3. The Zeroth Law of Reliability Generalized

You can reach almost any ambitious level if you are willing to sacrifice all the other attributes.

4. The Design-to-Price Principle

You can get more control over costs by designing to stay within interesting limits, than you can by passively trying to estimate the costs resulting from a design which gives priority to other objectives.

5. The Iterative Estimation Principle

You get more control over estimation by learning from evolutionary early-and-frequent result deliveries, than you will if you try to estimate in advance for a whole large project.

6. The "Quality Determines Cost" Principle

You cannot accurately estimate the costs of anything when cost determining quality attributes are unclearly defined.

7. The Natural Variation Principle

All system attributes can be expected to vary to some degree throughout their lifetime.

8. The Early Bird Principle

Any method which gives you early feedback and correction of reality is more likely to give you control over the final result than big-bang methods.

9. The Activist Principle

Estimation methods alone will not change a result which is off the track. Active correction must be a part of your methodology. (Action, not estimation, produces results.)

10. The "Future Shock" Principle

Data from past projects might be useful, but it can never be as useful to you as current data from your present project.

Changes in Closet

Mr. Blandings Builds His Dream House
"Four Little Flagstones", Chapter 22, at 1:22:00

   Okay, you've been working hard on this stuff, so now I'm going to tell you to take a break, and watch a movie. Every Systems Analyst must see *Mr. Blandings Builds His Dream House*, based on the book by Eric Hodgins, with Cary Grant as Jim Blandings, and Myrna Loy as Muriel Blandings. Although it was made in 1948, and is about building a house, not a system per se, it's probably the best movie on projects and systems ever made. I like to play the "Changes in Closet" sequence to my class at UC Berkeley Extension.

   The notation "Changes in Closet" is written on an outrageously large bill for modifications supposedly authorized by Mrs. Blandings. It turns out there were four pieces of flagstone left over from the porch that were going to be thrown away. Mrs. Blandings asked the contractor to put them on the floor of the pantry closet she called her "flower room". She said she wanted it to be nice and dry. "Well, you're the doctor" he said. The contractor interpreted "nice and dry" to require a drain. This needed a carpenter to rip out the floor, which went under the wall so they knocked that out, too. Then they needed to chop off a joist to make room for a cradle, weakening said joist, and requiring iron straps for a large pan to hold the cement. Because of the added weight, they needed a lally column to support the floor. The pan would sit on the hot and cold water pipes and the 220-volt electrical cable. So they needed a plumber to re-angle the drainpipes under the entire house and move the hot and cold water pipes, and an electrician had to reroute the 220-volt electrical cabling. Then a carpenter and a plasterer put the wall and floor back. The four old stones that were to be thrown away added something like 15% of what the entire house, including 35 acres of land, had cost!

   The lessons? A seemingly simple change can be very costly; and something that would have been trivial at the beginning is extremely expensive after a lot of work has been done. Don't forget technicians will assume the user knows what's involved when they ask for something, so beware.

---

[12] Gilb, Tom, Susannah Finzi (editor), *Principles of Software Engineering Management*, Workingham, England: Addison-Wesley (0-201-19246-2), 1988, Chapter 16, pp. 311-323.

15. Beyond Analysis
Classic Mistakes

People-Related Mistakes
1. Undermined motivation
2. Weak personnel
3. Uncontrolled problem employees
4. Heroics
5. Adding people to a late project
6. Noisy, crowded offices
7. Friction between developers and customers
8. Unrealistic expectations
9. Lack of effective project sponsorship
10. Lack of stakeholder buy-in
11. Lack of user input
12. Politics placed over substance
13. Wishful thinking

Process-Related Mistakes
14. Overly optimistic schedules
15. Insufficient risk management
16. Contractor failure
17. Insufficient planning
18. Abandonment of planning under pressure
19. Wasted time during the fuzzy front end
20. Shortchanged upstream activities
21. Inadequate design
22. Shortchanged quality assurance
23. Insufficient management controls
24. Premature or overly frequent convergence
25. Omitting necessary tasks from estimates
26. Planning to catch up later
27. Code-like-hell programming

Product-Related Mistakes
28. Requirements gold-plating
29. Feature creep
30. Developer gold-plating
31. Push-me, pull-me negotiation
32. Research-oriented development

Technology-Related Mistakes
33. Silver-bullet syndrome
34. Overestimated savings from new tools or methods
35. Switching tools in the middle of a project
36. Lack of automated source-code control

McConnell, Steve, *Rapid Development: Taming Wild Software Schedules*, Redmond, Washington: Microsoft Press (1-55615-900-5), 1996, pp. 40-49.

Technological Optimism

Henslowe: "Strangely enough, it all turns out well."
Shakespeare: "How?"
Henslowe: "I don't know—It's a mystery."

Techno-Optimism

There are other worlds and they are this one. —McKenzie Wark

Copyright © 2004 Patrick McDermott

UC Berkeley

Extension

pmcdermott@msn.com

I Sometimes Sound Cynical…

✓ Counter my Seeming Cynicism
✓ Despite Fuzzy Logic, We do Okay
✓ Berries & Tomatoes

Some would accuse me of being negative, but I'm not. Not to join Voltaire's Dr. Pangloss in novel *Candide*, or the best-of-all-possible-worlds Gottfried Leibniz he was based on, but we're doing pretty darn well. It's amazing how well. Most Utopians seem to think we are nowhere near our potential, but that's not true. Not to say we can't do better and shouldn't strive to, but we're no slouches either.

Make a Dif

To a jaded ear it might sound impossibly naive, but the people working on Chandler—like, in my experience, software developers everywhere—were motivated by the hope that their work might make a difference in people's lives. Perhaps the idealism most programmers share is a direct consequence of the toil and frustration of programming. If you're going to have to wrestle with daunting abstractions or squash armies of bugs, big ambitions can help pull you through the slog.

Rosenberg, Scott, *Dreaming in Code: Two Dozen Programmers, Three Years, 4,732 Bugs, and One Quest for Transcendent Software*, 2007, p. 33.

Brooks: Wonder, Excitement, Joy

"The computer-related intellectual discipline has exploded as has the technology. When I was a graduate student in the mid-1950s, I could read all the journals and conference proceedings; I could stay current in all the discipline. Today my intellectual life has seen me regretfully kissing subdiscipline interests good-bye one by one, as my portfolio has continuously overflowed beyond mastery. Too many interests, too many exciting opportunities for learning, research, and thought. What a marvelous predicament! Not only is the end not in sight, the pace is not slackening. We have many future joys."

Brooks, Frederick P., Jr., "Epilogue: Fifty Years of Wonder, Excitement, and Joy" in *The Mythical Man-Month: Essays on Software Engineering*, 1995, p. 292.

R.L. Glass

So what, in retrospect, have Parnas and Brooks said to us? That software development is a conceptually tough business. That magic solutions are not just around the corner. That it is time for the practitioner to examine evolutionary improvements rather than to wait—or hope—for revolutionary ones.

Some in the software field find this to be a discouraging picture. They are the ones who still thought breakthroughs were near at hand.

But some of us — those of us crusty enough to think that we are realists—see this as a breath of fresh air. At last, we can focus on something a little more viable than pie in the sky. Now, perhaps, we can get on with the incremental improvements to software productivity that are possible, rather than waiting for the breakthroughs that are not likely to ever come.

Can't Agree?

Conflict leads to Understanding

As Hermann Hesse's character quotes Siddhartha:

It pleases me and seems right that what is of value and wisdom to one man seems nonsense to another.

Hesse, Hermann, Hilda Rosner (translator from German), *The Journey to the East*, New York: Picador (0-312-42168-0), 2003 (1956), p. 7.

The Invisible Hand

As Adam Smith told us, an individual generally "neither intends to promote the public interest, nor knows how much he is promoting it … by directing [his] industry in such manner as his produce may be of greatest value, he intends only his own gain, and he is in this, as in many other cases, led by an invisible hand to promote an end which was no part of his intention. … By pursuing his own interest he frequently promotes that of the society more effectually than when he really intends to promote it."

Smith, Adam, *An Inquiry into the Nature and Causes of The Wealth of Nations*, London: W. Strahan & T. Cadell in the Strand, 1776, Book IV, Chapter 11.

Digital Harmony

Quantity Era	Quality Era	Harmony Era
Mechanical technology	Programmable control	Direct information access
Economies of scale	Economies of speed	Economies of convenience
Advance-planning emphasis	Customer feedback emphasis	Personalized emphasis
Hierarchical organizations	Team-based organizations	Architectural organizations
Value from volume	Value from performance	Value from coherence
Technology islands	Technology overlap	Technology merger
Environmental exploitation	Environmental concern	Environmental renewal

Penzias, Arno, *Digital Harmony: Business, Technology & Life After Paperwork*, New York: HarperBusiness (0-88730-785-X), 1996 (1995).

Our Lives

✓ We live Longer
✓ Most people choose Modern Life
  – So it must be good
✓ Less drudgery, more Interesting lives
IT Folks
  – The World Needs Both Art & Technology
    • Understand the Other Side
    • Diversity of Ideas
  – Get out there and Compute
  – Change the World, One Byte at a Time

Future, Tense…

? If you could live in the past, present or future, which would you choose?
⬠ The Past
  – *Success* was living to your 1st Birthday
The Future
  – We might be the last people who think 100 is old
  – I envy posterity, so I don't owe them anything

Flawed Species

Recognize that
We Are a Flawed Species
and
Get On With It

Dustin Hoffman, Interview,
The Charlie Rose Show, October 21, 2004.